Fatal Autonomy

Fatal Autonomy

ROMANTIC DRAMA AND

THE RHETORIC OF AGENCY

William Jewett

Cornell University Press

ITHACA AND LONDON

Copyright © 1997 by Cornell University

All rights reserved. Except for brief quotations in a review, this book, or parts thereof, must not be reproduced in any form without permission in writing from the publisher. For information, address Cornell University Press, Sage House, 512 East State Street, Ithaca, New York 14850.

First published 1997 by Cornell University Press.

Printed in the United States of America

Library of Congress Cataloging-in-Publication Data
Jewett, William.
    Fatal autonomy : Romantic drama and the rhetoric of agency / William Jewett.
      p. cm.
    Includes index.
    ISBN 0-8014-3352-5 (cloth : alk. paper)
    1. English drama—19th century—History and criticism. 2. Verse drama, English—History and criticism. 3. Political plays, English—History and criticism. 4. English drama (Tragedy)—History and criticism. 5. Autonomy (Psychology) in literature. 6. Agent (Philosophy) in literature. 7. Moral conditions in literature. 8. Romanticism—Great Britain. 9. Self in literature. I. Title.
PR719.V4J49 1997
822'.709358—dc21   97-12337

Cornell University Press strives to utilize environmentally responsible suppliers and materials to the fullest extent possible in the publishing of its books. Such materials include vegetable-based, low-VOC inks and acid-free papers that are also either recycled, totally chlorine-free, or partly composed of nonwood fibers.

Cloth printing   10 9 8 7 6 5 4 3 2 1

For Margaret

Contents

Preface ix

Introduction 1

Part One Tragic Agents and the Origins of Romanticism, 1794–1797

1. The Sublime Machine of History: *The Fall of Robespierre* and *Wat Tyler* 23
2. The Claim of Compulsion: *The Borderers* 58
3. Fancy and the Spell of Enlightenment: *Osorio* 99

Part Two Shelley, Byron, and the Body Politic, 1819–1822

4. Performing Skepticism: *The Cenci* 135
5. Fatal Autonomy: *Marino Faliero* 165
6. History's Lethean Song: *Charles the First* and *The Triumph of Life* 205

Index 255

Preface

This book describes an enduring moral puzzle and explains how it shaped, and was shaped by, a set of dramatic poems. The puzzle arises from language's power both to create and to suspend the habits of thought sustained by the belief that, on balance, we do more than is done to us. Most people will acknowledge, most of the time, that no moral calculus can find a just balance between passivity and activity, the two ways of understanding one's relation to things that happen. But our stubborn belief in such a balance can give us pause; and one name for that pause is tragedy. Tragedy, thus understood, binds itself intimately to drama because drama asks us—as lyric and narrative do not—to take pieces of language for persons, forcing us—out of a puzzlement that is inherently moral—to confront the ways in which our language grants us agency. The poets we call Romantic saw a moral challenge in that confrontation and followed its generic implications toward a new kind of poetry. That poetry provides the fundamental rationale for this book, which looks to Romantic drama to explain how Romantic poetry came to hold a permanent grip on our conceptions of moral life.

Few readers, however, are likely to be drawn to this book by the allure of the poetical dramas that form its main exhibits. Let me say, then, as succinctly as I can, why these texts matter. Several generations of writers have been led to follow the cardinal rule of freshman English—"Never use the passive where you can use the active"—out of a fear captured in George Orwell's "Politics and the English Language":

When one watches some tired hack on the platform mechanically repeating the familiar phrases—*bestial atrocities, iron heel, blood-stained tyranny, free people of the world, stand shoulder to shoulder*—one often has a curious feeling that one is not watching a live human being but some kind of dummy: a feeling which suddenly becomes stronger at moments when the light catches the speaker's spectacles and turns them into blank discs which seem to have no eyes behind them. And this is not altogether fanciful. A speaker who uses that kind of phraseology has gone some distance towards turning himself into a machine. The appropriate noises are coming out of his larynx, but his brain is not involved as it would be if he were choosing his words for himself.[1]

Who would not want to make sure of "choosing his words for himself" when the alternative is committing bestial atrocities like *"bestial atrocities"*? Only someone with blank discs where he should have eyes. The image seems marked by a hollow assurance characteristic of the World War II humanism that had critics of Romanticism deploying fantasies of automatism as readily as Orwell's hack marches out his clichés about the free world.[2] But the anxiety itself is less easily localized. It can be glimpsed, for example, in the deathly face of Keats's Moneta, which brings both dread and solace:

> But for her eyes I should have fled away.
> They held me back, with a benignant light,
> Soft mitigated by divinest lids
> Half closed, and visionless entire they seem'd
> Of all external things—they saw me not,
> But in blank splendor beam'd like the mild moon,
> Who comforts those she sees not, who knows not
> What eyes are upwards cast.[3]

The magnetic allure of Keats's image lies in its gracious condescension toward the form of life that knows it is not seen, yet can still take comfort in the "blank splendor" of that knowledge. Keats animates the "mild moon," using the active voice to make it an agent, dramatizing the process by which we grant it the power it holds for us. For the

---

1. George Orwell, *Collected Essays* (London: Secker & Warburg, 1975) 362–63, 367.
2. See, for example, Yvor Winters, *In Defense of Reason* (Chicago: Swallow Press, 1943) and Albert Guérard, "Prometheus and the Aeolian Lyre," *Yale Review* 33 (1944).
3. Keats, "The Fall of Hyperion" 260–61, 264–71; *Complete Poems*, ed. Jack Stillinger (Cambridge: Harvard University Press, 1982) 367.

power of the image lies in its ability to show us how, and why, we bring lifelessness to life, recognizing that life by reflecting upon our own power to bestow it. Keats shows us why we *need* the active voice and the belief it sustains, without either urging upon us, or chastising us for, our need.

The Romantic poets sought to understand that need by writing plays that explore what underlies our routine beliefs about the moral agency that brings us to life. But these plays also stage, with subtlety and grace, the anxiety Orwell arouses in attempting to make us feel a connection between politics and language. They do so out of political motives similar to Orwell's, although the circumstances that shaped those motives were very different. The force of circumstance was indeed acute at the two historical points through which this book approaches the relation between politics and language: 1794–97, the political turning point in the careers of the first-generation romantics, and 1819–22, the years in which the younger romantics wrote their most direct political poetry. And it is the force of circumstance that often triggers anxieties about agency. Unlike Orwell, however, who betrays an aversion to whatever threatens his beliefs about human freedom, the Romantic poets sought to understand the magnetic attraction exerted by those blank discs that seemed, just a moment ago, to be eyes. How could their dull sheen have been so easily taken for life? Romanticism's best answer underwrites Wittgenstein's famous aphorism: "To imagine a language means to imagine a form of life." All grammatical sentences, active or passive, convey an idea of agency; or, to put it in the passive voice, ideas of agency are produced by grammatical sentences. Keats taps that awareness briefly in imagining how one might draw comfort from the benevolently gleaming visage of a lifeless rock; Romantic drama explores it exhaustively.

"Agency" is a notoriously slippery term in contemporary theory, and it would be well to be clear about how and why I use it in this book. Paul Smith has set a standard for scrupulous usage in *Discerning the Subject,* but his abstract conception of agency as the locus of conflict within subjectivity "from which resistance to the ideological is produced" does little to suggest the historical variability of the problem the term will name here.[4] "Agency" is a term for which Coleridge had a

---

4. Paul Smith, "Note on Terminology," in *Discerning the Subject* (Minneapolis: University of Minnesota Press, 1988) xxxv.

hyperbolizing affection: his "Critique of *Bertram*" refers to "the superhuman entireness of Don Juan's agency," and his early contribution to Southey's *Joan of Arc* bore the subtitle "Preternatural Agency."[5] Coleridgean usage can hardly stand as a model of clarity, but even those who see Coleridge as a philosophical cuttlefish must admire the utility of a term that can bring him together with two of the period's plainest speakers: Thomas Reid, whose "common-sense" philosophy culminated in *Essays on the Active Powers of Man,* and William Hazlitt, who began his career with an *Essay on the Principles of Human Action.* Reid and Hazlitt inherit a problem Hume had posed in his analysis "Of the Idea of Necessary Connexion," where he addresses the difficulty of defining terms: "I begin with observing that the terms of *efficacy, agency, power, force, energy, necessity, connexion,* and *productive quality,* are all nearly synonymous; and therefore 'tis an absurdity to employ any of them in defining the rest." Hume argues that the idea of agency (under whatever name) originates not in reason but in particular experiences; but his awareness that we cannot *perceive* "the connexion between an act of volition, and a motion of the body" leads him to conclude: "We never therefore have any idea of power."[6] It remained for Hume's readers to explain their habitual recourse to the terms he lists.

I have given a privileged place to the term "agency" because Hume's other terms, in the usage of the Romantic period, all bear connotations that distract from the exploration of human action in the work of poets who were more famously concerned with "power" and "energy." Critics have turned from those terms and toward "agency" less on account of its currency in contemporary analytic philosophy than because its relatively colorless range of usages promises fewer distortions in mapping our concerns onto those of the texts we read.[7] If the revival of interest in agency can be understood as a reaction against Marxist and Structuralist critiques of the autonomous subject, the pervasive interest

---

5. Coleridge, *Biographia Literaria,* in *The Collected Works of Samuel Taylor Coleridge,* vol. 7, ed. James Engell and W. Jackson Bate (Princeton: Princeton University Press, 1983) 2:216 (subsequent references give volume, part, and page numbers); Robert Southey and Samuel Taylor Coleridge, *Joan of Arc* (New York: Woodstock, 1993) 37.

6. Hume, *A Treatise of Human Nature,* ed. Ernest C. Mossner (New York: Penguin, 1985) 206, 211.

7. Probably the most prominent among innumerable works of analytic philosophy employing the term is Donald Davidson's "Agency," in *Essays on Actions and Events* (Oxford: Clarendon, 1980).

throughout the Romantic period in the question of what can be known (or believed) about human action may have originated in a similar reaction against eighteenth-century materialism: the eighteenth-century fear that we are (only) our bodies has been replaced with the postmodern fear that we are (only) our words. Poststructuralism has given us critiques of the subject, of identity, of autonomy, even while its advocates have felt compelled to stake political agendas upon such terms as "performativity," "resistance," and "solidarity." These terms put a limit to the critique of the subject by calling upon us to say what, aside from our bodies and our words, allows us to think of ourselves as political beings who can be empowered or disempowered. "Agency," used to indicate the set of beliefs people hold about their relation to things that happen, thus serves to focus attention on the *consequences* of critiques of the subject for those who retain a sense of moral and political responsibilities that must be accepted or denied. Unlike Hume's "power," "force," and "energy," all of which have been tinted by aesthetic, economic, and other discourses, "agency" allows us to trace contemporary debates and anxieties to their origins in very different historical circumstances, and so to reflect on the genealogy of the beliefs by which we come to accept our places in history.

I am grateful for financial support I have received at Yale in the form of yearlong Lurcy and Morse Fellowships, and for research grants from Yale's Council for West European Studies, Enders Foundation, and Griswold Foundation. I also thank the staff librarians who have helped me in the libraries at Yale, the Olin Library at Cornell, Harvard's Houghton Library, the New York Public Library, and the Bodleian Library at Oxford. Parts of Chapter 1 appeared in *ELH* as "The Fall of Robespierre and the Sublime Machine of Agency," © 1996, The Johns Hopkins University Press, and are reprinted by permission; parts of Chapter 2 appeared in *Studies in Romanticism* as "Action in *The Borderers*," and are reprinted by permission of the Trustees of Boston University; parts of Chapter 4 appeared in *Texas Studies in Literature and Language* as "Strange Flesh: Shelley and the Performance of Skepticism," and are reprinted by permission of the University of Texas Press.

Many people have helped with the troubles this project has given me. My first debt is to Birgit Baldwin. Early versions of this book benefited from the advice of Alan Bewell, Leslie Brisman, Peter Brooks, Nora Crook, Paul Fry, Cyrus Hamlin, Geoffrey Hartman, David Kaufmann,

Alan Liu, David Marshall, Reeve Parker, and Donald Reiman. In its final stages, the project was sustained by generous criticism from Kevis Goodman, Alison Hickey, Victor Luftig, and Blakey Vermeule. The book might never have been finished without the support of my wife, Margaret Homans, to whom I dedicate it with love.

WILLIAM JEWETT

Guilford, Connecticut

Fatal Autonomy

Introduction

Romantic drama will not tell you what you need to know in order to act in this world. It can, however, make you intimate with that need; that is what it did for the poets who taught the value of such intimations. By locating that preoccupation of British Romanticism at the intersection of drama and moral inquiry, this book seeks to reverse the process by which the canonization of High Romanticism has effaced a constellation of anxieties from which some of our tradition's most valued writings emerged. To the extent that we remain in the grip of those anxieties, however, my literary-historical argument does double service as a theoretical exploration. My larger contention is that the minor canon of Romantic drama offers an opportunity to recover from one of the most volatile political moments in our cultural history some of our tradition's most sophisticated inquiries into the underpinnings of human action. Stephen Booth has remarked that "theories of the nature of tragedy are more important to us than theories of the nature of other things because theories of tragedy keep us from facing tragedy itself."[1] I see the plays written by the major Romantic poets as powerful and covertly influential efforts to explore the difficulty of "facing tragedy itself" and to trace the moral and political consequences of that difficulty. In this book I offer no theory of tragedy; I attempt to show how particular tragedies draw their restless energy from the moral and political anxieties that theories of tragedy put to rest.

1. Stephen Booth, *King Lear, Macbeth, Indefinition, and Tragedy* (New Haven: Yale University Press, 1983) 84.

My argument isolates a line of Romanticism that might be called "paratheoretical" in its focus on what compels people to adopt theories that compel them to act. "Romantic" appears in my title less as a blanket term for a period than as a name for the inclination within that period to probe the shadowy regions of moral life where discursive accounts of agency begin to work unanticipated effects. My readings begin to chart those regions by focusing on aspects of Romantic drama that respond to the tradition of informal moral inquiry in which Hazlitt, whose *View of the English Stage* is the most prominent survey of the theater by a contemporary, began his career as the author of an anonymous *Essay on the Principles of Human Action*. In that climate of opinion, even so thoroughgoing a skeptic as Sir William Drummond could judge Thomas Reid, founder of common sense philosophy and author of *Essays on the Active Powers of Man*, to be "a writer more profound than Kant."[2] This was also the intellectual milieu into which Coleridge sought to import the Kantian defense of "the autonomy of the will."[3] Readers have sometimes mistaken the tone of Coleridge's Kantianism in their haste to share Thomas Carlyle's despair over the droning intricacies of "omject" and "sumject," and it is partly as a result of such miscalculations that critics have failed to situate the period's dramatic writing in the line of practical moral reflection within which a term like "autonomy" would ultimately attain its modern currency. One purpose of this book is to show how the major Romantics used their plays to submit such apparently formal terms as "the principles of human action," "active powers," and "autonomy" to a kind of reality testing that imparted to their moral perplexities some of the political charge that characterized the popular theater. They knew better than we do how seldom literature's moral and political powers reach us in the form of propositional knowledge, and how even that small portion of knowledge can be homogenized by the formalisms of moral philosophy or compromised by the volatility of political theory. The authors of these plays seek to intimate how literary power entwines itself with the languages in which we explain to ourselves our moral and political beliefs to form the very fabric of our habits of thought and action—that is, of our characters.

The importance of what these plays can show us about moral and

---

2. William Drummond, *Academical Questions* (London, 1805) 381.
3. Coleridge, *Biographia Literaria*, in *Collected Works*, 7.1:154.

political agency has been overlooked, in some part because of the vagueness of the term "Romantic drama." Albert Guérard once praised Wordsworth's tragedy *The Borderers* as "one of the few satisfactory rejections of Romantic individualism," and it is not hard to imagine a text described in that way offering something of interest to the historian of moral discourses.[4] But will we really find in *The Borderers* anything of power that can also be found in other specimens of the genre? Do we really need "Romantic drama," and if so, what for? In this book I assume that an answer can be given only in the particulars of texts closely read. These texts examine moral and political problems of agency that arise from the conflict, or mutual limitation, of two generic features of drama that bring tragedy into a special relation with skeptical philosophy. Drama can facilitate skeptical thinking by assigning arguments to a variety of competing dramatic voices; but these voices must always be assigned to persons with bodies, real or imagined, and those bodies can always make demands on us that threaten the skeptical suspension of judgment. Problems in the representation of human agency mark the place where these two features meet.

A few examples might help to clarify the ways in which I do, and do not draw on philosophical traditions of moral inquiry. When Shelley declares that he wrote Beatrice Cenci's speeches to be delivered by the actress Eliza O'Neill, I am less interested in what Shelley knew of O'Neill's acting than in how his attempt to imagine it was conditioned by his compulsive reading in "Locke, Hume, Reid & whatever metaphysics came my way."[5] I do not mean to imply that when Shelley says "O'Neill," I strain to hear "Locke, Hume, Reid," for while the discourses of "metaphysics" may provide a useful framework for understanding Shelley's *concept* of the body, they will not help to describe the *attitude* toward bodies on stage that shaped his practice as a dramatist. I make no sustained attempt, then, to legitimate my readings, or the texts I read, by placing them explicitly within philosophical traditions. (In Part Two, however, I do keep my readings within the orbit of problems addressed by David Hume.) Rather, I try to weigh the lasting effect on each poet of the seemingly pervasive atmosphere of obstinate questioning in which Wordsworth describes himself "Dragging all pre-

---

4. Albert Guérard, "Prometheus and the Aeolian Lyre," *Yale Review* 33 (1944): 491.
5. Shelley, *The Letters of Percy Bysshe Shelley*, ed. Frederick L. Jones (Oxford: Clarendon Press, 1964) 1:303.

cepts, judgments, maxims, creeds, / Like culprits to the bar" (*Prelude* 1850 11:294–95).[6] When Wordsworth expressed, in the first version of that passage, his hope that "some dramatic story may afford / Shapes livelier to convey to thee, my friend, / What then I learned" (1805 10:878–80), he knew, as his "friend" Coleridge knew, that he had already summoned such shapes to act out those moral perplexities in *The Borderers*. Some critics have, accordingly, enshrined such perplexities as the deepest truths to which Wordsworth can lead us; but that is no more honest than to dismiss them as a temporary aberration.[7] Such value judgments ought to depend upon what can be learned by pondering the link Wordsworth makes between his conviction that he is looking back on moral perplexities and his desire to write drama. Some version of that link can be found in each of the poets I consider, all of whom drew upon such obstinate questionings as a source of poetic power only to find their misgivings pushing them toward dramatic form.

I have chosen not to emphasize the relations between this largely unperformed canon of plays and the theatrical world of early nineteenth-century London. That *demimonde,* which has held an enduring fascination in popular culture but which has until recently been neglected as a topic of serious literary research, might prove an invaluable resource for a study hoping to situate Romanticism's dramatic pretensions within a wider range of social phenomena. Others are better equipped to write that work than I. The poets I consider certainly thought about the skills of specific players and about the conventions dictated by the huge patent theaters when they contemplated yielding their words to the public embodiment projected by dramatic form. The prospect of seeing their characters take shape as autonomous persons loomed large among the anxieties stirred by the work of writing plays. But experts in other fields have now written at length about the culture of the Regency theater, and I could not hope to deepen our knowledge of these texts by proceeding directly on that front. For similar reasons, I do not undertake in this book a survey of Romantic drama in all its

---

6. All passages from *The Prelude* are quoted from the edition of Jonathan Wordsworth, M. H. Abrams, and Stephen Gill (New York: Norton, 1979), and come from the 1805 text unless otherwise noted.

7. See, for example, David Collings, *Wordsworthian Errancies: The Poetics of Cultural Dismemberment* (Baltimore: Johns Hopkins University Press, 1994).

Introduction

variety, a task begun by a number of scholars over the past decade.[8] My subject is at once wider, taking in broad moral and political issues of considerable significance for all kinds of writing in the Romantic period, and far narrower, being deliberately confined to claims that can be staked on particular texts.

The gap this book aims to fill is not, then, a matter of texts that have been overlooked, but of problems that have not been seen in those texts. My work bears few resemblances to a genre study such as Alan Richardson's *A Mental Theater: Poetic Drama and Consciousness in the Romantic Age* (1988), which remains, in the face of stiff competition, the most intelligent survey of the field. It is still less likely to be mistaken for an overview of the moral positions defended by the major figures of Romanticism; many years will pass before there can be a serious challenge to Laurence Lockridge's mapping of that terrain in *The Ethics of Romanticism* (1989). Although my project is contiguous with Richardson's and Lockridge's, it attempts to achieve breadth of scope by following out the ramifications of a single, specific problem: the fact that the poets accepted as the major voices of the Romantic self devoted their energies, at crucial turning points in their careers, to writing plays that complicate, contest, disrupt, anatomize, and otherwise render strange and unacceptable the routines by which people stake their conceptions of self upon their capacities to act. This oddity poses a vast problem of cultural diagnosis that entails a more limited task of critical description and analysis. I approach that critical task by explaining how assumptions and beliefs about such things as intentions, purposes, habits, motives, desires, constraints, and compulsions typically lead, in Romantic drama, to situations that exceed or defy routine ways of explaining how people do things.

I do not think the study of literature can either substantiate or disconfirm particular theories of agency. Anthony Giddens offers what is to my mind the most empirically plausible account of human agency; Paul Smith has done the most to explain postmodern theory's dissatisfaction with such accounts. The notion that literature is good for spinning such theories stems, I suspect, from the mistake of seeing the literary topos

---

8. Marilyn Gaull's *English Romanticism: The Human Context* (New York: Norton, 1988) contains an accessible survey (80–108) of the period's theater; Joseph W. Donohue's 1970 study *Dramatic Character in the English Romantic Age* remains exemplary in its integration of cultural and textual inquiry.

of uncertain agency as a pledge to solve problems that are, for most writers, not problems at all but opportunities. The critic who searches literature for such solutions is bound to end up disappointed with literature and anxious to conceal that disappointment—especially if his subject is Romantic drama, which has consistently been judged on the basis of exaggerated estimates, both high and low, of the period's understanding and presentation of action.[9] The tradition of dismissing Romantic drama as devoid of action, and of any serious understanding of that lack, has been overcompensated for by admiration of its texts as political "interventions" and of its audiences (especially when rioting, instead of watching plays) as powerfully "revolutionary."[10] That critics should want plays and their readings of them to count as actions, like the actions that plays stage, follows in part from the impatience one is bound to feel with one's own willingness to sit idly by as (say) Count Cenci torments his daughter. To damn oneself for such "passivity" is to embrace a radical narrowing of the range of what might count as "activity," a narrowing that the plays' authors studiously avoid. That studious avoidance of reduction is what I find valuable in these texts: valuable in a scholarly sense, for the fresh views the texts afford of their poets' more canonical writings; but valuable also in a moral sense, for the power with which they are able not merely to solve (or dismiss) but to focus attention on puzzles about human agency and on the effects of our puzzlement.

Debates about agency in contemporary theory typically fend off that puzzlement by observing a clean distinction between two conceptions of history: history as the sum of things that have actually happened, and history as an anthology of all the stories that have been told about who did those things. The distinction is observed by idealists and materialists alike, the former using it to shore up their claim to literary

---

9. Recent studies have only given further confirmation to Richard Fletcher's observation that "criticism of and complaints about Romantic drama depend in general on some variant remark about its lack of dramatic action, the absence in it of realism, and the like"; see Fletcher, *English Romantic Drama: A Critical History* (New York: Exposition, 1966) 13.

10. See Elaine Hadley, "The Old Price Wars: Melodramatizing the Public Sphere in Early-Nineteenth-Century England," *PMLA* 107 (1992): 524–37, and Gillian Russell, "Playing at Revolution: The Politics of the O. P. Riots of 1809," *Theatre Notebook* 44 (1990): 16–26. A sophisticated and useful history of the Old Price Wars is available in Marc Baer, *Theatre and Disorder in Late Georgian London* (New York: Oxford University Press, 1992).

Introduction

power, the latter using it to cement their claim to objective truth. A good example can be found in Perry Anderson's attempt to adjudicate between Louis Althusser and E. P. Thompson in their debate over the place of political agents in larger historical patterns. In order to secure an objective analysis, Anderson wants to put aside the question of the two writers' very different styles; yet he cannot help including in his analysis a discussion of rhetorical motives. In summarizing Thompson's arguments, Anderson demotes such pragmatic issues below theory even as he calls attention to Thompson's tendency to take different stances on a single issue in writing for different audiences:

> In *The Making of the English Working Class,* Thompson sought to uphold the creative activity and autonomy of English Radicalism against economic historians or sociologists bent on reducing the early working class to a passive object of industrialization. In "The Peculiarities of the English," he is concerned to defend the record of Left Labourism, by appealing for greater understanding of the ungovernable weight of circumstances compressing its capacity for action. The political intention is honourable in both cases. But when allowance has been made for it, the theoretical discrepancy remains insurmountable.[11]

Anderson's admission that theory can be shaped by "political intention" should be unsurprising in a book called *Arguments within English Marxism*. But it surprises Anderson into issuing a blanket disclaimer to his review of Thompson's arguments: "The part of agency in history cannot be adjusted ad hoc to fit particular forensic purposes." Anderson wants to treat "the part of agency in history" as one would treat demographic statistics or circulation numbers, because "agency" names for him an objectively ascertainable datum that had better not be falsified. But his own analysis shows that agency is not so readily categorized. His objection demands a counterobjection: What if forensic purposes are indeed always what determines the part of agency in history? What if that is just what historical agency *is:* a rhetorical device? For what we take to be *descriptions* of agency may indeed work more fundamentally as *ascriptions* of agency, preceding rather than following the establishment of knowledge about how history is made.

Anthony Appiah argues that such theoretical postulates as structural determination and subjective agency do not, in fact, combine in dy-

---

11. Perry Anderson, *Arguments Within English Marxism* (London: NLB, 1980) 48.

namic tension to organize the unfolding of history or even of historical knowledge, but rather organize different narratives that serve different purposes. "The understanding of agents and texts through the language of the subject," he writes, "is guided by different interests from the understanding that operates in the language of social structure, [and] these different interests make different idealizations appropriate, different falsehoods tolerable." Appiah mentions the recent argument that "in understanding people as intentional systems—as having the beliefs, desires, intentions, and other propositional attitudes of common sense psychology—we make a certain projection of rationality. We ascribe beliefs and desires to people in such a way as to 'make-rational' their acts."[12] Appiah treats this ascription of rationality as an idealization: rationality is something we grant, for example, to all fictional characters, until we are led to think otherwise. Outside the world of literature, however, rationality is merely what Appiah calls a "tolerable falsehood," a fiction we are willing to accept in the interest of behaving consistently with what ordinary language presumes about acting subjects. Indeed, we are even willing to suspend the discourse of the rational subject in cases—insanity pleas, for instance—in which the falsehood is no longer tolerable. The implication is that persons are constituted as agents neither truly nor falsely, only by other persons who grant them that status and who are in turn marked as agents by that ability to confer the status of agent.[13]

The value of Appiah's argument lies in the revelation that admitting the social production of agency, or recognizing its rhetorical functioning as the underpinning of a humanist discourse, does not necessarily tip the scales from subject to structure: it merely shows that there are no scales. Steven E. Cole has discerned this reciprocal constitution of agency in none other than Coleridge, who argues, in Cole's formulation, that "personhood is itself constituted by first, the capacity to recognize others as agents capable of having their behavior motivated by

---

12. Anthony Appiah, "Tolerable Falsehoods: Agency and the Interests of Theory," in *Consequences of Theory*, ed. Jonathan Arac and Barbara Johnson (Baltimore: Johns Hopkins University Press, 1991) 79, 75. See also Daniel C. Dennett, *The Intentional Stance* (Cambridge: MIT Press, 1989) for a fuller account of how people "decide to treat the object whose behavior is to be predicted as a rational agent" (17).

13. My thinking about this conception of agency follows from my having read, many years ago, H. L. A. Hart's essay "The Ascription of Responsibility and Rights," *Proceedings of the Aristotelian Society* 49 (1949): 171–94.

Introduction

ends, and second, the belief that others are similarly capable of recognizing my own motivation by ends rather than means."[14] Stanley Cavell offers a similar definition that can serve as a reminder of what was lacking in Appiah's discussion of "people as intentional systems," and of the way in which drama fills that lack. "Being human is the power to grant being human," Cavell writes; "Something about flesh and blood elicits this grant from us, and something about flesh and blood can also repel it."[15] Romantic drama does not merely offer puzzles of agency in the form of human bodies; it shows us our puzzlement *as* our bodies.

Romantic drama, then, helps us to see in its actual proportions what Cavell calls "flesh and blood." Wyndham Lewis once argued, in a somewhat sloppy recital of Nietzschean *ressentiment*, that weak people like tragedy because it opposes real action. He makes his point with the example of *Othello:* "Iago is the *small* destroyer, the eternal Charlie Chaplin figure of human myth, the gods on his side, their instrument in the struggle with the hero. . . . He is the ideal *little man* with the sling and the stone. Othello is the ideal human galleon, twenty storeys high, with his head in the clouds, that the little can vanquish."[16] Iago is little; we can choose to be little; perhaps we, too, will get our way. Why not just leave Othello to lumber along to his death? One can only respond that what Lewis objects to is not tragedy; and Romanticism plays a large part in what allows us to make that response. Tragedy shows Othello as neither too little, nor too big, but just my size. I can say this, however, only because Shakespeare belongs, for me, to a tradition that also includes Wordsworth. As Lionel Trilling once remarked, it is Wordsworth's valuing of the ordinary, his "passionate insistence on being, even at a very low level of consciousness, pride, and assertiveness, as well as at the highest level of quasi-mystic intensity, that validates a conception of tragedy, and a conception of heroism."[17] The critical tradition that sees Romantic drama as "the opponent of action"

---

14. Steven E. Cole, "The Logic of Personhood: Coleridge and the Social Production of Agency," *Studies in Romanticism* 30 (1991): 101–2.
15. Stanley Cavell, *The Claim of Reason: Wittgenstein, Skepticism, Morality, and Tragedy* (New York: Oxford University Press, 1979) 397.
16. Wyndham Lewis, *The Lion and the Fox: The Role of the Hero in the Plays of Shakespeare* (London: Grant Richards, 1927) 189; ellipsis and italics in the original.
17. Lionel Trilling, "Wordsworth and the Rabbis," in *The Opposing Self* (New York: Viking, 1955) 147.

shares with Lewis's bluster the conviction that tragic action must be somehow bigger than our ordinary affairs. It is the distinguishing and disturbing recognition of Romantic drama that such is not the case, and never was.

This book inevitably shares some of the textual, generic, and historical concerns of Renaissance New Historicism, which has attained an undisputed hegemony, at least in English departments, as a model for the study of drama. Renaissance New Historicism, with its efforts to locate individual agents within systematic accounts of "discourse" and "social energy," has been very explicit about questions of agency. In a criticism that seeks to generalize a mode of historical responsibility for literary texts, figures of uncertain agency tend to appear in moments when the critic turns back on his method to wonder why he has been so preoccupied with ascribing agency to linguistic constructs embedded in historical contexts. Louis Montrose diagnoses the problem as a professional anxiety:

> Many of those who profess "the Humanities" see themselves and their calling as threatened by marginalization within a system of higher education increasingly geared to the provision of highly specialized technological and preprofessional training. In its anti-reflectionism, its shift of emphasis from the formal analysis of verbal *artifacts* to the ideological analysis of discursive *practices,* its refusal to observe strict and fixed boundaries between literary texts and critical texts, the emergent historical orientation in literary studies is pervasively concerned with writing as a mode of *action.* I do not believe that it compromises the intellectual seriousness of this concern to see it as impelled by a questioning of our very capacity for action— by a nagging sense of professional, institutional, and political impotence.[18]

Montrose suggests that we rummage through the archive in search of texts that exemplify the active power of words because we have no other way of confirming our hope that our own words might help *us* act. That hope, we feel, is thrown into doubt by the embeddedness of writing in social contexts that render all our beliefs about autonomy uncertain—as though words could act apart from social contexts! Montrose concludes by tempering this uncertainty with a hope for a qualified critical agency, one that would give him something to be

18. Louis Montrose, "The Elizabethan Subject and the Spenserian Text," in *Literary Theory / Renaissance Texts,* ed. Patricia Parker and David Quint (Baltimore: Johns Hopkins University Press, 1986) 332.

responsible for: "in reflecting upon my own practice . . . I am aware of a strong stake, not in any illusion of individual autonomy but in the possibilities for limited and localized agency within the regime of power and knowledge that at once sustains and constrains us" (333). The desire to discover one's own mode of action in texts hauled up from the archive, and to capture something of that possibility for action in one's own writing, is bravely acknowledged. The stakes are high, but the efficacy of the game remains uncertain.

Alan Liu sees the same problem not in Renaissance New Historicism but in Romantic studies. His classic essay "The Power of Formalism: The New Historicism" draws attention to what Liu calls "a genuinely undecidable crux":

> Do literary or even historical subjects *do* anything? Does the plural movement of a carnival or a satire, for example, truly *subvert* dominant authority? Or to cite the so-called "escape-valve" theory, does the dominant merely release a little gas through the Bakhtinian "material body lower stratum," thus acknowledging movement within itself but also containing that movement? Indeed, what kind of movement is subversion anyway— the single action still allowed in a New Historicist universe become like a gigantic, too-quiet house within which, somewhere, in one of the walls, perhaps, insects chew? Given New Historicism's prejudice for synchronic structure—for the paradigmatic moment-in-time in which the whole pattern of historical context may be gazed at in rapt stasis—is any action conceivable at all?[19]

Liu nicely parodies the attractive openness of New Historicist campaigns to void the category of agency by avoiding assertions (which necessarily misassign agency) in favor of rhetorical questions that tumble out in a spectacle of infinite productivity. But his Swiftian vision of historical action reduced to flatulence expresses a fear, visible throughout the tradition of critical commentary on Romantic drama, that certain modes of historicist thought may have the power to destroy the historical subject's ability even to *conceive* action and, in doing so, may eliminate the first condition of action itself. Liu evokes that fear to justify his call for a change in the direction of research, which he insists must undertake the study of "action *qua* action—of action, that is, seen

---

19. Alan Liu, "The Power of Formalism: The New Historicism," *ELH* 56 (1989): 734.

as an alternate ground of explanation definitive of what we mean by identities and their coercive representations" (735). Liu's rejection of "the purely theatrical 'action' of New Historicist unrealpolitik" resembles Hamlet's criticism of the Players in its implication that to be convinced that all possibilities for action are established only within a self-enclosed space of representation is to forfeit both the understanding and the capability of "action *qua* action." But it implies that we should then search for something we may have no means of finding: the evidence we require to substantiate the faith that action can occur outside the space of representation.

Liu does, however, take a significant step in tracing the origin of such apparently debilitating critical constructs as "Foucault's agentless archive" and "New Historicism's paradigms uncertain in their Subject and Action." He locates this origin "in the Romantic period between the classic and symbolist: the period in which history originally became a *historicism*":

> Caught in the flux of such historicist and literary transition, the very notion of the Subject had to be rethought in the shape of that strangely unmotivated or unconsciously motivated being haunting both literary and historiographical Romanticism: the Folk with its post-Hegelian Spirit. So, too —as demonstrated in England's self-consciously defensive posture during the invasion scares of the Napoleonic wars or in such excruciatingly inactive characters as Mortimer in Wordsworth's *Borderers*—Action had to be rethought. Action, as Michelet, Burckhardt and other historicists demonstrated, occurred on many quieter, social fronts flanking the obvious political or military event. (738)

Liu views the genesis of historicist thought, then and now, as the birth and rebirth of a power to recognize newly capacious categories of subjectivity and agency. Historicism thus appears to underwrite enabling forms of language born of the very debilitation brought on by acknowledging the weight of history. Liu's qualified hope matches Montrose's, and the realization of possibilities for action is similarly uncertain in both critics. But the Wordsworthian example cited by Liu at least shows us where to look for the satisfaction of Montrose's longing for "possibilities for limited and localized agency" that might be realized in a historicism capable of counteracting the crushing weight of historical reflection. Although this book is by no means conceived as a stage in Liu's pursuit of "action *qua* action," I do offer Romantic drama as a

Introduction

glass in which we can see how we come upon empowering and disempowering beliefs about what we can do.

Two things we feel sure we can do are read and go to the theater. But do we know what we are doing when we do these things? Alexander Welsh, having raised a similar question in his 1963 study *The Hero of the Waverley Novels*, allowed his detailed commentary on Walter Scott's passive heroes to imply an answer. "Reading itself is a passive act," Welsh writes, "more so than aural attention to the same narrative, and presumably much more so than attending 'old romance' expressly intended for the ear. Possibly readers of the long prose narrative by definition enjoy fancying themselves acted upon rather than acting." Such an argument makes a nice match for Welsh's brilliant exposition of Scott's "proper heroes" and of their submissive postures toward "prudence and the superiority of civil society." The problem examined in this book is related to Welsh's study of Scott's passive heroes, one of whom (Nigel Olifaunt) significantly berates himself, with the phrase Wordsworth used to dismiss Coleridge's Ancient Mariner, as "a thing never acting but perpetually acted upon."[20] Welsh's suggestion that our relation to culture replicates our willingness to submit to the liberal state is a provocative one. But what might that hypothesis allow us to conclude about the passivity or activity engendered by drama (whether viewed in the theater or read in the closet) and thus, presumably, sought after in dramatic heroes?

Stanley Cavell, to whom the present study is indebted in a number of ways, has devoted much effort to unraveling that question. Cavell's famous essay on *King Lear* explains our connection with dramatic characters in terms of our inhabiting their time, as we cannot inhabit the time of characters in narrative. His arguments may help to explain why the Romantic poets chose to write plays rather than novels. A contemporary review of Coleridge's tragedy *Remorse* complained that its plot was "sufficiently long and complicated to form the basis of a novel in four volumes"; why, then, did Coleridge not put it to that use?[21] Attempts have been made to answer such questions with infor-

---

20. Alexander Welsh, *The Hero of the Waverley Novels* (New Haven: Yale University Press, 1963) 57; compare Wordsworth's 1800 "Note on the Ancient Mariner," cited below, 82.

21. *The Christian Observer*, quoted from *The Romantics Reviewed: Contemporary Reviews of British Romantic Writers*, ed. Donald H. Reiman (New York: Garland, 1972) A:1:287.

mation about the lives of the poets and about the culture in which they wrote, but these accounts tell us little about what remains compelling in their choice of drama or about what we would miss had they chosen otherwise. Cavell offers a very different approach in his notion that drama produces a freedom *from* action that invites theater audiences (and readers of drama) to take onto themselves the burden of tragedy:

> Kant tells us that man lives in two worlds, in one of which he is free and in the other determined. It is as if in a theater these two worlds are faced off against one another, in their intimacy and their mutual inaccessibility. The audience is free—of the circumstance and passion of the characters, but that freedom cannot reach the arena in which it could become effective. The actors are determined—not because their words and actions are dictated and their future sealed, but because, if the dramatist has really peopled a world, the characters are exercising all the freedom at their command, and specifically failing to. Specifically; not exercising or ceding it once and for all. They are, in a word, men and women; and our liabilities in responding to them are nothing other than our liabilities in responding to any person—rejection, brutality, sentimentality, indifference, the relief and the terror in finding courage, the ironies of human wishes.[22]

Acknowledging one's absention from the sphere of agency, in Cavell's account, prepares one to enter that sphere: not because that acknowledgment relieves one from action, but because it *is* an action, the first action, from which all else follows.

Cavell's emphasis on an audience's (or reader's) lack of agency pointedly denies the escapist idea of theater voiced by the Shelley character who compares stage illusions to "skiey visions in a solemn dream, / From which men wake as from a Paradise / And draw new strength to tread the thorns of life"; it is far closer to what Keats looked for in "Sitting Down to Read King Lear Once Again": "when I am consumed in the fire, / Give me new phoenix wings to fly at my desire." The theatrical experience that appears to offer an escape from the sphere of agency is, for Cavell, actually an intensification: "The conditions of theater literalize the conditions we exact for existence outside—hid-

22. Stanley Cavell, "The Avoidance of Love: A Reading of *King Lear,*" in *Disowning Knowledge in Six Plays of Shakespeare* (New York: Cambridge University Press, 1987) 88–89.

Introduction

denness, silence, isolation—hence make that existence plain. Theater does not expect us simply to stop theatricalizing; it knows that we can theatricalize its conditions as we can theatricalize any others. But in giving us a place within which our hiddenness and silence and separation are accounted for, it gives us a chance to stop" (104). To stop seeking hiddenness, silence, and isolation is to stop avoiding the acknowledgment of human separateness, to recognize the solitary burden of action in such a way as to end one's solitude. Cavell draws from this recognition the moral that theater offers an experience of human solidarity grounded in nothing more than this separateness: "If I do nothing because there is nothing to do, where that means that I have given over the time and space in which action is mine and consequently that I am in awe before the fact that I cannot do and suffer what it is another's to do and suffer, then I confirm the final fact of our separateness. And that is the unity of our condition" (110).

The value of Cavell's humanist paradox is, I think, plain. I do not mean to impugn it, but rather to enhance it, by asking: *Whose* condition is thus unified? "Our condition," if we are to discover its unity as Cavell says, can only be ours to the extent that we are citizens of modern liberal polities. Such, at least, would be the answer of Richard Rorty, the foremost contemporary apologist for postromantic liberalism, hinting that what Cavell offers as a universal humanism is actually contingent on particular historical circumstances. Rorty would not take this to be a damning criticism, since his "fundamental premise" is that "a belief can still regulate action, can still be thought worth dying for, among people who are quite aware that this belief is caused by nothing deeper than contingent historical circumstance."[23] The criticism does, however, demand a further refinement of Cavell's position.

Since my subject is *Romantic* drama, I am interested in the contingencies that, in that period, lent a historically specific political charge to the surrender of agency in Cavell's theater. Those contingencies might be approached by considering what theatergoers in the early nineteenth century might have made of Thomas Nashe's remark that a crowd watching a play would, at least, not be hatching a rebellion.[24] Romanticists might object that rebellions were most likely to be hatched *by*

23. Richard Rorty, *Contingency, Irony, and Solidarity* (New York: Cambridge University Press, 1989) 189.
24. Cited in Stephen Greenblatt, *Shakespearean Negotiations: The Circulation of Social Energy in Renaissance England* (Berkeley: University of California Press, 1988) 18.

theater audiences, offering the 1809 Old Price Riots at Covent Garden as a case in point. But if the O. P. Riots did anything in venting the rage of that revolutionary class the bourgeoisie, they contained rather than liberated political agency, allowing theatergoers to inflict upon the theater the same submission to contractual obligation they themselves might have been practicing within the theater. How are we to weigh the relative progressiveness of the riot at the opening of the new Covent Garden in 1809 against what the audience did not do that night—sit and watch a performance of Kemble's *Macbeth*, the most famous regicide play of this politically volatile period?[25]

The balance tips only in the eyes of those who are sure that one way of spending time counts as political action while another does not. The poets considered in this book were not so sure. The Romantic poets wrote and read dramas to understand how we come to take others, and ourselves, as moral and political agents, and why we sometimes refuse to do so. For drama, by countering the ironic dispersion of voices with the solidity of bodies on stage, is able to demonstrate, as neither narrative nor lyric can, the possibility of turning our passive consumption of literature into a means of recovering a sense of ourselves as practical agents. The Romantic poets may have written plays to make money, or to achieve fame, or to reform the English stage. But the only motive that should matter is their wish—a wish they invite their readers to share—to probe, and to tap, literature's resources for bringing people to an awareness of their active powers, of their origins and limitations. Writers in the later nineteenth century came to develop these resources most fully in genres other than drama—primarily the novel—but drama offers the most direct way of discovering how these writers arrived at an awareness of literature's power to shape beliefs about the power to act. It is impossible to say why other genres (and forms of culture other than literary) came to seem better for this purpose without considering what was done, and what could not be done, in poetic drama.

The mid-eighteenth-century novel, as Catherine Gallagher argues, met a range of social needs by allowing its readers to *practice* having an emotional life, allowing readers to sympathize with disembodied

25. Mary Jacobus gives an excellent and wide-ranging account of the politics of the Romantic Macbeth in " 'That Great Stage Where Senators Perform': *Macbeth* and the Politics of Romantic Theater," *Studies in Romanticism* 22 (1983): 353–87; Jonathan Bate examines the narrower role of *Macbeth* in the O. P. Riots in *Shakespearean Constitutions: Politics, Theatre, Criticism 1730–1830* (Oxford: Clarendon Press, 1989) 42–45.

persons as they could not sympathize with real people.[26] Gallagher asks why it should have been *fictional* persons that were created to arrange this effect. My question is what difference it makes to have such fictional persons live not in narrative but on stage, where they have, or speak from, or are, or become, *bodies*. In Gallagher's account, the conditional emotions of the novel reader become available precisely because fictional persons have no bodies; drama complicates that account by making us ask what emotions become available when these fictional persons *do* have bodies. Theatergoers, unlike readers of novels, experience *in their own persons* the collective voluntary submission to civil society that renders them, for a time, not agents; they give up their positive freedom to do as they please so that they may be protected from the aggressions of those on the stage. The same holds true for those who merely read drama, and the major Romantic poets found no disadvantage in having to oblige readers to ask themselves, as theater audiences need not ask, what it means to experience in one's own person.

In attempting to identify and explain agency problems, I look primarily at poetic and rhetorical textures, and secondarily at the logic of plots, with an eye to the pragmatic effects of characters' unstated beliefs. In doing so, I have tried, to the extent that it is possible, to avoid using swatches of poetry to work through my own beliefs, some of which I can state and some of which I cannot. This is not so much a method as an attempt to heed what I take to be warnings encoded in the texts lying open before me, without making myself an unwitting dupe of Jerome McGann's "Romantic Ideology." The balancing act is more challenging than it may appear, for there is every reason to want to endorse what one's reading makes attractive without stopping to consider the needs served by such endorsements. Marxist and deconstructive critics have no particular reason to ask themselves what needs are met by affirming, as Marx did, that "men make their own history, but not in circumstances of their own choosing" or by claiming, as Nietzsche did, that "the 'doer' is merely a fiction added to the deed."[27] But the need for phrases that excuse (rather than resolve) ambi-

---

26. See Catherine Gallagher, *Nobody's Story: The Vanishing Acts of Women Writers in the Marketplace* (Berkeley: University of California Press, 1994), chap. 4, esp. 170–71.

27. Karl Marx, *The Eighteenth Brumaire of Louis Bonaparte*, quoted from *The Marx-Engels Reader*, ed. Robert C. Tucker (New York: Norton, 1978) 595 (translation slightly modified); Friedrich Nietzsche, *The Genealogy of Morals*, chap. 13, trans. Francis Golffing (Garden City: Doubleday, 1956), 178.

guities in the assignment of agency looms large in critical discourse, and we ignore it at our peril. Such, at least, is the warning I have heard in the texts I consider here. I doubt that any of the writers conventionally called Romantic lacked the awareness conveyed in Marx's pronouncement, or Nietzsche's; but the need answered differently by those two theories of agency prompted another *kind* of response among the British romantics. It gave rise to complex dramatic structures hardly less intelligent, provocative, or influential—though certainly less well known—than the theories of Marx, Nietzsche, and the numerous traditions founded in their names. This book, then, begins a genealogy of contemporary debates about agency by showing how the plays of the major Romantic poets respond to the same pressures and anxieties that continue to drive much recent theorizing. Yet even the subtlest theoretical explorations of agency will blind us if we expect literary texts to argue or instantiate claims about agency. In this book I treat that temptation as evidence not of a wish to understand but of a desire to ward off anxieties that Romantic drama seeks to arouse and sustain. Marx and Nietzsche, seen from within the tradition of Romantic drama, seem to tell us less about the nature of action than about the conflicted emotions of longing and self-reproach that resonate in their verdicts on agency: to remind oneself (with Marx) that one's acts are conditioned is to admit one's wish that it were not so, while to regret (with Nietzsche) the subjective limits we place on action is to acknowledge the compulsion to submit to those limits. These emotions elicit a sententious wisdom that forecloses the skepticism it intimates. Romantic drama aims to forestall such wisdom, encouraging us not to assume the self-evidence of "history" or "the deed." In the place of such abstractions, it promotes an ethos of active reflection on the anxieties such plain speaking might cover over. But it goes one step further: by allowing one to suppose that "history" may not be the sum of human actions, or that "the deed" may be as fictional as the doer, Romantic drama shows *what would follow* if one were to sustain that kind of skepticism, the kind Marx, Nietzsche, and their heirs are compelled to bring to a halt.

My argument unfolds in two stages. Part One draws primarily on plays written by Wordsworth and Coleridge in the 1790s to examine the pressures of history upon familiar, routine, or inherited models of moral action. The early poetry of these writers is complicated by strug-

Introduction

gles to reconcile political aspirations with moral misgivings; such complications appear in their plays as puzzles about agency. Those puzzles lingered on to shape the moral agendas of their later work, but their immediate result was a dramatic literature of the morally anomalous, exhibiting a variety of ways in which agency can be decentered from individuals into collusions, compulsions, accidents, uncanninesses, conjurations, or spectacles. Part Two focuses the first generation's lessons about agency on a sequence of dramatic texts written by Byron and Shelley toward the end of their careers, in implicit dialogue with each other. The problem I address is the way in which dramatic form tests skeptical critiques of identity and agency, as they either facilitate and enhance, or impede and unravel, the forms of political agency each poet sought to develop by writing plays. My aim is to show how these plays, particularly their channeling of political debate through bodies on stage, might help pry open political problems in the larger canons of the two poets.

The two pieces of my argument sketch a beginning and an end for a Romanticism both like and unlike the period that organizes most teaching and research on these writers. The point is not to change that work by proving that Romantic drama is, after all, good. The point is to show that it was good *for something*, something we must care about deeply if we care about Romanticism.

Part One

TRAGIC AGENTS AND THE ORIGINS OF ROMANTICISM, 1794–1797

1

The Sublime Machine of History: *The Fall of Robespierre* and *Wat Tyler*

> There is something to be said, indeed, for the nature of the political machinery, for the whirling motion of the revolutionary wheel which has of late wrenched men's understandings almost asunder....
>
> —HAZLITT, "On Consistency of Opinion"

Some of Coleridge's most influential work originated in his special genius for making unwieldy social interactions—what Stephen Greenblatt has called "the circulation of social energy"—converge in the moral problems of individual persons. Every piece of language, Greenblatt reminds us, is at some level collectively produced; but dramatic language acknowledges the social currents on which it floats, as the language of the novel, whose reader "withdraws from the public world of affairs to the privacy of the hearth," need not. The closet dramas of Romanticism pose a special problem, however, for in them the dramatic openness to social energies is challenged by a withdrawal from the theatrical forum in which those energies circulate. Greenblatt reads Shakespeare to see how "collective beliefs and experiences" are transposed into "specially demarcated zones ... invested with the power to confer pleasure or excite interest or generate anxiety." Such transpositions are Coleridge's chosen specialty, and his mission begins on the public–private border straddled by closet drama.[1]

---

1. Greenblatt, *Shakespearean Negotiations* 4–7.

Coleridge writes with great density and complexity whenever he considers how public questions of political action intrude into the more private realms of moral and aesthetic decision. In an essay for *The Friend* (8 February 1810) he addressed the relation between political agency and the morality of art by considering a controversy that appears in his *Notebooks* as early as 1803:

> At Florence there is an unfinished bust of Brutus, by Michael Angelo, under which a Cardinal wrote the following distich:
>
>> Dum Bruti effigiem sculptor de marmore finxit,
>> In mentem sceleris venit, et abstinuit.
>> *As the Sculptor was forming the Effigy of Brutus, in marble, he recollected his act of guilt and refrained.*
>
> An English Nobleman, indignant at this distich, wrote immediately under it the following:
>
>> Brutum effinxisset sculptor, sed mente recursat
>> Multa viri virtus; sistit et obstupuit.
>> *The Sculptor would have framed a Brutus, but the vast and manifold virtue of the Man flashed upon his thought: he stopped and remained in astonished admiration.*

"Now which," he asked, "is the nobler and more moral Sentiment, the Italian Cardinal's or the English Nobleman's?"[2] The apparently rhetorical question subsumes several genuine questions of moral, political, and aesthetic judgment and challenges the reader to say which of these judgments is to be given priority. For the Italian cardinal, the main concern is Brutus's moral guilt; for the English nobleman, it is his political virtue. That conflict of values is staged as a contest of interpretations that debates not the value of Brutus's act but the meaning of a work of art. The significance of that work is found in the work its artist *did not do*—Michelangelo did not finish the bust—and each interpretation converts that nonaction into an (aesthetic) act that follows from, and expresses, a judgment either reversing or confirming the judgment that prompted Brutus's (moral or political) act. The epigram-

---

2. Coleridge, *The Friend*, in *Collected Works*, vol. 4, ed. Barbara E. Rooke (Princeton: Princeton University Press, 1969) 2:317–18; subsequent textural references are given in parentheses. For details on the bust, including its relation to the assassination of Alessandro de' Medici, see Charles de Tolnay, *Michelangelo: Sculptor, Painter, Architect* (Princeton: Princeton University Press, 1975) 61–63 and 212–13.

matic commentaries thus attempt to finish the unfinished artwork by accounting for the artist's agency according to the same criteria by which the artist is presumed to have accounted for the agency he failed, or declined, to commemorate.

Coleridge's use of this figure can be clarified by comparing another use to which it was put. Some thirty years later, Thomas Medwin used the Michelangelo touchstone in his attempt to explain why his friend Shelley had left his drama *Charles the First* incomplete. Medwin informs his Victorian readers that "the poet was not so great a republican at heart as Mrs. Shelley makes him out."[3] "Shelley could not reconcile his mind to the beheading of Charles," whom he considered, Medwin claims, "as the purest in morals, the most exemplary of husbands and fathers,—great in misfortune, a martyr in death" (342). Medwin's Shelley is a Stuart hagiographer unable to reconcile his newfound conservatism with his earlier work. (In 1819 Shelley had called Charles I "one of those chiefs of a conspiracy of privileged murderers and robbers whose impunity has been the consecration of crime.")[4] "He seemed tangled in an inextricable web of difficulties," Medwin deduces from the blurred manuscripts; "it was clear that he had formed no definite plan in his own mind, how to connect the links of the complicated yarn of events that led to that frightful catastrophe, or to justify it" (341). Shelley, it seems, was *unable* to reconstruct as dramatic necessity the events that led to Charles's tragic dénouement because he was *unwilling* to justify the course of history. Medwin thus takes Shelley's failure as a sign of moral nobility, and points his argument with Coleridge's example: "There is in the Uffizzi gallery, at Florence, an unfinished bust by Michael Angelo, of Brutus, on which is written an epigram, the point of which is, that the great sculptor wisely abandoned the task from disgust at the traitor; might not similar influences have raised an obstacle in the mind of Shelley, to the completion of his unwelcome undertaking?" (341). Medwin's interpretation does to Shelley's play what both epigrams do to Michelangelo's bust: it aims to complete the fragment by focusing its conflicting energies in a comfortingly univocal exemplum.

3. Thomas Medwin, *The Life of Percy Bysshe Shelley* (1847; repr. New York: Oxford University Press, 1913) 343; subsequent references are given in parentheses.
4. Shelley, *A Philosophical View of Reform*, quoted from *Shelley's Prose, or The Trumpet of a Prophecy*, ed. David Lee Clark (Albuquerque: University of New Mexico Press, 1954) 232.

Medwin's assurances, however, beg the question: Why did Shelley not convert his alleged disgust into a finished play of royalist sympathies? The analogy between a drama that can present a complete action from various points of view and a statue that can only monumentalize an agent suggests that a play becomes like a statue whenever it yields to the temptation of monumentalizing history. Shelley's failure to complete *Charles the First* can stand as evidence of his political wariness only because it exhibits his resistance to the monumentalism so pathetically evoked in the statuary conceit of "Ozymandias." Medwin's analogy suggests that Shelley refused to monumentalize his not-so-republican sympathies for the same reasons he declined to give a false monumental form to his former republican convictions: *Charles the First* is a fragment, and in Medwin's view a noble failure, because Shelley refused to turn history into a public monument of his private sympathies. Lucien Goldmann once described Pascal's *Pensées* as "achieved by inachievement"[5]; Medwin is saying that the "shattered visage" of *Charles the First* is peculiarly Shelley's achievement, its unreconciled confusions the best index of his inviolable integrity.

How does Coleridge's meditation on Michelangelo's Brutus, and on the web of moral, political, and aesthetic judgments woven around it, differ from Medwin's? Coleridge starts by focusing not on the artist's act but on the act of Brutus, as it is understood in the competing epigrams. He imagines the Cardinal thinking that a monument to Brutus might help to justify any action, provided its agent could imagine himself as Brutus. "If one man may be allowed to kill another because he thinks him a tyrant," Coleridge has the Cardinal reason, "religious or political phrenzy may stamp the name of tyrant on the best of kings: regicide will be justified under the pretence of tyrannicide, and Brutus be quoted as authority for the Clements and Ravillacs" (318). The Cardinal would maintain that the commandment "Thou shalt not kill" is more sound than the human judgment that presumes to tell kings from tyrants, vulnerable as that judgment is to "religious or political phrenzy." The Englishman, however, will not admit such special cases as evidence of a universal vulnerability of judgment. "No!" he objects; the killing of a tyrant is justified "not because the patriot *thinks* him a

---

5. Quoted from Marjorie Levinson, *The Romantic Fragment Poem: A Critique of a Form* (Chapel Hill: University of North Carolina Press, 1986) 6, which quotes from Thomas McFarland, *Romanticism and the Forms of Ruin* (Princeton: Princeton University Press, 1981) 3.

tyrant; but because he *knows* him to be so, and knows likewise, that the vilest of his slaves cannot deny the fact, that he has by violence raised himself above the laws of his country—because he knows that all good and wise men equally with himself abhor the fact!" (318). If it is denied that such communal values establish a clear distinction between tyrannicide and regicide, then, the Englishman would ask, as Coleridge asks: "*What* actions can be so different, that they may not be equally confounded?" (319).

Coleridge imagines this dispute to make a more general point. He has been arguing that our awareness of situation and circumstance keeps us from being confused by "apparent resemblances between the good action we were about to do and the bad one which might possibly be done in mistaken imitation of it"; for, "alter the circumstances and a similar set of motions may be repeated, but they are no longer the same or similar action" (316). The very thought of such confusion makes Coleridge as indignant as his imaginary Englishman: "As if an action could be either good or bad disjoined from its principle! as if it could be, in the christian and only proper sense of the word, an *action* at all, and not rather a mechanic series of lucky or unlucky motions!" (315).[6] The Cardinal has imagined a man who would commit a murder without first making the judgment that would make it count as an action. Such a murder, the Englishman would retort, is not a bad action but no action at all; the religious or political fanatic making the motions that *appear* to be those of an agent is not a bad man but no man. Such cases, then, do not call for the Cardinal's affected delicacy, for the unprincipled regicide is as little defensible as the unprincipled tyrant: "Do you hesitate to shoot a mad dog," Coleridge asks, "because it is not in your power to have him first tried and condemned at the Old Bailey?" (319).

The Cardinal's view of Michelangelo's Brutus is thus presented as exploiting the force of moral law to avoid recognizing a more fundamental political distinction that may be understood by anyone who can tell the human from the inhuman. For the Englishman, the ability to understand the virtue of Brutus's tyrannicide is a criterion for judging what counts as fully human, although Coleridge seems to suspect it may be only a criterion for judging what counts as genuinely English.

---

6. Coleridge's derisive words "lucky or unlucky" offer a loose thread that would be worth tugging at in the manner of Bernard Williams in *Moral Luck* (New York: Cambridge University Press, 1981) 20–39 or Dennett in *Elbow Room: The Varieties of Free Will Worth Wanting* (Cambridge: MIT Press, 1984) 92–100.

The function of art, and of its interpretation, is to make the more universal criterion available to consciousness; it is the ability of art to manifest the human fate of political autonomy that gives it the sublimity Michelangelo commemorated when the bust "flashed upon his thought" the inextricable bond between the human and the political, so that "he stopped and remained in astonished admiration."[7]

Coleridge concludes with a request "that the preceding may not be interpreted as my own settled judgement on the moral nature of Tyrannicide" (320). The firm convictions represented by the Cardinal and the Englishman (and by Michelangelo and Brutus) reveal a defensive hesitancy in Coleridge's anecdotal (rather than aphoristic) exposition. Coleridge may be backing away from what had seemed so certain because he secretly shares the hypocritical moralism with which he sees the Cardinal cloaking his political misgivings, or because he sees the Englishman's absolute certainty as culturally produced. But I think his hesitation is more likely to have stemmed from his awareness that the artifact he has been evaluating is not an *action* with a moral, political, or aesthetic agent, but an *assemblage* of materials, circumstances, interpretations, and reinterpretations produced not by a single agent but through the interaction and collaboration of many. The defaced bust that bears the name "Brutus" is a palimpsestic social text left behind as a trace of the "circulation of social energy." What makes the example so striking for Coleridge is that this collaborative assemblage looks exactly like a person.

Coleridge's persistent feelings of awe before art's power to testify to the nature of the human were qualified only by his ability to feel anxiety about the processes by which individuals constitute themselves out of social energies.[8] His preoccupation with these themes begins with the first text to appear in his name, the 1794 "historical drama" he wrote with Robert Southey and published as *The Fall of Robespierre*. It is not insignificant that Coleridge's careerlong fascination with the intertwining of moral, political, and aesthetic beliefs starts with a text written by several hands and featuring an interplay of multiple voices. This

---

7. In the *Dialogues* of Donato Giannotti, Michelangelo is made to say: "He who kills a tyrant kills not a man, but a fierce beast in human form ... and so Brutus and Cassius did not commit a sin by killing Caesar" (quoted from de Tolnay, *Michelangelo*, 63).

8. The observation is cast in a humanistic light by Anya Taylor in *Coleridge's Defense of the Human* (Columbus: Ohio State University Press, 1986).

collaborative drama, apparently so atypical of Coleridge and of Romanticism, offers a revealing glimpse of beliefs and anxieties about agency that continued to motivate both for years to come.

I.

The Fall of Robespierre opens a wide range of questions about the place of agency in history, the first of which arises from the ambivalent stance of the play's collaborating authors toward the concept of individuality. On the one hand, the play can be read as an apotropaic defense of the individual, warning against the root causes of a politics committed to the destruction of individuality. As such, it would prefigure Edmund Burke's denunciation of French totalitarianism in *Letters on a Regicide Peace:* "To them the will, the wish, the want, the liberty, the toil, the blood of individuals is as nothing. Individuality is left out of their scheme of government. The state is all in all."[9] On the other hand, as a collaborative play about conspiracy, it rejects individualism as an organizing principle. Clearly it cannot be counted among the modern dramas John Hamilton Reynolds dismisses in his praise of Elizabethan dramatic collaborations: "We have no example in later times of these friendly conjunctions of genius. A fondness for individuality has long been popular, and mankind, in literature as in life, seem to have ceased to be social."[10] Any text can position itself, in different contexts, both "for" and "against" the sanctity of individuals, but that potential ambiguity is never far from the surface in Romantic drama. Some critics have wanted to position Romanticism itself in this way: Gerald Izenberg, for instance, defines Romanticism in terms of the belief that "individuality is not only compatible with infinity, it is the very vehicle for realizing the union with infinity."[11] Such paradoxes, however, allow the vague reference of "individuality" to disguise difficulties that arise in

---

9. Edmund Burke, *Letters on a Regicide Peace,* in *Works in Twelve Volumes* (London, 1887) 5:375.

10. John Hamilton Reynolds, "On the Early Dramatic Poets, I.," *The Champion* (7 January 1816); repr. in *Selected Prose of John Hamilton Reynolds,* ed. Leonidas M. Jones (Cambridge: Harvard University Press, 1966) 30.

11. Gerald Izenberg, *Impossible Individuality: Romanticism, Revolution, and the Origins of Modern Selfhood, 1787–1802* (Princeton: Princeton University Press, 1992) 15.

the narrower conception of the individual *agent*. One virtue of Romantic drama is that it drives questions about agency inexorably toward the specific and the concrete.

The Fall of Robespierre turns the analysis of potential fissures in the conception of the individual—presented as the problem of where to locate the origins of action—into a *vade mecum* of political rhetoric. It asks both how people do things with words—words being the means by which actions are both performed and represented within a dramatic text—and how words themselves act, sometimes uncooperatively, in the company of those people. That double question marks the crossroads of the individual and the collective, where *The Fall of Robespierre* places the interaction (on the level of plot) between the words of individuals and collective ideologies, even as (on the level of composition) the play's apparently well-individuated poetic diction emerges as indistinguishable from anonymous sources in the popular press. It is hard to say what the text *does* in addressing the problem of individual versus collective agency if we cannot know whether to ascribe to it a singular or a plural agency. *The Fall of Robespierre* derives its interest from a dramatization of historical and aesthetic questions about political language, but we cannot with certainty attribute this interest to Coleridge, or to Southey, or even to some collaborative agent Coleridge-Southey, since it is equally possible to view the appearance of this thing done with words as an accidental conjuncture of innumerable social energies.[12]

12. *The Fall of Robespierre* has not received anything like the critical attention given to the Revolution books of *The Prelude*. Richard Holmes dismisses it as "a farrago of rhetorical bad verse," written only "to raise money" for the Pantisocracy scheme (*Coleridge: Early Visions* [New York: Viking, 1990] 74, 73), as Southey himself said: "Surely I can write enough to clear 200 pounds before March and more would not be wanted" (21 August 1794; *New Letters of Robert Southey*, ed. Kenneth Curry [New York: Columbia University Press, 1965] 1:69). Kenneth Curry finds the play interesting only "as an historical document preserved in literary form" ("The Literary Career of Robert Southey to the Year 1796," diss., Yale University, 1935, 172–73). From Coleridge's defensive letter of 6 November 1794 it appears that contemporary readers were equally reductive (*Letters of Samuel Taylor Coleridge*, ed. Earl Leslie Griggs [Oxford: Clarendon Press, 1956] 1:125–26). The notion of "an historical document preserved in literary form" calls attention to *The Fall of Robespierre* as historical evidence of the rise of historical documentation, for the play provides early testimony of the encroachment of a new kind of newspaper reporting, developed from the creation of foreign correspondents in the early 1790s, upon the traditional terrain of dramatic literature. James Perry, who began sending reports from Paris to the *Morning Chronicle* in 1789, is generally regarded as the first foreign correspondent, and in 1792 *The Times* set up a Paris reporter and

The problem of individual agency arises even on the title page, which bears the name of a single author. Coleridge explained this to Southey in a letter of 19 September 1794: "I shall put my name because it will sell at least a hundred copies in Cambridge. It would appear ridiculous to print two names to *such* a work. But if you choose it, mention it and it shall be done. To every man who praises it, of course I give the true biography of it . . ."[13] The pretense of single authorship is explained as commercial necessity: Coleridge's name will sell. His anxiety about being ridiculed for naming two authors betrays a similar concern for the value of the name: two authors could be expected to produce a play at least twice as good as this one; each would be devalued by his association with the other. If the play is praised, however, the relative distinction between good and twice-as-good will be overridden by the absolute value of a textual life that will itself provide a subject for "true biography."

Coleridge's incantatory repetition of the pronoun "it" signals a desire for the text to remain impersonal and objective. This desire, together with the text's theme of collective and individual agency, should be seen as historically inflected. Written in August, 1794, in Bristol, *The Fall of Robespierre* is as closely bound to its historical moment as any of the many dramatizations of events in Revolutionary France. More important, it is quick to portray this present moment *as* historical: Coleridge's prefatory letter calls the play "an historical drama," even though the events it dramatizes occurred only three weeks prior to its composition. The power struggles of the Thermidorean reaction were matched in England by domestic repression that both poets associated with the French Terror, and these conditions (along with the poets' personal circumstances) required that their play appear immediately as an active intervention in current debates. Southey's hopes for the Pantisocracy project were closely intertwined with his expectation of violent revolution in England: "The storm is gathering and soon must break," he

---

initiated its own courier service; before then, foreign news had been collected abroad and distributed to the domestic papers by the General Post Office. The GPO likely assembled the reports quoted from the *London Chronicle* in this chapter. For helpful sketches of the rise of the popular press during the period of the Revolution, see Elie Halévy, *A History of the English People in 1815* (New York: Routledge and Kegan Paul, 1987 [1924]) 145–49; Raymond Williams, *The Long Revolution* (New York: Columbia University Press, 1961) 184–90; and Robert W. Desmond, *The Information Process: World News Reporting to the Twentieth Century* (Iowa City: University of Iowa Press, 1978) 54–57.

13. Coleridge, *Letters* 1:85.

warned Horace Bedford; "you must all come when the fire and brimstone descend."[14]

But the immediacy of historical events tended to complicate rather than clarify their significance. "The death of Robespierre is one of those events on which it is hardly possible to speak with certainty," wrote Southey, speaking for a wider range of young Englishmen than might once have been assumed.[15] Other reactions to the death of Robespierre, particularly those of Coleridge and Wordsworth, have been documented in Nicholas Roe's *Wordsworth and Coleridge: The Radical Years*. The securely celebratory lines that Wordsworth addressed to Coleridge in book 10 of the 1805 *Prelude* are familiar: "O friend, few happier moments have been mine / Through my whole life than that when first I heard / That this foul tribe of Moloch was o'erthrown, / And their chief regent levelled with the dust" (10:466–69). Roe contrasts these lines about the leveled leveler with Southey's report of Coleridge's sentiments: "Coleridge says 'he was a man whose great bad actions cast a dis[astrous] lustre over his name.' He is now inclined to think with me that the [actions?] of a man so situated must not be judged by common laws, that Robespierre was the benefactor of mankind and that we should lament his death as the greatest misfortune Europe could have sustained . . ."[16] The reactions of Wordsworth and Coleridge seem straightforward and irreconcilable; yet Coleridge's later denials, together with Wordsworth's own vacillations, lead Roe to propose a connection between the two poets in the suggestive idea that "both Coleridge and Wordsworth discovered in Robespierre an alarming, distorted version of themselves."[17]

Wordsworth and Coleridge thus seem to collaborate, even before they meet, in using Robespierre as a means of reflecting on their own poetic aspirations to power—turning him into a distorting mirror, to use that master trope of Romantic drama. The gesture is the same whether the death of Robespierre is being celebrated by Wordsworth through a process of identifying with the chastising power gained by the Thermidoreans, or lamented by Coleridge through a process of

14. Southey, *New Letters* 1:87, 66; 12 November 1794 (echoing 20 July 94); 1 August 1794.
15. Ibid. 1:73, 7 September 1794.
16. Ibid. 1:73, 22 August 1794; quoted in Nicholas Roe, *Wordsworth and Coleridge: The Radical Years* (Oxford: Clarendon Press, 1988) 206.
17. Roe, *Wordsworth and Coleridge*, 210.

identifying with Robespierre's lost power to benefit mankind. For both poets, power can be seen as generating ambivalence more than celebration or regret, an ambivalence Wordsworth expresses in *The Prelude*:

> So did some portion of that spirit fall
> On me to uphold me through those evil times,
> And in their rage and dog-day heat I found
> Something to glory in, as just and fit,
> And in the order of sublimest laws.
> And even if that were not, amid the awe
> Of unintelligible chastisement
> I felt a kind of sympathy with power—
> Motions raised up within me, nevertheless,
> Which had relationship to highest things.
> (10:409–18)

The diction of "sublimest laws," "motions raised up," and "highest things" makes this passage read like others in which Wordsworth stands confronted by the power of the Imagination. Yet the syntax of "even if" and "nevertheless" conveys an ambivalence at the heart of a "sympathy with power" that must be felt as "unintelligible chastisement." Wordsworth is less comfortable than Hazlitt would be with the affinity between poetry and power: he seems to be chastising himself for the aggression that buys him his sense of autonomy, by directing that aggression against himself.[18] Wordsworth's celebration of Robespierre's death can thus be read as a masochistic containment of "sympathy with power," yielding him a new and undying power that is still

---

18. See Jean Laplanche, *Life and Death in Psychoanalysis,* trans. Jeffrey Mehlman (Baltimore: Johns Hopkins University Press, 1976), esp. chap. 5: "Aggressiveness and Sadomasochism," 85–102. Izenberg reads Wordsworth's *Borderers* in similar terms, sketching how Mortimer's "desire for vengeance turns his thoughts back upon himself in terror" (*Impossible Individuality,* 206); but his psychobiographical argument traces Wordsworth's guilt at having disowned and sublimated his feelings of aggression, rather than at suffering them pleasurably, as confessed in these lines. I do not mean to submit authors and characters to amateur psychoanalysis, but only to suggest that the cultural aftermath of early revolutionary fervor is one of the origins of the conception of character that led to psychoanalysis. For further arguments along those lines, see Alexander Welsh, "Hamlet Arrested and Psychoanalyzed," in *Strong Representations: Narrative and Circumstantial Evidence in England* (Baltimore: Johns Hopkins University Press, 1992) and Welsh, "Patriarchy, Contract, and Repression in Scott's Novels," in *The Hero of the Waverley Novels, With New Essays on Scott* (Princeton: Princeton University Press, 1992).

defended in the 1850 *Prelude* as "Motions not treacherous or profane, else why / Within the folds of no ungentle breast / Their dread vibration to this hour prolonged?" (1850; 10:458–60) A similar "dread vibration" of self-assertion and self-denial—the endlessly self-replicating Oedipal vacillation between a "sympathy with power" and an "unintelligible" sympathy with the power to chastise it—can be seen in Coleridge's later anxiety about his youthful Jacobinism ("Once a Jacobin, Always a Jacobin"). The pattern's complexity warns against reading a dramatic text like *The Fall of Robespierre* as simple evidence either of sympathy or of denial.

The play was reviewed favorably in the *Critical Review*, though its reviewer noted dryly that the composition could not have taken more than a few hours and that the speeches drew heavily from newspaper reports. ("Poor Robespierre!" wrote Southey; "Coleridge and I wrote a tragedy upon his death in the space of two days!"[19]) The reviewer may have had this information from the authors. Personal acquaintance may explain why the reviewer acknowledged that "a writer who could produce so much beauty in so little time, must possess powers that are capable of raising him to a distinguished place among English poets." The first act, which is Coleridge's alone, is said to be "by far the most finished," bearing out Southey's later claim that Coleridge "rewrote the first act at leisure."[20] The review concludes by reproducing several passages with the remark that the events being too recent to furnish an interesting plot, one ought to pay attention to the language of the speeches.[21]

19. Southey, *New Letters* 1:72, 3 September 1794.
20. *The Life and Correspondence of Robert Southey*, ed. Charles Cuthbert Southey (London, 1849) 1:217.
21. *Critical Review*, second series, 12:260 (November 1794). Since Coleridge did not join the staff of the *Critical* until 1796 (Holmes, *Coleridge* 133) we should resist the temptation to think that the review could have been written by Coleridge himself. Garland Greever claims that Coleridge *was* writing for the *Critical Review* prior to August 1794, when an anonymous review of *The Mysteries of Udolpho* appeared; see *A Wiltshire Parson and His Friends: The Correspondence of William Lisle Bowles* (London: Constable, 1926) 165–67. Greever argues for an identity between the "we" that opines in Coleridge's 1797 reviews and the "we" of the 1794 review, on the grounds that the former makes reference to the latter; but there is no other evidence for considering the editorial "we" of the *Critical* as a substantial or self-identical subject. In spite of Michael Gamer's clever extension of these arguments in *The Wordsworth Circle* 24 (1993): 53, the best authority on such matters remains David V. Erdman, "Immoral Acts of a Library Cormorant: The Extent of Coleridge's Contributions to the Critical Review," *Bulletin of the New York Public Library* 63 (1959): 433–54.

This critical procedure follows the lead of Coleridge's dedicatory note: "In the execution of the work," he wrote, "as intricacy of plot could not have been attempted without a gross violation of recent facts, it has been my sole aim to imitate the empassioned and highly figurative language of the French orators, and to develope the characters of the chief actors on a vast stage of horrors." Coleridge's emphasis on the "highly figurative language" of a dramatic moment, at the expense of a complex historical plot, matches later statements about how we should come to know things, presumably including history. Chapter 16 of the *Biographia Literaria* affirms the dictum of the *Gorgias:* " 'I think that what Plato has said in the Gorgias is indeed true: "Anyone who knows words will know things too." ' " This affirmation is quoted from the German philosopher Daniel Sennert, who further suggests that a failure to know words, to control their meaning, will lead to a failure to know things, to control the course of history: " 'Alas, what great calamities have misty words produced, that say so much that they say nothing—clouds, rather, from which hurricanes burst, both in church and state.' " The power of "misty words" lies in their ability to turn wayward signification into disruptions in the course of history, as is clear from Coleridge's additional quotation from Hobbes: " 'Notice how easily men slip from improper use of words into errors about things themselves.' " These figures for the aberrantly generative power of figurative language have a prominent place already in *The Fall of Robespierre,* which seems to dramatize another maxim from chapter 18 of the *Biographia* characterizing figures of speech in terms that others had used for the forces driving the Revolution: as "originally the offspring of passion, but now the adopted children of power."[22]

The play begins with an example of "highly figurative language" used by one character to diagnose another's "highly figurative language." The speaker is Barrere, the traitor who shuttles between the Robespierre group and the Thermidorean conspirators. He describes Robespierre's "soul" with metaphors that echo the bursting firestorms of

22. Coleridge, *Biographia Literaria*, in *Collected Works*, 7.2:31, 65. See also the figure in *Conciones ad Populum* (1795): "Strange Rumblings and confused Noises still precede these earthquakes and hurricanes of the moral World" (*Lectures 1795 On Politics and Religion*, in *Collected Works*, vol. 1, ed. Lewis Patton and Peter Mann [Princeton: Princeton University Press, 1971] 36). Such figures can be found in other early writings by Coleridge; see Robert Sayre, "The Young Coleridge: Romantic Utopianism and the French Revolution," *Studies in Romanticism* 28 (1989): 403.

Southey's letters and that forecast the *Biographia*'s fixation on clouds and hurricanes:

> The tempest gathers—be it mine to seek
> A friendly shelter, ere it bursts upon him.
> But where? and how? I fear the Tyrant's soul—
> Sudden in action, fertile in resource,
> And rising awful 'mid impending ruins;
> In splendor gloomy, as the midnight meteor,
> That fearless thwarts the elemental war.
> (1.1–7)[23]

Here, as elsewhere in more directly political speeches, the present is made historical by being made Miltonic. Coleridge alludes to book 1 of *Paradise Lost,* where Milton tells how Satan

> above the rest
> In shape and gesture proudly eminent
> Stood like a tower; his form had yet not lost
> All her original brightness, nor appeared
> Less than archangel ruined, and the excess
> Of glory obscured. . . .
> (1:589–94)[24]

Roe, who identifies the allusion, does not comment on the indirections of Coleridge's Miltonism, even though the lines issue a warning about disguise. Coleridge's attempt to strike a Miltonic note might be assimilated to the undeniably sincere Miltonisms of his 1794 "Sonnets on Eminent Characters." Yet for Coleridge to have begun by imitating *this* passage, which Edward Young had used in his *Conjectures on Original Composition* to characterize the greatness that lingers on in the imitation of an original, signals a high degree of self-consciousness about adopting another's language.[25] Coleridge is playing a game with claims

---

23. I use the text of *The Fall of Robespierre* printed in the second volume of *The Poems of Samuel Taylor Coleridge,* ed. Ernest Hartley Coleridge (London: Oxford University Press, 1927). Parenthetical references give act and line numbers.

24. John Milton, *Complete Poems and Major Prose,* ed. Merritt Y. Hughes (Indianapolis: Bobbs-Merrill, 1957); see also Roe, *Wordsworth and Coleridge* 207.

25. Edward Young, *Conjectures on Original Composition* (1759), in *The Great Critics: An Anthology of Literary Criticism,* ed. James Harry Smith and Edd Winfield Parks (New York: Norton, 1967) 424.

and attributions of original power, in which his Miltonizing of political discourse counts not as an effort to recanonize the stilted and anachronistic classicism of French political rhetoric, but as the English historical drama's readiest means of parodying it.

This "highly figurative language" does not just make Robespierre appear as sublime (or as secondary) as Satan; it exposes the process by which that appearance is engineered, the rhetorical moves by which the lines construct the historical agent as a sublime figure. First comes a confession of fear; fear then seems to generate, as its justification, a sublime diction. Barrere's lines reveal a pattern, one that will scarcely be limited to his character, whereby an internal anxiety about one's own power is projected onto another whose description occasions the language of the Miltonic sublime. This link between anxiety and the sublime bears out Steven Knapp's contention that "the sublime depends on an ideal of perfect, self-originating agency that no one really expects or wants to fulfill," and that sublime experience therefore involves no wish "to identify *oneself* with a transcendental ideal of pure subjective power, but rather to entertain that ideal as an abstract, fantastic, unattainable possibility."[26] Barrere's speech offers just such a fantasy: the hypothesis of a pure power that must belong to someone else.

The sequence generating sublimity from projected anxiety recurs throughout Act 1. When Barrere exits, the pattern asserts itself in the voice of Tallien, leader of the Thermidorean conspiracy. As Barrere fears Robespierre, so Tallien fears Barrere; but Tallien proceeds to diagnose Barrere's anxiety. The mix of fear and perceived fear again appears in the language of the Miltonic sublime, marked by the distinctive Miltonic "hung" later celebrated by Wordsworth, here introduced in what would become Wordsworth's signature enjambment:

> 'Twas all-distrusting guilt that kept from bursting
> Th'imprisoned secret struggling in the face:
> E'en as the sudden breeze upstarting onwards
> Hurries the thundercloud, that pois'd awhile
> Hung in mid air, red with its mutinous burden.
> (1.20–24)

26. Steven Knapp, *Personification and the Sublime: Milton to Coleridge* (Cambridge: Harvard University Press, 1985) 3, emphasis added.

How can Tallien read Barrere's mutinous intentions if their signs have been swept off his face? How do the "pois'd" signs of uncertainty yield interpretive certainty? Mutinous intentions seem to become legible here only by virtue of their dominance in the mind of the play's principal mutineer, Tallien himself; the intent read off Barrere's blank face is equally (perhaps initially) Tallien's own, projected onto Barrere and then depersonalized in a repetition of Barrere's sublime dispersion of mutinous intent to the prevailing winds.

The pattern recurs when the Robespierre group enters. St. Just uses similar language to describe Collot d'Herbois, historically a playwright and actor as well as a member of the Committee for Public Safety:

>   He is one
> Who flies from silent solitary anguish,
> Seeking forgetful peace amid the jar
> Of elements. The howl of maniac uproar
> Lulls to sad sleep the memory of himself.
> A calm is fatal to him—then he feels
> The dire upboilings of the storm within him.
> A tiger mad with inward wounds!—I dread
> The fierce and restless turbulence of guilt.
>   (1.82–90)

There is again a significant Miltonic imitation here, specifically of *Paradise Lost* 4:13–26, where Satan's attempt to initiate action leads to an inward recoiling from his own agency.[27] Once again, Coleridge is playing self-subverting tricks with his rhetorical verse, the subtlety of its perceived function depending on the recovery of origins far more banal than the Miltonic subtext. For these lines assume an uncanny power when we realize that St. Just is quoting a description Coleridge had

---

27. Knapp comments that the Miltonic recoil is also a subtext for Collins's "Ode to Fear," specifically for the account of "Fear's reaction to his own agency" (89). Joanna Baillie's *DeMonfort* offers another dramatic imitation of these lines:

> A distant gath'ring blast sounds through the wood,
> And dark clouds fleetly hasten o'er the sky:
> O! that a storm would rise, a raging storm;
> Amidst the roar of warring elements
> I'd lift my hand and strike! but this pale light,
> The calm distinctness of each stilly thing,
> Is terrible.

See *The Dramatic and Poetical Works of Joanna Baillie* (London, 1851) 94–95.

recently given of himself. Speaking through the mask of one "Silas Tomkyn Comberbache," unhappy volunteer private in the 15th Light Dragoons, S.T.C. had confessed in a letter: "I fled to Debauchery—fled from silent and solitary Anguish to all the uproar of senseless Mirth!" (February 1794).[28] That St. Just's description of Collot d'Herbois should turn out to be the exalted figurative double of Coleridge's sordidly literal account of himself provides strong grounds for recognizing a link in Coleridge's mind between self-analysis, rhetorical inflation, and the contagion of fear.

These lines dramatize something more specific than, say, the romantic disturbance of Wordsworth's Pedlar, who "wished the winds might rage / When they were silent."[29] While St. Just confesses a fear of Collot d'Herbois, what he seems specifically to fear, in diagnosing Collot d'Herbois's "guilt" as self-fear, is an identical fear within Collot d'Herbois himself. As the fear of another ("I dread") is revealed as a fear of another's fear of fear ("He is one / Who flies from silent solitary anguish"), St. Just appears to fall into "the fierce and restless turbulence" of a *mise en abîme* whose name is given as "guilt." The sublime "storm within" seems to be generated as a figure of the abyssal projection onto another of the speaker's fear of his own agency—the same projection that Wordsworth enacts in the Revolution books of *The Prelude* "amid the awe / Of unintelligible chastisement." But while indulging in this now familiar pattern, St. Just also provides a way of understanding the structure of the sublime. When Collot d'Herbois is said to seek external storms to avoid recognizing the storms within, it seems as though external storms *originate* in the fear of internal storms. If the political arena has a sublime fearfulness, the speech suggests, this sublimity originates in a fear of oneself that leads to a fear of others and then to a general cosmic fearfulness.

It is not quite true that there is nothing feared here but fear itself. What is most fearful is the *mechanism* by which one character's avoidance of agency is projected, in a whirling *mise en abîme* of aversion from aversion, onto another. For the apparently nonsubjective mechanicity of fear has the real effect of generating a sublime poetry whose own further effects are the responsibility of no one in particular. These

---

28. Coleridge, *Letters* 1:67–68.
29. Wordsworth, "The Pedlar," MS. M, 305–6; *"The Ruined Cottage" and "The Pedlar,"* ed. J. Butler (Ithaca: Cornell University Press, 1979) 405.

effects begin in the reduction of all possible political dangers to the fantasized power of individual agents—reversing radical irresponsibility into universal guilt—and culminate in the sacrifice of the single individual who touches off the chain of sublime visions.

The Fall of Robespierre makes this rhetorical pattern seem all-pervasive in Revolutionary Paris, although Coleridge closes act 1 with a very different domestic scene between Tallien and his wife. That scene's formal incompatibility with the rest of the play is the first acknowledgment of a critical resource that the play will later exploit more fully: namely, the drama's generic power to acknowledge the "space of historical and personal difference" that Tilottama Rajan has seen as deconstructing, by a multiplication of incompatible viewpoints, the "transcendental privacy" promised by the Romantic lyric.[30]

After providing this perspective on the rhetorical generation of political conspiracy, the play moves back, in act 2, to the pattern of sublime fearfulness, in speeches that Southey admitted having versified directly from the newspapers.[31] Southey counterbalances the rhetorical trickery of Coleridge's first act with a far greater emphasis on the business of plot: Robespierre is condemned for restricting free speech and for substituting the rule of an individual for the rule of law. As Roe convincingly argues, the target here is not Robespierre but Pitt, who had passed seditious libel laws and suspended *habeas corpus* a few weeks before similar measures took effect in France.[32] What is most important for the structure of the play, however, is the way in which the speeches in Act 2 carry forward the first act's construction of the individual as the locus of historical power. The attacks on Robespierre are made in the name of the people against the tyranny of the individual, but they

---

30. Tilottama Rajan, "Romanticism and the Death of Lyric Consciousness," in *Lyric Poetry: Beyond New Criticism*, ed. Chaviva Hosek and Patricia Parker (Ithaca: Cornell University Press, 1985) 206.

31. "It was written with newspapers before me as fast as newspapers could be put into blank verse" (*Life and Correspondence of Robert Southey,* 1:217). For details on the use of news reports, see Curry, *Literary Career* 164–72, and Carl Woodring, *Politics in the Poetry of Coleridge* (Madison: University of Wisconsin Press, 1961).

32. Roe, *Wordsworth and Coleridge* 200–206. Act 2 could thus have been enlisted by the defense in the propaganda war surrounding the trials of John Thelwall, Thomas Holcroft, Horne Tooke, and others in the fall of 1794; Southey refers to their impending trial in his letter of 12 October 1794 (*New Letters* 1:81). For more detailed information on treason and sedition trials in the 1790s, see John Barrell, "Imaginary Treason, Imaginary Law: The State Trials of 1794," *The Birth of Pandora and the Division of Knowledge* (Philadelphia: University of Pennsylvania Press, 1992) 119–43.

voice the same self-centered anti-individualism one hears in *Julius Caesar* when Brutus gives his reasons for killing Caesar: "I know no personal cause to spurn at him, / But for the general. He would be crowned" (2.1.11–12).[33] The Shakespearean "general" appears in *The Fall of Robespierre* as "generale," an archaic term for "the people." Yet if the accusations against Robespierre are made in the name of the people rather than in the name of individuals, they nonetheless uniformly adopt the language of Act 1, which moves from a dispersed and impersonally mechanistic fearfulness to a projection of decisive agency onto sublime individuals.

Attacking individuals now becomes a ritual that elevates rather than demotes the individual's significance. The climax comes in a stylized version of the newspaper reports on Billaud Varennes' denunciation:

>Who spar'd La Valette? who promoted him,
>Stain'd with the deep dye of nobility?
>Who to an ex-peer gave the high command?
>Who screen'd from justice the rapacious thief?
>Who cast in chains the friends of Liberty?
>Robespierre, the self-stil'd patriot Robespierre—
>Robespierre, allied with villain Daubigné—
>Robespierre, the foul arch-tyrant Robespierre.
>
>(2.228–35)

In the newspaper reports, which are similarly riddled with rhetorical questions, Billaud Varennes reconciles the charge of conspiracy with his emphasis on "one man alone" by scapegoating another solitary individual who can stand for all: "I accuse him [Robespierre] of being surrounded by a band of ruffians, among whom it is only necessary to mention the infamous name of Daubigny." The casual naming of Daubigné cannot mitigate the charge against a *single* individual agent, upon whom all responsibility must be placed—Robespierre. The play thus

---

33. The newspapers report Tallien modelling his denunciation of Robespierre after Brutus's denunciation of Caesar: "like Caesar," Tallien is reported to have said, "the name of King was only wanting to him, for the full establishment of his power." The stock allusion to Brutus would probably have struck Southey less than the self-consciously dramatic manner in which the newspapers reported it: "I invoke the shade of the virtuous Brutus [*fixing his eye upon the bust*]." *London Chronicle*, 16–19 August 1794, 173–74; all newspaper reports are cited from this or adjacent columns in the same number.

aligns its dramatic development with "the illusion of politics" François Furet finds at the heart of Revolutionary ideology: "like mythical thought, it peoples the objective universe with subjective volitions, that is, as the case may be, with responsible leaders or scapegoats."[34] *The Fall of Robespierre* seems disinclined to distinguish between these two cases; mythical thought is woven into the very fabric of a plot in which one individual, Robespierre, falls, and another, Tallien, rises to take his place. This portion of the play is thus entirely devoted to the fate of individuals, authorized by a sublime rhetoric that makes history originate in individual power. Yet there remains something that cannot quite be pinned to any single individual agent. We do not yet know the origin of the fear generating the language of sublime origins.

If the speeches of act 2 attempt to *present* a rather unsubtly ordered discursive chaos, act 3 *reports*—attempts to make distant—the true chaos of the Robespierrist counterinsurrection. What was, historically, largely a crowd phenomenon is captured in Act 3's attempt to represent —or rather, to dramatize *without* representing—a new form of historical agency. For the emergence of a new order with new individual leaders is made to depend upon the chaotic interruption of distant crowd noise. If acts 1 and 2 attempt to present history in confrontations between individuals who construct one another as sublimely powerful agents, act 3 gestures toward the frenetic action of historical events themselves, as something that cannot be presented.

The play's genre shifts markedly here. We might expect a summary trial to round out the rhetorical survey begun in the first two acts, or perhaps a private scene focused on the fate of the fallen heroes in their domestic spheres; both feature, for example, in the dénouement of Georg Büchner's *Dantons Tod*. Up to this point, rhetorical form has fully coincided with historical content, as the dramatic action has consisted entirely in the exchange of words. Now, however, the dramatic action has no access to the stage: the individual protagonists of the night of 9–10 Thermidor never again appear; we hear of their fates from a series of messengers. Thus while act 3 completes the play's action, it also contains far fewer lines than either of the preceding acts, as political rhetoric is marginalized in favor of narrative reports and offstage noise. The brevity of act 3 may seem to serve a mimetic aim,

---

34. François Furet, *Interpreting the French Revolution,* trans. Elborg Forster (New York: Cambridge University Press, 1981) 26.

capturing the haste with which the Robespierrists were hurried off to execution. But the generic divergence from the preceding acts suggests that Coleridge and Southey meant to organize their climax around a deliberate refusal to represent decisive historical events in terms of individual agents who could step onstage. Or so we might conclude, if we were able to speak with confidence of an author whose actions could be called "deliberate."

We learn what happens to Robespierre partly from act 3's pivotal stage directions, which, though they are few, become oddly prominent considering that we see no action. These point typically to activity offstage and dictate not decisive actions but dispersed expressions such as "Violent applauses from the galleries" or "Shouts without." Their peculiarity arises from their dual origin: some stage directions are Southey's renderings of reportorial narrative, while others merely reproduce what had already taken the form of italicized stage directions in the newspaper reports, which are peppered with stagey interpolations like *"(Loud Applauses.)."* The play thus exhibits itself as art by means of a condensing and distancing of historical action that would have gone unmarked in the newspaper sources, which lacked the stage's conventional capacity to reproduce actions. Since drama, by definition, must be capable of representing things done, it is striking that Southey refuses that capability, clinging instead to the textbound feel of his sources.

If act 3 moves toward history, then, it does so by gesturing toward an agent that cannot be presented onstage or in a script because it is, in effect, the audience. It makes historical action diffuse by having the onstage continuity of the Convention's speeches disrupted by something not so easily represented in a dramatic text. What remains onstage is a development of the abyssal structure of fear seen in the earlier acts. It reappears here, significantly, in the voice of Barrere, who had inaugurated the pattern: "What means this uproar! if the tyrant band / Should gain the people once again to rise— / We are as dead!" (3.96–98). And again: "Hark! how the noise increases! through the gloom / Of the still evening—harbinger of death, / Rings the tocsin! the dreadful generale / Thunders through Paris" (3.115–118). When the factional conflict is resolved and Robespierre is carted off to the scaffold, Barrere can switch from speaking out of a fear of the people to speaking in the name of the people; he can even make himself into the individual embodiment of the people, troping "we" as "I" in recalling "that day /

When, on the guilty Capet, I pronounced / The doom of injured France" (3.176–178). In the meantime, however, the play's formal shift has produced an origin for the fear generating the rhetoric of sublime individualism by refiguring it as a fear of the crowd. The play thus moves from a rhetoric of individual agency affiliated with an anachronistic Miltonism toward a different focus that disrupts that affiliation: the stage directions that acknowledge the clamor of an outside world of "news" more than a dramatic tradition of popular discord.[35] Throughout act 2, each of the individual orators sought to appear more moral than his predecessor, at least more eager to talk about morality. In act 3, we see this contagion of individualist moral discourse not as a reaction against the immorality of the named protagonists of history, but as a reaction against the feared amorality of a historical movement that has no protagonist.

In its dispersed focus on the crowd, act 3 moves away from the heroic reductions of history that were characteristic of early Revolutionary dramas. This formal shift attacks the reduction of political history to the moral decisions and acts of autonomous subjects, a reduction some historians have wanted to ascribe to Robespierre's ideal of a "Republic of Virtue" and one that Coleridge himself came to see as the chief error of Jacobinism.[36] Thus *The Fall of Robespierre* already shows signs of Coleridge's later frustration with the difficulty of finding a mode of individual action capable of affecting history. The allure of passivity in the well-known song to "Domestic Peace" in act 1 is thus intimately bound to the undermining and dispersal of individual agency that act 3 effects by replacing heroic protagonists with the concealed agencies of history Coleridge would conjure up a year later in speaking against "massacres *mechanized* into Revolution."[37]

Coleridge's fear of unfathomable political machinations consuming the fuel of human freedom acts out a pattern Hannah Arendt identifies in describing the historical force of the impoverished masses: "The less

---

35. The dramatic tradition is studied in Lucy De Bruyn, *Mob-Rule and Riots: The Present Mirrored in the Past* (New York: Regency, 1981).

36. Laurence Lockridge has argued that, in later years, "Coleridge thinks the literal extension of individual ethics to the political affairs of nations is the subversive error of the Jacobins" (*The Ethics of Romanticism* [New York: Cambridge University Press, 1989] 20). Cf. Robespierre's maxim: "Liberty would have been long since affirmed among us if individuals were as pure as the mass of the nation"; quoted from Carol Blum, *Rousseau and the Republic of Virtue: The Language of Politics in the French Revolution* (Ithaca: Cornell University Press, 1986) 200.

37. Coleridge, *Conciones ad Populum*, in *Lectures 1795, Collected Works* 1:48.

we are doing ourselves, the less active we are, the more forcefully will this biological process assert itself . . . and overawe us with the fateful automatism of sheer happening that underlies all human history."[38] But *The Fall of Robespierre* does not merely embrace a fatalism that would excuse the absorption of individual agency into mass movement. For if its dénouement gives history back to the masses, it does so only by refusing to represent those masses. That refusal cannot, however, be recuperated as one moment of a dialectic, as would be possible in earlier and later popular dramas representing the Revolution. Coleridge's and Southey's theater of absence differs essentially, for example, from the earlier London spectacles whose purpose was, in Jeffrey Cox's words, to "celebrate mass action and trace a movement from the enclosed spaces of the past . . . to the open spaces of a liberated future."[39] It absents itself equally from a tradition that was to flourish across the nineteenth century and that culminated in Romain Rolland's 1890s "Théâtre du Peuple," which sought to bring to the stage the "dramatic sense of the crowds."[40]

The Fall of Robespierre, by contrast, strives for a dramatic actualization of something like the efficient unrepresentabilities hypothesized in mid-twentieth-century critiques of psychic and historical causality: Lukács's "totality," Althusser's "absent cause," Lacan's order of "the Real." Coleridge's and Southey's nonrepresentation of the masses as the concealed prime mover of history cannot, therefore, be reduced to the terms of a sociology of the crowd.[41] Yet this failure of representation does have an important historical correlate in the fact that there was no

---

38. Hannah Arendt, *On Revolution* (New York: Penguin, 1982) 59.

39. Jeffrey Cox, "Ideology and Genre in the British Antirevolutionary Drama of the 1790s," *ELH* 51 (1991): 582. Cox's argument deals with plays that parody the "Jacobin" ideological "belief in action by the people" (585), above all the efforts in the *Anti-Jacobin* "to replace the image of mass action with conspiracy theories of isolated, ambitious men manipulating the foolish people" (587). The positing of conspiratorial agents behind what seemed mass action was, of course, a strategy available to interests across the political spectrum.

40. Untraced comment by Rolland, quoted from David James Fisher, "Romain Rolland and the French People's Theatre," *Drama Review* 21 (1977): 88. Rolland's method was basically dialectical: in *Le Quatorze Juillet* "the People are the protagonist, and the taking of the Bastille afforded . . . ample opportunity for utilizing them," while "in *Les Loups* and *Le Triomphe de la Raison* they hover in the background and determine the course of events: they are always near at hand, although they do not appear on the stage" (Barrett H. Clark, Preface to Romain Rolland, *The Fourteenth of July and Danton: Two Plays of the French Revolution,* trans. Clark [New York: Henry Holt, 1918] 10).

41. As, for example, in George Rudé, *The Crowd in the French Revolution* (1959; repr. New York: Oxford University Press, 1972).

fixed means in British public discourse, let alone the Constitution, for representing what was sometimes called "the mobility" (*mobile vulgus*, or "mob"), the vast nonclass of those ranking below "the people," which included only ratepayers and householders who could lay claim to political representation.[42] The play's negative representation therefore has a positive function, and the necessary lack of historical information for analyzing it cannot justify undervaluing that function.

What historical circumstances might have motivated the technique of *The Fall of Robespierre*? One need look no further than to the play's sources in the popular press to find what contemporary writers identified as a manipulative and deadening mass medium. Late twentieth-century criticisms of mass culture find a striking antecedent, for example, in Wordsworth's fear of "a multitude of causes, unknown in former times, [that] are now acting with a combined force to blunt the discriminating powers of the mind, and, unfitting it for all voluntary exertion, to reduce it to a state of almost savage torpor."[43] Wordsworth's defense of the mind's threatened autonomy might be traced to the popular experience in Revolutionary Paris, during the brief cessation of censorship, when an explosion of theater and propaganda (both revolutionary and counterrevolutionary) inundated the masses with simulated information, neutralizing and silencing them by removing their ability to tell their own agency from its simulation. The functions of theater and newspaper had become closely intertwined.[44] But Wordsworth's anxiety also had a specific source in England, in newspapers pandering to the masses. Jonathan Arac sees Wordsworth's condemna-

42. On the various terms for the underclass, see R. J. White, *Life in Regency England* (New York: Putnam, 1963) 43, and Raymond Williams, *Keywords: A Vocabulary of Culture and Society*, rev. ed. (New York: Oxford University Press, 1983) 193. Williams also reports that usage of the term "mass" remained "indeterminate, until the period of the French Revolution. Then a particular use was decisive. As Southey observed in 1807: 'the levy in mass, the telegraph and the income-tax are all from France.' Anna Seward had written in 1798: 'our nation has almost risen in mass' " (193–94).

43. Wordsworth, "Preface" to *Lyrical Ballads* (1800), in *The Prose Works of William Wordsworth,* ed. W. J. B. Owen and Jane Worthington Smyser (Oxford: Oxford University Press, 1974) 1:128.

44. The official reports of Thermidor in the *Moniteur Universel* were immediately followed, on each day, by a schedule of *spectacles*. Plays about Revolutionary festivals were staged on the evening of the festival day, and, as Marvin Carlson notes, war news from the front sometimes reached the theatergoing public before it was in print (*Theatre of the French Revolution* [Ithaca: Cornell University Press, 1966] vi). There are many examples of quasi-journalistic attempts to bring theatrical representation so close to ongoing events that it might actually precede and forestall them.

tion of "the increasing accumulation of men in the cities, where the uniformity of their occupations produces a craving for extraordinary incident, which the rapid communication of intelligence hourly gratifies" as identifying a vicious circle of mass behavior turning on the centralization of mass communication: "conurbation and mechanization created crowds, news then galvanized those crowds into mobs, and they performed the acts of agitation that provide the stuff for more news."[45]

One of the most important aspects of Thermidor, as *The Fall of Robespierre* affirms, was the novel agency of the crowd: its strategic nonact of refusing to serve as a personifiable agent. It was perhaps the first time that the revolutionary crowd declined to play the role of the people, so that it decided the course of events not by intervening as an actor but by standing by as disaggregated spectators. One can imagine British onlookers following the process by which agencies of representation aiming to unite the masses into the people—the rising popular press, generally, and on this occasion also the enforced spectatorship of Robespierre's Festival of the Supreme Being, which preceded Thermidor by a short two weeks—reversed field to turn the people back into the masses, depriving the people of the identity and mission that had been manufactured for it. Victor Hugo would later see the theater's virtue in its power to work a magical "transformation de la foule en peuple, profond mystère!"[46] But magical powers cannot always control their effects. Jean Baudrillard observes as much in the logic by which the twentieth-century mass media, in marketing specific forms of bourgeois individualism, end up exhibiting the subjective philosophical categories of desire, will, and responsibility as simulacra that can readily be replaced by "a sort of radical antimetaphysics whose secret is that the masses are deeply aware that they do not have to make a decision about themselves and the world, that they do not have to wish, that they do not have to know, that they do not have to desire."[47]

The same logic might have been recognizable as a legacy of the Revolutionary theater—or indeed, the popular press—feeding back to the

---

45. Wordsworth, *Prose* 1:129; Jonathan Arac, *Critical Genealogies: Historical Situations for Postmodern Literary Studies* (New York: Columbia University Press, 1987) 180.
46. Victor Hugo, *Littérature et philosophie mêlées*, quoted from Anne Ubersfeld, *Lire le théâtre* (Paris: Éditions sociales, 1978) 14.
47. Jean Baudrillard, "The Masses: The Implosion of the Social in the Media," trans. Marie Maclean, *New Literary History* 16 (1985): 585.

masses their own image as the people. Coleridge's and Southey's refusal to represent the masses that resolve the action of their play may amount to such a recognition: a critical awareness of what is today called "massification," which Raymond Williams has paired with the "mass media" as "modes of disarming or incorporating the working class," "of alienation and control, which prevent and are designed to prevent the development of an authentic popular consciousness." The odd discontinuities of *The Fall of Robespierre* could, then, be understood as a strike against the dramatic manipulation of the people as simulacrum, or as a movement of the imagination in the direction of Williams's vision of "a mass uprising against mass society, or a mass protest against the mass media, or mass organization against massification."[48]

If a literary form can thus be read as an action in itself, how do we speak of the *agents* of such an action? In this case, one can hardly say that Coleridge and Southey wanted to defend the crowd, which to English radicals in 1794 would have meant reactionary church and king mobs. The point is rather that, once it has been shown that great men are not the prime movers of a historical process, one cannot simply look for another sublime agent and find it in "the people," which one then depicts as acting like a great man. Coleridge would later declare that the idea of collective will "applies to no one Human Being, to no Society or assemblage of Human Beings, and least of all to the mixed multitude that makes up the PEOPLE."[49] The tendency of his early writing is to imply that, while the people can be figured as sublime, the crowd cannot. The crowd might better be seen as an instance of countersublimity, figuring neither a power that can be harnessed by representation, nor something that exceeds representation, but merely the machinery of history as it continues to grind away. In *The Fall of Robespierre*, as it moves toward a clash between its speaking heroes and the invisible crowd, the opposite of the sublime turns out to be not the beautiful, as in the passing lyrical idyll named "Domestic Peace," but rather the disruptiveness of random noise. In the banal stage directions of act 3, the unthinking and anarchic crowd does its deconstructive work even if, or rather because, it does not speak or even appear in the play.

48. Williams, *Keywords* 196–97. Williams adds that "the distinction that is being made, or attempted, in these contrasting political uses, is between the masses as the subject and the masses as the object of social action."
49. Coleridge, *The Friend*, in *Collected Works*, 4.1:193.

Can we still, then, find in the play an agency that can be localized, even by a displacement substituting the crowd as nonindividual "character" for the text's nonindividual "author"? Or does close attention to its literary form force us to acknowledge kinds of historical agency that are more truly problematic, because not so readily deciphered by our familiar critical tools? Sublime representations of the crowd familiar from Revolution historiography produce results very different from what I have tried to identify in Coleridge and Southey as a nonrepresentational countersublimity. It would be misguided to present their *bagatelle* either as a novel political intervention or as an aesthetic experiment, as though the critique of individual agency in political history were bound to reinstate that agency in the augmented, superindividual strength of collaborating poets. The critical force of *The Fall of Robespierre* surely prohibits us from blithely congratulating its authors, for the text's structural modulations are calculated to suspend the reduction of politics to the agency of autonomous individuals.

Yet neither author could ensure that suspension. Indeed, their reputations were significantly shaped by later episodes in which they were made to assume personal responsibility not just for their own earliest political writings, but for large chains of consequences that followed from them uncontrollably.

2.

Southey's investment in the critique of agency staged in *The Fall of Robespierre* can be traced in another play he wrote two months later. The agent of that act would return with an uncanny power when Southey was most certain it was dead.[50] His three-act Jacobin squib *Wat Tyler* lay neglected in the shop of the London publisher Ridgeway until 1817, when it was published, widely circulated, and debated in the House of Commons as part of a campaign to discredit the Laureate. That episode provides a striking illustration of the process by which the circulation of social energy is effaced when a single work or person is chosen to represent its crosscurrents, for the question of Southey's per-

---

50. Leigh Hunt, in a hilarious parody of Southey's attempt to defend himself in the *Wat Tyler* scandal, has Southey's dead body rise and deliver a long speech, until at last "the didactic dust and ashes" falls silent and "relapse[s] into his proper mortality." See "Extraordinary Case of the Late Mr. Southey," *Examiner* 11 May 1817.

sonal integrity drew attention away from the many cultural tendencies that converged to make *Wat Tyler*. The play itself devotes attention not only to the power of such disembodied energies, but also to the process by which they are focused in a protagonist whose "treason" is punished in a ritual dismemberment of the body politic. *Wat Tyler* takes as its prime mover not an actor but a speaker, the radical preacher John Ball, whose message—not just in 1381, but in 1794 and again in 1817—is that social change can never be reduced to the actions of individuals. "The electric truth shall run from man to man," he prophesies, "And the blood-cemented pyramid of greatness / Shall fall before the flash!"[51] "Audacious rebel!" responds Sir John Tresilian, before delivering the sentence with which the play concludes:

> you shall be hanged by the neck,
> But not till you are dead—your bowels open'd—
> Your heart torn out and burnt before your face—
> Your traitorous head be sever'd from your body—
> Your body quarter'd, and expos'd upon
> The city gates—a terrible example—
> And the Lord God have mercy on your soul!"
> (68)

How did Southey himself, in 1817, come to be exposed as "a terrible example"? His scapegoating followed in large part from his own insistence that political evils must be laid to the account of individual agents. Southey's habit of choosing easy targets encouraged his critics. The introduction to the pirated *Wat Tyler* noted that, "though Coleridge and Wordsworth had also been obnoxious as Jacobin Poets," their subtlety or simplicity allowed them to evade criticism; Southey, by contrast, "was always committing himself in a tangible shape," as though committing a crime that lay him open to public scrutiny and condemnation (xi). In Hazlitt's words, Southey could "comprehend but one idea at a time, and that is always an extreme one, because he will neither listen to nor tolerate any thing that can disturb or moderate the petulance of his self-opinion." Southey must, says Hazlitt, nonetheless acknowledge "the hypostatical union between the Quarterly Reviewer

---

51. [Robert Southey], *Wat Tyler* (Oxford: Woodstock, 1989) 66; further page references are given in parentheses.

The Fall of Robespierre and Wat Tyler

and the Dramatic Poet," for, as he recalls from Wordsworth, "The child's the father of the man."[52]

What did most to bring upon Southey the wrath of the Opposition was his idea that Reform writers must bear all responsibility for political unrest. Here is the passage from Southey's *Quarterly Review* essay "On Parliamentary Reform" that was read on the floor of the House of Commons:

> When the man of free opinions commences professor of moral and political philosophy for the benefit of the public—the fables of old credulity are then verified—his very breath becomes venomous, and every page which he sends abroad carries with it poison to the unsuspecting reader. We have shown, on a former occasion, how men of this description are acting upon the public, and have explained in what manner a large part of the people have been prepared for the virus with which they inoculate them. The dangers arising from such a state of things are now fully apparent, and the designs of the incendiaries, which have for some years been proclaimed so plainly, that they ought, long ere this, to have been prevented, are now manifested by overt acts.[53]

After quoting this specimen of witch-hunting rhetoric, William Smith, Opposition MP for Norwich, read out one of the speeches Southey had written for John Ball, just such a "man of free opinions." Southey's childhood friend Charles Wynn stood to defend him, citing the genre of historical drama as proof against assigning John Ball's opinions to

---

52. William Hazlitt, unsigned review in the *Examiner* (9 March 1817), quoted from *Robert Southey: The Critical Heritage,* ed. Lionel Madden (Boston: Routledge and Kegan Paul, 1972) 233. Hazlitt habitually read the inconsistencies of his conservative enemies as exploding their claims to be integral persons. For example: "I can hardly consider Mr. Coleridge as a deserter from the cause he first espoused, unless one could tell me what cause he ever heartily espoused, or what party he ever belonged to, in downright earnest. He has not been inconsistent with himself at different times, but at all times" (*The Complete Works of William Hazlitt,* ed. P. P. Howe [London: Frank Cass, 1967] 17:29). Or again: "Mr. Burke, the opponent of the American war—and Mr. Burke, the opponent of the French Revolution, are not the same person, but opposite persons—not opposite persons only, but deadly enemies" (1817 "Review of Biographia Literaria," in *Works* 16:130). Hazlitt's canonical commentary on such matters is his 1821 essay "On Consistency of Opinion" (*Works* 17:22–34), which opens with this astounding gambit: "Many people boast of being masters in their own house. I pretend to be master of my own mind. I should be sorry to have an ejectment served upon me for any notions I may chuse to entertain there. Within that little circle I would fain be an absolute monarch."

53. *Hansard's Parliamentary Debates* (14 March 1817), quoted from *Southey: Critical Heritage* 236.

Southey. Coleridge echoed that defense in the *Courier:* "*Wat Tyler* is a poem, and a dramatic Poem, and ... it is both unfair and absurd to attribute to the Poet, as a man all the sentiments he puts in the mouth of his characters."[54] He went on to claim that those sentiments, far from being contagious, worked to "inoculate" readers in the modern sense, to preserve them from the danger of owning such generally-circulated opinions. John Ball's speeches were written in an attempt to represent a political milieu, Coleridge judged, "as the natural sentiments of such men in such circumstances, at the utmost as *exaggerated* truths, characteristic of heated minds; and not as his own convictions, much less as his wish or will" (3.2:458). *Wat Tyler,* written not for the Spa Fields crowd of 1817 but for the discerning intellectual of 1794, will be found, Coleridge insists, "an admirable burlesque on the pompous extravagancies of the demagogues of the day. It affords us just such amusement in respect of politics as Tom Thumb does in respect of Tragedy" (3.2:453).

It seems unaccountable that anyone could serious deny that the effect of *Wat Tyler* had become divorced from its author's "wish or will." Such a divorce between intention and consequence was Southey's own concern in his attack on the reformers whose "very breath *becomes* venomous" only when it reaches "the unsuspicious reader." That *Wat Tyler* was being circulated by the radical press allowed sophisticated readers to imagine its effect on the unsuspicious reader, even to imagine themselves *as* that unsuspicious reader. Such a reader simply would not understand what Coleridge meant in saying that "*Wat Tyler* is a poem, and a dramatic Poem," because he would not understand the kind of agency Coleridge describes as characteristic of the poet. "On the sub-stratum of their general feelings [the poet] is to act by general truths, general emotions," Coleridge writes; "the grandeur of liberty, compassion for the oppressed, indignation against the oppressors, are as natural to him, when these are his subject, as fidelity, loyalty, the majesty of law, and devotion, even to the death, for friend, or King, or Country are, in his next Poem, perhaps" (3.2:470).[55] To fail to understand this is to fail to see that the moral quality of actions is to be judged from their circumstances; he who cannot see this is no more

---

54. Coleridge, *Essays on His Times*, in *Collected Works*, vol. 3, ed. David V. Erdman (Princeton: Princeton University Press, 1978) 2:457; further references are given in parentheses.

55. Coleridge sometimes speaks of the poet as an inert organ for the transmission of social energy; see, for example, *Letters* 4:718–19.

human than the fanatic who cannot tell regicide from tyrannicide. Coleridge's rejoinder to the Cardinal who feared the effects of art on those who cannot understand it was that such persons are, in fact, not fully persons. His rejoinder to Southey's critics, and to Southey himself, is likewise that there simply is no "unsuspicious reader," not at least until someone deliberately brings him into being. As he put it in a private letter: "who in the Devil's Name ever thought of reading Poetry for any political or practical purposes till these Devil's Times that *we* live in?"[56] The *Wat Tyler* debate, then, turns on the power of representations to bring the "unsuspicious reader" into being, making it possible for unbound social energies to be bound to the intentions of individual agents and passed on to others as the "electric truth" Southey's John Ball helped to conduct "from man to man."

How do social energies idling about "in the air" come to be bound to individual agents capable of unleashing them as collective action? That process was, ironically, what Southey had plotted in *Wat Tyler*, although that does not mean that *Wat Tyler* was not also intended to set the process in motion. Southey's John Ball aims to turn the appeal to conscience into a force of solidarity by speaking in such a way as to hold individual peasants together as a collective agent. That aim is clear in a scene at the center of the play:

> *John Ball.*   In good truth
>   Ye have cause for anger: but, my honest friends,
>   Is it revenge or justice that ye seek?
> *Mob.* Justice, justice!
> *John Ball.*   Oh then remember mercy:
>   And tho' your proud oppressors spar'd not you,
>   Shew you excel them in humanity.
>   They will use every art to disunite you,
>   To conquer separately, by strategem,
>   Whom in mass they fear—but be ye firm—
>   Boldly demand your long-forgotten rights,
>   Your sacred, your inalienable freedom—
>   Be bold—be resolute—be merciful!
>
>   (32–33)

---

56. Coleridge, *Letters* 4:713. Coleridge goes on to complain that "the Root of Evil is *a Public*—and take my word for it, this will wax more and more prolific of inconvenience, that at length it will scarcely be possible for the State to suffer any truth to be published, because it will be certain to convey dangerous falsehood to 99 out of a hundred."

This speech also poses a question about how the actions of one man can come to figure the cause of many. For Ball's rhetorical question "revenge or justice?" recapitulates the question from which Southey's plot begins: how did Wat Tyler's "revenge" become the crowd's "justice"?

The contingent nature of Wat Tyler's actions was important enough to Southey that he enshrined their agent, rather than his protagonist, in the play's title. The plot is set in motion when Wat Tyler, seeing his daughter insulted by a representative of the king, instantly picks up his hammer and *"knocks out the Tax-gatherer's Brains."* "A just revenge," says the young plowman Piers, to which Tyler mournfully responds: "Most just indeed; but in the eye of the law / 'Tis murder—and the murderer's lot is mine" (16–7). Before the law can overtake natural justice, however, a mob enters crying "Liberty! liberty!—No Poll-tax! —No War!" How has a solitary act of revenge become a social movement? When the peasant leader Hob Carter brings the news, Wat Tyler is as mystified as anyone:

> Hob. We have broke our chains—we will arise in anger—
> The mighty multitude shall trample down
> The handful that oppress them.
> Tyler.   Have ye heard
> So soon then of my murder?
> Hob.   Of your vengeance.
> Piers ran throughout the village—told the news—
> Cried out, To arms!—arm, arm for Liberty!
> For Liberty and Justice!
>   (18–19)

Wat Tyler tries to calm the mob by speaking of his solitary burden of guilt, but in asking them to disregard his private cause (thus echoing *The Fall of Robespierre,* act 2) he cannot help rallying them to the collective cause it represents:

> Oh do not call to mind my private wrongs,
> That the state drain'd my hard-earn'd pittance from me;
> That, of his office proud, the foul Collector
> Durst with lewd hand seize on my darling child,
> Insult her maiden modesty, and force

> A father's hand to vengeance; heed not this:
> Think not, my countrymen, on private wrongs;
> Remember what yourselves have long endur'd.
> Think of the insults, wrongs, and contumelies,
> Ye bear from your proud lords—that your hard toil
> Manures their fertile fields—you plow the earth,
> You sow the corn, you reap the ripen'd harvest,—
> They riot on the produce!—That, like beasts,
> They sell you with their land—claim all the fruits
> Which the kindly earth produces as their own.
> The privilege, forsooth, of noble birth!
> On, on to Freedom; feel but your own strength,
> Be but resolved, and these destructive tyrants
> Shall shrink before your vengeance.
>
> (21–22)

It is Tyler alone, up to the point in act 2 where he is stabbed to death, who is able to control the "giddy multitude" (53). At that point John Ball steps in to turn the mob away from Wat Tyler's vengeance ("His mangled feelings prompted the bad act," 50) toward the aim of "reformation" (51).

Act 1 thus traces the formation of a political movement from an *acte gratuit,* exposing both the contingent circumstantiality of such collective agencies and their underlying rationality. John Ball's function is to provide that social process with a unifying consciousness that may be owned by anyone wishing to be a free agent and not merely an instrument either of the rebel leaders or, as formerly, of the feudal landowners. By act 3, his imperative of unity has become a call for political enfranchisement. What that means to John Ball becomes clear when King Richard grants those political rights in a charter written to trick the rebels into dispersing:

> Herald. Now then depart in quiet to your homes.
> John Ball. Nay, my good friend—the people will remain
>   Embodied peaceably, till Parliament
>   Confirm the royal charter: tell your King so:
>   We will await the Charter's confirmation,
>   Meanwhile comporting ourselves orderly
>   As peaceful citizens, not risen in tumult,
>   But to redress their evils.
>
> (55–56)

"We must remain embodied," he repeats to Hob Carter, knowing that the king's only hope is to turn the "peaceful citizens," for whom John Ball speaks as "We," back into a tumultuous mob. John Ball is left alone on stage for a moment's reflection, but before he can mount his pulpit again, the people begin to disperse offstage, and the king's soldiers start hewing away. Piers reports that "they are murdering / Our unsuspecting brethren: half unarm'd, / Trusting too fondly to the tyrant's vows, / They were dispersing:—the streets swim with blood." At this point the soldiers enter and seize John Ball: *"They lead off John Ball—the tumult increases—Mob fly across the stage—the Troops pursue them—loud cries and shouts"* (60, s.d.).

The meaning of John Ball's insistence that the people must remain "embodied" is illustrated in this sequence, in which, within a minute, a solitary man soliloquizing on stage is led off to be ritually dismembered and is replaced on that stage by a disorderly "Mob." Political agency is produced whenever social energies can be "embodied" by a man speaking on stage; it is undone whenever those energies revert to the free circulation unbounded by such conditions. *Wat Tyler* thus offers the embodied tragic subject as both emblem and guarantor of political freedom: without it, the "peaceful citizens" are merely a disaggregated mob of what Southey would later call "unsuspicious readers." John Ball gives a precise inflection to the claim that political power is theatrical, in a scene at the very center of the play where he is told that Jack Straw has gone to seize the king. "It was well judg'd," he says:

> fain would I spare the shedding
> Of human blood: gain we that royal puppet,
> And all will follow fairly: depriv'd of him,
> The nobles lose their pretext, nor will dare
> Rebel against the people's majesty.
>
> (39)

The embodiment of aristocratic will—"that royal puppet"—is all that grants the nobles their power, just as embodiment will turn out to be all that grants the people their majesty. This can hardly count as Southey's insight, although he can be made to bear the burden of it in 1817, just as he could, in 1794, make John Ball bear the burden in 1381.

A comment in the *Black Dwarf*'s review of *Wat Tyler* displays in concentrated form some of the powerful ambiguities that were bound to arise when writers could so transparently manipulate the opacity of political agency. "Mr. Southey seems to have been employed," it was said, "as the agent and the instigator of the whole conspiracy."[57] The name "Southey" figures at once the origin of collective action and the process by which the need for an origin calls into being an individual agent whom everyone acknowledges to be a puppet. The paradox that makes the wielder of dramatic language into a political agent, the better to rob him of agency, lies beyond demystification, for everyone knows perfectly well what is happening. But the moral problem that appears in aesthetic form retains, all the same, its power to stir political energies, to make things happen. Coleridge and Southey, who were among the first to bring that knowledge to the public, tapping its power to produce political agency, were also among the first to understand why the ghostly aftereffects of that agency cannot be laid to rest.

57. Quoted from *Southey: Critical Heritage* 239.

2

The Claim of Compulsion:
The Borderers

> The need for punishment functions like the driving force that propels a machine with a certain power, which, if it increases above a certain measure, destroys the machine.
> —THEODOR REIK, *The Compulsion to Confess*

At the climax of Wordsworth's 1797 tragedy *The Borderers,* the villain Rivers confesses to the hero Mortimer both his own past crime and the fact that he has just choreographed Mortimer's re-enactment of it. In his youth, Rivers killed an innocent older man by abandoning him at sea under the delusion that he was executing justice. In the play, he has arranged for Mortimer to kill another old man—Herbert, father to Mortimer's beloved, Matilda—under the same delusion. Rivers wants his confession to express confidence in the freedom of will he thinks he has now recovered, but it hints instead at his uncertainty over how to tell action from compulsion:

> *Rivers.* Ay, we are coupled by a chain of adamant;
> Let us be fellow-labourers, then, to enlarge
> Man's intellectual empire. We subsist
> In slavery; all is slavery; we receive
> Laws, but we ask not whence those laws have come;
> We need an inward sting to goad us on.
> *Mortimer.* Have you betrayed me? Speak to that.
> *Rivers.* The mask,
> Which for a season I have stooped to wear,
> Must be cast off.—Know then that I was urged,

> (For other impulse let it pass) was driven,
> To seek for sympathy, because I saw
> In you a mirror of my youthful self;
> I would have made us equal once again,
> But that was a vain hope. You have struck home,
> With a few drops of blood cut short the business;
> Therein for ever you must yield to me.[1]

Rivers's placid moralizing only intensifies Mortimer's nightmare, even as his recital of motives clarifies for the audience the play's main themes. The smooth surface is disturbed only once by the ripple of concealed currents, which Wordsworth ropes off with parentheses: "(For other impulse let it pass)." Coleridge once said that parentheses contain "the very drama of thought";[2] but what is being dramatized here? Is that a bad angel dictating to Rivers? Is it a repressed voice? As his account of urges and drives gives way to a fleeting anxiety about his motive in giving that account, Rivers seems to slip helplessly toward a vortex of compulsion spinning furiously just out of sight. What moves him?

Rivers wants Mortimer to "know" how a perception of likeness has compelled him to bind his captain with the "chain" he calls "sympathy." He wants it known that he "was urged" by an impulse that is "other," "was driven" by the external compulsion that is the business of lawyers and exorcists rather than the internal compulsion that is the business of psychiatrists. But the imperative in that aside—"let it pass"—expresses his awareness that such distinctions can at best *pass* as knowledge. Rivers admits that he cannot say whether his compulsion is external, as he seems to hope, or internal, as he seems to fear. He can confess it truthfully only by confessing that he does not know how to avoid lying: for if such differences are only rhetorical positions, then his confession can only be wishful, and his parenthetical aside comes to count as truth —even as it justifies a cynical indifference to truth—only by exposing that wishfulness.

---

1. *The Borderers,* ed. by Robert Osborn (Ithaca: Cornell University Press, 1976) 243; 1842 text, lines 1854–69. Subsequent citations refer to this edition, with quotations from the 1797 text followed by act, scene, and lines numbers, and quotations from the 1842 text followed by line number. Citations for other poems by Wordsworth refer to the De Selincourt and Darbishire edition (Oxford: Clarendon Press, 1967); *The Prelude* is quoted from the Wordsworth, Abrams, and Gill edition (New York: Norton, 1979).

2. Letter to Thomas Poole, 28 January 1810, in *Collected Letters of Samuel Taylor Coleridge,* ed. E. L. Griggs, vol. 3 (Oxford: Clarendon Press, 1959) 282.

But what drives Rivers to confess his confession's wishfulness? His aside might be taken as evidence of Wordsworth's incompetence as a dramatist or, more generously, as an indication that the poet felt unsure of his ability to convey his meaning in words given to another person. Such judgments overlook how effectively the aside performs the very suspension of agency Rivers is confessing, raising doubt about what prompts these words. Psychology can provide only a limited range of explanations: one might suppose that Rivers does not know what he is confessing or to whom, that he does not recognize it as a confession, that he has no idea why he has said what he has said; perhaps he is unconsciously administering to himself a punishment that has been withheld, to win from himself the love ("sympathy") such punishment would signify; or perhaps, having tried unsuccessfully to confess in the narrative just concluded, he now resorts to acting out. Such speculations, however satisfying, stray from the essential question: what drives him to express himself?

I have quoted Rivers's confession from Wordsworth's 1842 revised text, where it seems to do double service as a confession of what Wordsworth himself had done in his youth—in 1797, when he wrote the play—and of what he is now suffering in submitting himself to a reenactment of that deed. To say that Rivers expresses himself because he is a man on a stage is merely to push the question back toward the more fundamental question: Why is there a man on the stage? What, that is, drives *Wordsworth* to express himself? That drive toward expression seems, not only here but in all of act 4, indeed in much of Romantic drama, to override all other considerations, most obviously the conventions of verisimilitude. Peter Brooks has traced the compulsion to confess from the early tradition of melodrama back to Rousseau and Sade, "who were obsessed by the idea that they must say all, *tout dire,* that nothing of the possible human response must be left unexpressed, that writing must be a continual overstatement."[3] His term "obsessed" hints at a psychoanalytic explanation for this generic feature of melodrama, one that might follow Wilhelm Stekel's diagnosis of the compulsive

---

3. Peter Brooks, *The Melodramatic Imagination: Balzac, Henry James, Melodrama, and the Mode of Excess* (New York: Columbia University Press, 1985) 67. Rivers's overstatements make him more an allegorical Vice than a subject with full psychological interiority—an example, that is, of the "motiveless malignity" Coleridge saw in Iago. See Bernard Spivak, *Shakespeare and the Allegory of Evil: The History of a Metaphor in Relation to His Major Villains* (New York: Columbia University Press, 1958).

doubter: "He stages a play in which he acts the part of the perfect human being. However, he doubts the genuineness of his play. Within himself he knows that he is a hypocrite and he must repeat everything because he strives towards his ideal of goodness."[4] If this sounds like a description of Rivers, it also sounds uncannily like a description of Wordsworth, the compulsive autobiographer. One might conclude from this fearful symmetry that what drives Wordsworth to express himself in a play is the wish to secure a space of inconsequence or neutrality for his own compulsive doubt to run wild, so that it will not express itself as Rivers's does. In such an account the play would work, like psychoanalytic transference, to "render the compulsion harmless, and indeed useful, by giving it the right to assert itself in a definite field," converting neurosis into transference neurosis and exchanging Wordsworth's actual suffering for "an artificial illness" accessible to the therapeutic powers of self-awareness.[5] The writing of the play would then have allowed Wordsworth to think of himself—to *know* himself—as having actively mastered, as art, what he had once passively suffered, as history.

Such an account is inadequate in one respect: it does not take seriously the power of Rivers's words to undermine the therapeutic distinction between active and passive. It would not help Rivers to acknowledge his active role in making his fate, for he regards the distinction required for any such acknowledgment as wishful and factitious. Could Wordsworth have taken control of his own obstinate questionings by imagining a character for whom moral responsibility has become inconceivable? Rivers seems driven by his very insistence on external compulsion to admit that internal and external are only manners of speaking, ways of insisting. His desire to "say all" cannot be gratified within his moral vocabulary; it can only be acted out. But we cannot take the play itself both as Wordsworth's acting out and as a map of his moral and imaginative recovery without giving credence to Rivers's persuasion that the fate of the compulsive is enlightenment.

Readers who grant the play's dark powers the homeopathic virtue Rivers sees in his own poisonous manipulations assume that Words-

---

4. Wilhelm Stekel, *Compulsion and Doubt,* trans. Emil A. Gutheil (New York: Liveright, 1949) 1:294.
5. Sigmund Freud, "Remembering, Repeating and Working-Through," *Standard Edition of the Complete Psychological Works of Sigmund Freud,* trans. James Strachey (London: Hogarth, 1973) 12:154.

worth shares that persuasion. It is hard to overcome the temptation of such a reading without first trying to carry it as far as possible; in what follows I will try to make out a best case for it. But to follow out the political consequences of the play's psychological involutions means passing from the apparent autonomy Rivers shares with his creator to the discourse of social compulsion glimpsed in *Wat Tyler,* where "freedom" is not just the peasants' rallying cry but also the false pledge of smirking aristocrats: "Aye, there's nothing like / A fair free open trial," Southey had written at the height of the 1794 Treason Trials, "where the King / Can chuse his jury and appoint his judges" (*Wat Tyler* 61). Wordsworth's conversion of psychological compulsion into dramatic structure, I will argue, reveals his intense awareness of the social and economic pressures exerted on individual agency and of the ways in which beliefs about freedom ignore those pressures to the cost of every agent. The apparent loss of control on the part of the enlightened compulsive works, I propose, to criticize the delusion that it is possible to experience an uncompromised positive freedom.[6] I must show how Wordsworth dramatizes this position before I can explain why he does so and what it meant for the development of Romanticism.

The Fall of Robespierre and *Wat Tyler* find power in condensing the transition usually mapped across the careers of Coleridge and Southey, from a youthful "Jacobinism" to a mature renunciation of "sympathy with power," into an anxious ambivalence about the status of individual agents. *The Borderers,* whose composition spans Wordsworth's career more literally, finds a similar power in dramatizing what Wordsworth's late note calls "transition in character" (815).[7] All three plays link complications in the understanding of agency to beliefs about the power of language. But where the 1794 plays offer only brief ironic glimpses of language's amoral power over its anxious users, *The Bor-*

---

6. I understand "positive freedom" along the lines established in Isaiah Berlin's essay "Two Concepts of Liberty," in *Four Essays On Liberty* (New York: Oxford University Press, 1970).

7. The complete sentence in the 1843 Fenwick note explains that the play's preface was written "to preserve in my distinct remembrance what I had observed of transition in character & the reflections I had been led to make during the time I was witness of the changes through which the French Revolution passed" (815). I agree here with E. P. Thompson's claim that Wordsworth and Coleridge drew poetic power from their political vacillations, but I suspend judgment on his condemnation of Coleridge's "apostasy." See "Disenchantment or Default? A Lay Sermon," in *Power and Consciousness,* ed. Conor Cruise O'Brien and William Dean Vanech (London: London University Press, 1969).

derers is arranged to sustain a focus on that power. The resulting intensity and complexity has allowed modern readers to take *The Borderers* as an important achievement whose significance is not to be limited to the light (or shadow) it casts on later poetry. It was long valued mainly by critics seeking to chart Wordsworth's career by focusing on early, transitional works. Stationed on the threshold of the "Great Decade," it looks both forward and backward, the precariousness of its position signaled in stylistic fluctuations between an oblique understatement worthy of "The Ruined Cottage" and a melodramatic excess reminiscent of the "gross and violent stimulants" Wordsworth would condemn in "sickly and stupid German Tragedies."[8] The play's dramatic turns were taken, partly on the poet's authority, as representing the Revolutionary "transition" by which the self—Wordsworth's self—breaks its ties to nature by falling into radical action, losing its innocence but gaining the mastery required to document that loss. This critical tradition culminates in Gerald Izenberg's pinpoint diagnosis: "This is the Wordsworth of 1796–97 mercilessly exposing the Wordsworth of 1792–93 through the Wordsworth of 1794–95."[9]

Could any of those Wordsworths have been quite so single-minded? The complexity of *The Borderers* has increasingly prompted readers to ask that question. In affirming the habit of obstinate questioning Wordsworth condemns in describing himself "Dragging all precepts, judgments, maxims, creeds, / Like culprits to the bar" (*Prelude* 1850 11:294–95), readers have confirmed his hope that "some dramatic story may afford / Shapes livelier to convey to thee, my friend, / What then I learned" (1805 10:878–80). The poet knew that such shapes had already been summoned to act out those moral perplexities in *The Borderers:* even as he tries to confine them within a passing develop-

---

8. Wordsworth, "Preface" (1800) to *Lyrical Ballads,* in *Prose* 1:128. Stephen Gill offers a good example of the rhetoric of transition: "By comparison with *The Borderers, Adventures on Salisbury Plain* seems very limited. The poem closes a movement in Wordsworth's intellectual life. The play begins the exploration of themes which are to absorb him till his death." See *William Wordsworth: A Life* (Oxford: Clarendon Press, 1989) 101.

9. Izenberg, *Impossible Individuality* 203. Some biographical readings reduce *The Borderers* to "a document in the history of Wordsworth's mind," illuminating his moral and intellectual rather than his poetic development; see, for example, R. F. Storch, "Wordsworth's *The Borderers:* The Poet as Anthropologist," *ELH* 36 (1969): 341. Others offer highly refined psychological insights; see particularly Geoffrey Hartman, "Wordsworth's *The Borderers* and 'Intellectual Murder'," *Journal of English and Germanic Philology* 62 (1963): 761–68.

mental phase, Wordsworth cannot help acknowledging their persistent, conflicted grip on him.

Two strands of criticism can be seen as acting out a conflict in Wordsworth's own understanding of the play, which seemed to him both to reveal general laws of social psychology and to conceal idiosyncratic vexations of deeply personal significance. The conflict between biographical or personal readings and sociohistorical or theoretical readings persists among the play's readers because critics have failed to acknowledge the ways in which the play itself attempts to mediate between private confession and the general laws of human nature. *The Borderers* may seem to tilt rather precipitously toward confession; it strikes every reader as a play of self-reflection, built around a plot in which selves are not just examined, but constructed and manipulated, as in an autobiography.[10] When Rivers claims that he sought to make Mortimer into a "mirror" of his youthful self, it is hard not to take this as a confession that Wordsworth was, in some more complex way, doing the same. The "strange repetition" in *The Borderers* is easily assimilated to that of *Tintern Abbey:*

> in thy voice I catch
> The language of my former heart, and read
> My former pleasures in the shooting lights
> Of thy wild eyes. Oh! yet a little while
> May I behold in thee what I was once . . . .
> (116–120)[11]

The figure of Dorothy allowing William to read himself is not quite the same as the figure of Mortimer allowing Rivers to sympathize with himself. But the two texts do seem to mirror each other in providing

---

10. David Collings speaks of Rivers's "narcissistic pleasure in manipulating himself, as in the mode of autobiography" (*Wordsworthian Errancies* 66). He claims to make primary reference here to Jean-Pierre Mileur; elsewhere he footnotes my earlier reading, "Action in *The Borderers*," *Studies in Romanticism* 27 (1988): 399–410.

11. "Strange repetition" is Wordsworth's phrase in "Guilt and Sorrow" for the return of one's own crime in a form that one can witness. In that revision of "Adventures on Salisbury Plain," which Wordsworth was finishing as he revised *The Borderers,* the Sailor who returns to the scene of his crime sees an abused child and imagines that another is repeating his own act: "a groan the Sailor fetched / As if he saw—there and upon that ground—/ Strange repetition of the deadly wound / He had himself inflicted" (489–92; *The Salisbury Plain Poems of William Wordsworth,* ed. Stephen Gill [Ithaca: Cornell University Press, 1975] 261).

specular confrontations to help locate and recover elusive former selves. Before Wordsworth could look back to his period of active political engagement and write "I cannot paint / What then I was" (*Tintern Abbey* 75–76) he must, one might assume, have tried his hand at "painting his former self," the autobiographical act for which Wordsworth's preface to *The Borderers* grants Rivers true "greatness."[12]

The Borderers can, indeed, be read productively with Wordsworth's later semi-autobiographical poetry. Its treatment of action may, for example, help to illuminate the Solitary's imitation of Hamlet in *The Excursion*:

> my business is,
> Roaming at large, to observe, and not to feel,
> And therefore, not to act—convinced that all
> Which bears the name of action, howsoe'er
> Beginning, ends in servitude—still painful,
> And mostly profitless.
>
> (3:891–96)

The Borderers can help show why "the name of action" leads one astray and why, as might also be observed in book 10 of *The Prelude*, it may be necessary to muffle the stark memory of a revolutionary break with literary allusions. Yet the play clearly dramatizes the *danger* of trying to paint one's former self. It is not concerned to evaluate Wordsworth's own past actions, disguised or displaced; it stages actions to illuminate the idea and the discourses of action generally considered. The fiction of *The Borderers* borders on autobiography not because it tells us about a particular nonfictive self and its acts, but because it examines the act of reflection and self-construction that establishes a position from which the Solitary (or Hamlet, or Wordsworth) can examine and dismiss his former self and its acts.

The play is not essentially a study of character, then, as psychological interpretations assume, but a parable about the possibility of crossing the divide between talking about action and taking action. *The Borderers* shows what happens when one breaches the wall

---

12. The preface says that Rivers "frequently breaks out into what has the appearance of greatness; and in sudden emergencies when he is called upon by surprize and thrown out of the path of his regular habits, or when dormant associations are awakened tracing the revolutions through which his character has passed, in painting his former self he really *is* great" (65).

separating an enlightened moral discourse from the actions it codifies. More specifically, it shows this border being transgressed as another is effaced: the line separating the abstract and impersonal space projected by Rivers and Mortimer, in their talk of action, from the space of historically specific social relations. For the abstract moral discourse Wordsworth gives to Rivers assumes that "the measure of justice" can be found by "diving into our own bosoms" (3.5.24–25), so that the actions of one man can provide a basis for abstract reflection on man in general.

Wordsworth's objective is not to confess something but to examine the ways in which Enlightenment moral discourse allows one to move at will between the personal and the general. He thus joins forces with Burke to enlighten his countrymen about the misuses of enlightenment.[13] But the epigraph affixed to the early text immediately casts doubt on the possibility of such enlightenment. The well-chosen lines (35–38) from Pope's "To Cobham" read:

> On human actions reason though you can,
> It may be reason, but it is not man;
> His principle of action once explore,
> That instant 'tis his principle no more.

These lines convey Wordsworth's difficulty in knowing what claim *The Borderers* can make to illuminate a "principle of action" motivating its characters if, as soon as we explore their reasonings on action, we are stuck with our own principles and not theirs. The lines from Pope stand out in front of the play to remind readers why it is so difficult to talk about the "arguments" or "claims" made by a play. The claims of *The Borderers*, like those of any drama, are staked upon the ways in which characters act and the ways in which they reason on action. This drama, however, is devoted from these first words to examining self-consciously the extent to which ways of acting are nothing but ways of talking, and to showing the recursive effect of those ways of talking upon further actions. In displaying the effects of a discourse of motive upon its users, *The Borderers* ventures into a no-man's-land between the private and the communal, the individual and the general, between what is experienced and what is known. The problem it discovers there,

---

13. He understands his project, naturally, as anti-Burkean: "I have endeavoured," he writes, "to shake this prejudice" (67).

although it cannot appear apart from psychology or history, lies within neither discourse but rather at the crossroads of the moral and the political.

1.

No motive in *The Borderers* is allowed to float free of conditions or consequences, for Wordsworth is careful to situate even the most abstract and apparently detached thoughts within a chain of actions. Consider, for example, the play's most famous lines:

> Action is transitory, a step, a blow—
> The motion of a muscle—this way or that—
> 'Tis done—and in the after vacancy
> We wonder at ourselves like men betray'd.
> Suffering is permanent, obscure and dark,
> And has the nature of infinity.
>
> (3.5.60–65)

Harold Bloom has said that all Romantic poets think this, except Blake.[14] Perhaps they all did, at some point, but I quote Rivers here to make a more specific observation. Every element of this sententious formula—action, a blow, after vacancy, betrayal, suffering—reappears in the narrative segment of Rivers's personal confession in act 4. That later scene thus belatedly reveals the famous lines on action and suffering to be not merely true, in some universal way, but also—or rather—autobiographical. They bring into play a dramatic *Nachträglichkeit* that compels the audience to account for its approval of the lines that are later revealed to have passed off a sociopath's reminiscence as a moral discovery. If anyone in the audience manages to miss the point, Rivers explains it point-blank: "we receive / Laws, but we ask not whence those laws have come."

Rivers's deceptions claim no purpose beyond making Mortimer into a living canvas on which Rivers can "paint his former self." His stage-managing of the tales with which the Female Vagrant brings Herbert

---

14. Harold Bloom, *The Visionary Company* (Ithaca: Cornell University Press, 1971) 75; Bloom adduces the passage as he claims that Blake's Los is "the only Romantic hero whose primary role is activity rather than passive suffering."

into suspicion with Mortimer (1.3), along with the recycled *Othello* motifs of sexual jealousy and invidious ambition, contribute less to the shape of the plot than the idea of an intellectualized moral discourse capable of generating, or regenerating, real actions. This neater ideal plot appears in the lines of the confession from which I began: "I saw / In you a mirror of my youthful self; / I would have made us equal once again" (1865-67). The mirror *seems* to be a suitable figure for a plot that replicates acts by replicating agents; yet what Rivers says next —"that was a vain hope" (1868)—suggests that the figure lies. In acting out Rivers's crime, Mortimer was to hold up a mirror to Rivers's nature, enabling Rivers, by playing his own spectator, to sympathize with himself. Rivers learns, however, that Mortimer cannot be *made* to serve this purpose without his forfeiting the freedom of action Rivers hopes to resume, however vicariously. Rivers has polished his mirror with abstract slogans about "the moral shapes of things" so that he might see in it not merely himself but a general figure bodying forth "the shape of man" (2.5.104, 5.2.53).[15] That vision, he hoped, would absolve him with the knowledge that he is not alone. Now, however, he successfully recognizes the failure of that compulsive drive for self-recognition and for sympathy; but he still does not know *where* his moral abstractions have failed him. By the end of act 4, then, *The Borderers* has exhibited the necessity and the coercive power, but also the failure of a moral discourse that would enable the hero, and with him the audience, to recognize a universal freedom of action. Now it must show *why* the specular recognitions offered by drama are condemned to failure.

That is the purpose of a scene in which the shattering of Rivers's mirror is heard echoing beyond the claustral space of the protagonists' moral debates: the scene in act 5 between Mortimer and an impoverished cottager, in which Mortimer first guesses that Herbert may have died as a result of his own criminal neglect. (He had meant to abandon Herbert to a providential trial on the waste; he had not meant to walk off with the old man's food.) Mortimer cannot, however, learn to shoulder the burden of solitary guilt until he has tested the possibility of a shared guilt. Unable to see himself as having collaborated with the man

---

15. The rationalist metaphor of universally valid truth as geometric "shape" is one constant of Rivers's language that will echo in Mortimer's voice. Cf. 2.1.100 ("shapes of things") and 4.2.108 ("shape of action").

who betrayed him into his crime, he alights on the perfect substitute: an innocent bystander named Robert, who has simply declined to imperil himself by rescuing the old man.

This neglected minor character walks in from the world of *Wat Tyler* holding the key to the much-debated social, political, and historical meanings of *The Borderers*. Before act 5, Robert and his wife Margaret have appeared only on the outer edges of the main action—in 4.1 and 4.3, the stormy heath scenes that frame the tragedy of consciousness Rivers unfolds to Mortimer in 4.2, in which the storm (and the rest of the world) falls silent. Those melodramatic outer scenes, by recalling the social and natural environments in which all action unfolds, have already begun to pull Rivers's interior drama outward. By exhibiting social rather than moral reasons preventing a poor laborer from leading a blind old man to safety, they prepare Robert to play, in act 5, a role modeled after that of Gloucester's old tenant in act 4 of *King Lear*, who offers the sole indication in Shakespeare's notionally feudal world of the range of positions available in a class structure.[16] Wordsworth uses Robert's social position—not the class consciousness of Southey's John Ball, but a class-specific unconsciousness—to remind his audience of the social world framing Mortimer's tragedy. Robert's reluctant stepping to the fore thus offers our best clue for a historical understanding the moral vortex that is trying to suck him in.

Robert might be imagined as haunted by Gloucester's words to his tenant: "Thy comforts can do me no good at all; / Thee they may hurt" (*King Lear* 4.1.16–17). Robert's wish to save Herbert runs up against his fear of an arbitrary authority: "I have no friend," he reasons to his wife; "I am spited by the world—if I had brought him along with me and he had died in my arms.—Hush! I am sure I heard something breathing" (4.3.67–70). These lines sound like a test run for the *Pre-*

---

16. *King Lear*'s remoteness from mimetic realism has posed for Shakespearean historicists the same problem that *The Borderers* poses for romantic historicists. John Turner, remarking on the "early feudal" setting of *Lear*, argues that "Shakespeare has imagined worlds of kings and barons, without legal, ecclesiastical or parliamentary structures, without merchants, artisans, or labourers" ("The Tragic Romances of Feudalism," in *Shakespeare: The Play of History*, ed. Graham Holderness, Nick Potter, and John Turner [Iowa City: University of Iowa Press, 1987] 87). Richard Halpern, quoting Turner, mentions Gloucester's tenant as the exception proving the rule: "his appearance only reinforces our sense of a fully agrarianized feudalism at whose summit sat the king" (*The Poetics of Primitive Accumulation: English Renaissance Culture and the Genealogy of Capital* [Ithaca: Cornell University Press, 1991] 224).

lude's account of the after-vacancy following the episode of autumnal trap-robbing: "when the deed was done / I heard among the solitary hills / Low breathings coming after me, and sounds / Of undistinguishable motion, steps / Almost as silent as the turf they trod" (1805 1:328–32). Robert's terror, like the child's, expresses an inchoate moral sensibility; it is prompted not by some misdemeanor, however, but by the moral puzzle Gloucester broaches. Yet Robert's problem is not, as problems tend to be in *Lear*, purely moral. While the mythic realm of *Lear* may allow for an unproblematic juxtaposition of social and moral themes (feudal obligation being indistinguishable, here, from human kindness), the historical setting of *The Borderers* calls for a more delicate handling of their potential conflict. Wordsworth makes an effort to display the subtle forces exerted by class differences on the waxing and waning of conscience, so that he may put forward, at this precarious moment when his plot is teetering toward a dénouement, an unanticipated political argument.

Mortimer's scene with Robert (5.2) stages a bizarre parody of sympathy that allows us to see both our desire for mirrors in which we can recognize our own free agency and the ways in which circumstance can shatter those mirrors. The force of circumstance comes into focus very slowly this late in a play that has seemed, so far, to have little historical dimension. The scene seems to unfold in a purely moral register, with both Mortimer and Robert trying to evade responsibility for Herbert's death: "*Mortimer:* That was no work of mine. . . . *Robert:* Nor mine, God knows." The frenetic pacing of this dark slapstick prepares a moment when the play comes to a dead stop, the moment of Mortimer's hallucinatory recognition of his own "crimes" in the figure of Robert:

> *Robert.*   I am in poverty
>   And know how busy are the tongues of men.
>   My heart was willing, Sir, but I am one
>   Whose deeds will not stand by their own light,
>   And though it smote me more than tongue can speak—
>   I left him.
> *Mortimer (looks at him for some time).*
>   I believe that there are beings
>   For unknown ends permitted to put on
>   The shape of man, and thou art one of them.
>   But human things have pressed so hard on me—
> *Robert.* My wife and children came into my mind—

> *Mortimer.* Oh monster! monster! there are three of us
> And we shall howl together.
>
> (5.2.46–57)

In this brief moment of confusion, Mortimer uses the moral abstractions he has learned from Rivers ("the shape of man") to send Robert down to the hell of remorse he and Rivers already occupy. He quickly breaks down, however, unable to sustain his identification with Robert: "My crimes," he stammers, "have brought a judgment / On this innocent man" (5.2.58–59). David Bromwich has declared that the scene offers "no suggestion that the reader may take [Mortimer's accusation] with a degree of irony." Irony, it is true, does not describe what is happening here; but it cannot be assumed, as Bromwich concludes, that "the author has here joined cause with his hero." [17] For Wordsworth is choreographing Mortimer's confusion to pose a question about the ways in which which we attempt to recognize our human freedom.

This scene historicizes the character of Robert in order to show how Mortimer's education in moral abstraction has made him unable to acknowledge the otherness Robert represents. *The Borderers* has usually been read as though its action, like that of *Wat Tyler,* had no historical context other than the general atmosphere of radical politics in the 1790s.[18] Wordsworth's own notes encourage this tendency. In the 1843 Fenwick Note he claims that he searched for a historical setting that would allow his plot to unfold in a purely moral region beyond history: "As to the scene and period of action," he said, "little more was required for my purpose than the absence of established Law and Government—so that the Agents might be at liberty to act on their own impulses" (814). Wordsworth seems to think that, in writing the play, he had taken the "stride at once / Into another region" which the *Prelude* places "in the minds of all ingenuous youth" at the moment

---

17. David Bromwich, "Revolutionary Justice and Wordsworth's *Borderers,*" *Raritan* 13 (1994): 20. Bromwich is reviving the debate about what the play does with Godwin; for background, see Donald G. Priestman, "*The Borderers:* Wordsworth's Addenda to Godwin," *University of Toronto Quarterly* 44 (1974): 56–65.

18. Reeve Parker's speculations about the genesis of the play in Girondin circles are a special case. Parker's work on *The Borderers,* at the time of this writing, consists of three essays: "'Oh Could You Hear His Voice!': Wordsworth, Coleridge, and Ventriloquism," in *Romanticism and Language,* ed. Arden Reed (Ithaca: Cornell University Press, 1984) 125–43; "Reading Wordsworth's Power: Narrative and Usurpation in *The Borderers,*" *ELH* 54 (1987): 299–331; and "'In some sort seeing with my proper eyes': Wordsworth and the Spectacles of Paris," *Studies in Romanticism* 27 (1988): 369–90.

when Britain declared war on Revolutionary France (1805 10:240–41, 232). His plot, he believes, opened a gap in his writing no less real than the gap opened in the social order by Robespierre's death, in *The Prelude*'s account: "To Nature, then, / Power had reverted: habit, custom, law / Had left an interregnum's open space / For her to stir about in, uncontrolled" (1805 10:609–12). The rhetoric on display here retained its appeal for the author of the 1850 *Prelude* ("yet I feel . . . / The aspiration, nor shall ever cease / To feel it"; 11:255–58); it retains its allure today for those who find the radicalism of Wordsworth's psychological drama compromised by his need to situate it historically. That enthusiasm is not foreign to *The Borderers,* but Wordsworth means his play to show what would happen, in a concrete social setting, if such thoughts were consistently maintained. For the fantasy of an "uncontrolled" "liberty to act" appears to have had less influence over Wordsworth's choice of a setting than over Rivers's discourse of radical freedom, in which he idealizes the borderlands to legitimate his quest for total self-determination: "Happy are we / Who live in these disputed tracts that own / No law but what each man makes for himself. / Here justice has indeed a field of triumph!" (2.1.51–54). His libertarian utopia is scarcely realized in the course of the play; any lingering doubts are put to rest in the late scene between Mortimer and Robert.

One cannot help wondering whether Wordsworth, looking back on his work, might have confused his own aesthetic decisions with the rhetoric of a character whom those decisions were calculated to condemn. For it is hard to avoid seeing in Robert a character who is *not* "at liberty to act on [his] own impulses." The constraints upon his liberty of action reveal his character as essentially a product of Wordsworth's historical imagination, unlike other characters in the play who receive more or less historical coloring. Most readers, however, have overlooked the historical conception of Robert's character; even Mary Moorman, who vividly depicts the poverty surrounding the Wordsworths at Racedown, declares that "*The Borderers* has no concern with social evils, just as it has no definite historical setting."[19] She is wrong

---

19. Mary Moorman, *William Wordsworth: A Biography* (Oxford: Clarendon Press, 1957) 1:283–84 and 303. Among recent critics only Marjean D. Purinton has explicitly addressed the play's setting, in *Romantic Ideology Unmasked* (Newark: University of Delaware Press, 1994) 31–34. Purinton raises the issue only to dismiss it: "actions and historical events are merely the outward symbols of mental structures and processes" (34).

on both counts but right to connect the two points. Robert's poverty has subjected him to legally sanctioned torture and false imprisonment, and Wordsworth carefully traces these to the play's "scene and period of action," set, as the opening stage direction states, in the middle of the thirteenth century, immediately after the baronial wars. The polemical currency of constitutional history in the 1790s would have ensured the audience's awareness that this was the point in English history when the chartered rights granted by Magna Carta were first commanding broad observance, but not yet for any man "of whatever state or condition he may be"—not, that is, for a "cottager" like Robert.

The scene's historical specificity deserves some emphasis. When Wordsworth identifies Robert as a "cottager" in the *dramatis personae,* he means to indicate a specific class position within a well-defined economic system: "a peasant who occupies a cot-house or cottage belonging to a farm . . . for which he has . . . to give or provide labour on a farm, at a fixed rate, when required."[20] In the 1790s, "cottier" was becoming current as a term for those subject to such arrangements; the term used by historians writing about the feudal period dramatized in *The Borderers* was "bordar." Such economic arrangements were quickly becoming outmoded, except in the Lake District. Michael H. Friedman writes that, in spite of Wordsworth's explicit worry that "capitalism was eroding the traditional affective relations," the *Lyrical Ballads* show that such "patriarchal, feudal relations were more persistent in Westmoreland and Cumberland than elsewhere."[21] David Simpson notes that in the Lake District, around 1794, "only one-third of the land was freehold, the rest held 'by that species of vassalage called customary tenure; subject to the payment of fines and heriots, on alienation, death of the lord, or death of tenant, and the payment of certain annual rents, and performance of various services.'"[22] Robert's circumstances may be imagined in terms of Elie Halévy's account of feudal remnants in the economy of the Lake District:

20. See "Cottar, cotter," in *The Compact Edition of the Oxford English Dictionary,* 1979 ed.; see also "cottier."
21. Michael H. Friedman, *The Making of a Tory Humanist: William Wordsworth and the Idea of Community* (New York: Columbia University Press, 1979) 11. Friedman also notes that "Heriot, a feudal duty or tribute due, under English Law, to a lord upon the death of a tenant, lasted there into the first quarter of the nineteenth century."
22. David Simpson, *Wordsworth's Historical Imagination: The Poetry of Displacement* (New York: Methuen, 1987) 84; quoting John Bailey and George Culley, *General View of the Agriculture of the County of Cumberland* (London, 1794) 11.

In the North of England and the South of Scotland a contract of service prevailed in virtue of which the agricultural labourer, the hind as he was called, not only received part of his wages in cash but was in addition lodged in a cottage of his own, given a piece of land, and supplied with a certain amount of fuel and oats. In return for these advantages the hind entered into an obligation to work for his master the whole year round. This bondage system was perhaps simply an attenuated form of ancient serfdom.[23]

Wordsworth was certainly familiar with these remnants of serfdom and with their impact, for good and for ill, on the lower classes. Alice Chandler argues, for example, that Goody Blake's nocturnal thievery can be seen as an "exercise [of] her traditional rights of turbary, or wood-gathering."[24] Wordsworth had openly condemned the cottage system in *Adventures on Salisbury Plain:* "Then rose a mansion proud our woods among, / And cottage after cottage owned its sway" (300–301). Others, including Southey, Arthur Young, and William Cobbett, would advocate the cottage system as an improvement of the general condition of English laborers; and Wordsworth himself would come, in 1818, to praise the same residually feudal arrangements in his cynical advice to Lord Lonsdale that "the feudal power yet surviving in Eng-

23. Halévy, *A History of the English People in 1815* 213. As Arnold Bennett noted in his story "The Elixir of Youth," a Scottish collier was "legally enslaved to his colliery, legally liable to be sold with the colliery as a chattel, and legally bound to bring up all his sons as colliers, until the Act of George III [actually two acts, passed in 1775 and 1796] put an end to this incredible survival from the customs of the Dark Ages" (Bennett, "The Elixir of Youth," in *The Matador of the Five Towns and Other Stories* [New York: Doran, 1912] 32). For further details see Martha Vicinus, *The Industrial Muse: A Study of Nineteenth Century British Working-Class Literature* (London: Croom Helm, 1974).

24. Alice Chandler, *A Dream of Order: The Medieval Ideal in Nineteenth-Century English Literature* (Lincoln: University of Nebraska Press, 1970) 98. Chandler also explains how such remnants of feudalism became important to Scott: "In the Scotland of his youth, where ancient fortifications still dominated the landscape, many aspects of feudal land tenure still prevailed. Scottish peasants paid their rent with services as well as money—with arriages or ploughings, bounages or reapings, carriages or carting. Wordsworth's Highland reaper, singing of 'old unhappy far-off things, / And battles long ago,' could have been a real figure in his archaic world" (25). She recognizes that this was Wordsworth's world as well: "In the area surrounding the Lake District, somewhat similar conditions existed, although the machinery of land tenure was somewhat different. For all his sturdy independence, the northern yeoman was in some respects a villein still. His land was burdened with dues and heriots; his time cut into by the 'boon days' on which, if summoned, he might have to fetch and carry the lord's peat, plough or harrow his fields, reap his corn, make his hay, or carry his letters. Particularly in Cumberland, antique customs tended to prevail long after they had died out elsewhere" (58).

land is eminently serviceable in counteracting the popular tendency to reform."[25]

In 1797, however, Wordsworth wished to show the terrible consequences of the fact that, in the late feudal context of *The Borderers*, Robert does not own his labor. He comes upon the dying Herbert because he is out late on the heath; he is there because he tends someone else's flocks; he tends someone else's flocks because he does not own his labor; and the alienation of his labor entails the alienation of his liberty to act on Herbert's behalf. Wordsworth, then, uses Robert to represent a specific (and to some extent current) economic arrangement that robs the poor of their "native freedom."[26] But the mimetic realism of that representation is relatively unimportant. It is the structure of Wordsworth's plot, as it plays out Mortimer's compulsion to identify his free agency in Robert, that allows him to bring out a historical contradiction: while Robert may be a free agent in moral and theological discourses, he is not a free man in thirteenth-century law. His dilemma in not knowing whether to help Herbert, or even whether to acknowledge his lack of benevolence, would, in the context of the 1790s debates over the rights of man, have brought to mind certain social conditions that followed upon the establishment of Magna Carta. The provision that applies to Robert's case is cap. 39: "No *free man* shall be taken or imprisoned . . . except by lawful judgment of his peers or by the law of the land."[27] *Habeas corpus,* after Pitt suspended it in 1795, became perhaps the single most contested liberty among radical and moderate pamphleteers, and the historical genesis of this chartered liberty is

---

25. See Chandler, *Dream of Order* 77, 99, and Letter, 28 Nov. 1818 in *Letters of William and Mary Wordsworth,* ed. Ernest de Selincourt, 2d ed., *The Middle Years, Part II, 1812–1820,* rev. by Mary Moorman and Alan G. Hill (Oxford: Clarendon Press, 1970), 508. The elder Lord Lonsdale, retainer of Wordsworth's father, was characterized by DeQuincey as "a true feudal chieftain." See Thomas DeQuincey, "William Wordsworth," in *Tait's Edinburgh Magazine,* 1839; repr. in *Recollections of the Lakes and the Lake Poets,* ed. David Wright (New York: Penguin, 1985) 149.

26. See C. B. Macpherson, *The Political Theory of Possessive Individualism* (New York: Oxford University Press, 1975) 146; and C. E. Searle, "Custom, Class Conflict and Agrarian Capitalism: The Cumbrian Customary Economy in the Eighteenth Century," *Past and Present* 110 (1986): 106–33. The idea became a staple of Reform literature, as in Shelley's *Philosophical View of Reform:* "Labor, industry, economy, skill, genius, or any similar powers honorably and innocently exerted are the foundations of one description of property, and all true political institutions ought to defend every man in the exercise of his discretion with respect to property so acquired" (Shelley, *Prose* 250).

27. Magna Carta 1215 cap. 39, emphasis added; quoted from J. C. Holt, *Magna Carta* (Cambridge: Cambridge University Press, 1965) 327.

clearly marked in *The Borderers,* both in Robert's background and in the date of the action. *The Borderers* is set at the precise time when this cornerstone of English law was first made secure, for the baronial wars were significant chiefly (as one historian specifies) for hastening "the decay of the old feudal forms of justice—trial by ordeal of battle or of torture."[28] To know this is to acknowledge more than gothic sensationalism in Margaret's exclamation to her husband: "in my dreams a thousand times have I heard the cracking of your joints upon that dreadful engine" (4.3.85). Her fears diagnose Robert's inability to act as a consequence of his having been subjected to that genuinely external compulsion to confess, "trial by ordeal of torture."

Such historical details make a strange contrast to the predominantly moral framework in which Rivers would have his actions understood. For the "other impulse" bearing down on Robert can be called external with a certainty quite unlike the assurance Rivers uses to mask his ambivalence. If one were to apply to Robert the same interpretive criteria I applied to the confession of Rivers, one would have to say that the threat of torture *may* compel Robert to act (or not act) in certain ways, or it *may* simply allow him to deny his freedom. But those criteria are cancelled by the sense that Wordsworth dated the action of his play to construct a parallel between the recently abolished structures of French ancien régime society and the unreformed legal apparatus that sustained an ancien régime feudalism in England. Moral discriminations seem to be overridden by the suspicion that Robert is put on stage to refresh a memory of exploitation and abuse that, for those unable to afford theater tickets, had hardly decayed in the 1790s.[29]

This memory is what comes between Robert and Mortimer in their scene together. The general theme of economic distress hindering benevolence was clear already in 4.3, as Theresa M. Kelley has noted: "Robert leaves Herbert to die because, as a poor man with a family to feed, he fears reprisal should he end up with a dead man on his hands. His

28. Bonamy Dobrée, *English Revolts* (London: H. Joseph, 1937) 39.
29. On Magna Carta and "chartered rights," see E. P. Thompson, " 'London'," in *Interpreting Blake,* ed. Michael Phillips (New York: Cambridge University Press, 1978) 5–10; on such related figures as "the free-born Englishman" and "Saxon liberties," see Thompson, *The Making of the English Working Class* (New York: Vintage, 1966). Technically, the liberties granted in cap. 39 had long since been extended to all classes; the qualification "no free man" was changed in 1354, in response to social pressures, to read: "no man of whatever estate or condition he may be" (Holt, *Magna Carta* 9; quoting from 28 Edward III, cap. 3).

The Borderers

wife . . . reasons that the old man may be rich or well placed and that he or his heirs may reward them."[30] But Robert's scene with Mortimer dramatizes something more specific: the disruption of consciousness Peter Szondi calls "alienated conditionality," a feature of later naturalist drama foreshadowed in *The Borderers* as the link between forfeiting one's labor and forfeiting one's freedom of action.[31] The theme of "alienated conditionality" contrasts with Godwin's materialist ethics in allowing us to historicize not the material forces that make us act, but the material basis of a social system that inhibits potential agents. Robert's complicity in Herbert's death, we are encouraged to think, stems not from moral but from social causes: the legal abuses to which he has been subjected have entirely destroyed his ability to act, and all that remains for him is to equivocate.

It need not be claimed that Robert's poverty *compels* his conduct. It is enough to see how poverty justifies *for him* the claim to compulsion. His rationalizations follow the pattern of Romeo's scene with the Apothecary:

> *Romeo.* Need and oppression starveth in thy eyes,
> Contempt and beggary hangs upon thy back:
> The world is not thy friend, nor the world's law;
> The world affords no law to make thee rich;
> Then be not poor, but break it and take this.
> *Apoth.* My poverty, but not my will, consents.
>
> (5.1.70–75)

Southey, recalling this last line in his 1807 *Letters from England*, comments that the condition of the working classes in the north of England might allow half of England's criminals the same extenuation. And the Southey of 1807, by his own avowal, was no longer the Southey of 1794.[32]

The interpretive hypothesis of "alienated conditionality" diagnoses social causes for moral or psychological effects. Whether it is *Wordsworth*'s hypothesis can be tested upon the manner in which Mortimer

---

30. Theresa M. Kelley, *Wordsworth's Revisionary Aesthetics* (New York: Cambridge University Press, 1988) 76.
31. Peter Szondi, *Theory of the Modern Drama*, ed. and trans. Michael Hays (Minneapolis: University of Minnesota Press, 1987) 35–41.
32. [Robert Southey], *Letters from England: by Don Manuel Alvarez Espriella. Translated from the Spanish*, ed. Jack Simmons (London: Cresset, 1951) 200.

takes Robert as his mirror. Mortimer has actively abandoned Herbert because, being beyond history in Wordsworth's view, he is free to administer this radical form of justice. Robert has abandoned Herbert because, like so many characters in English Jacobin literature, historically specific social pressures have robbed him of his freedom to act.[33] Robert can serve as Mortimer's mirror because, paradoxically, he is subject to social conditions which Mortimer, occupying an ideal region on the borders of society, has escaped. At this point in Wordsworth's play, however, the contradiction is purposefully suspended in an uncanny moment of horrid sympathy between the perpetrator of one injustice and the victim of another.[34]

This pseudo-recognition scene demands a reappraisal of the technique Wordsworth later thought he had used in abstracting his play's moral themes from historical specifics, in light of what now appears to be a thoroughly considered historicism, calculatedly limited to a single minor character. Robert figures the return of a historical realism that had to be repressed in the moral tribulations of Rivers and Mortimer. As a result, Mortimer's misrecognition of his own free agency in Robert exposes that free agency as having been a misrecognition all along. Yet it is important to see that Mortimer now, for the first time, recognizes the structure of misrecognition into which Wordsworth shows him falling; his dawning insight may be understood as the source of his verbal confusion or incipient madness. Mortimer, as his strange lines suggest, now realizes that his recognition depends on Robert's being reduced from a historicized character to an abstract figure of the freedom that now haunts Mortimer himself. He sees how he has reduced a man—as he has himself been reduced—to a manifestation of "the shape of man."

What kind of drama can make a space of absolute repression mirror a space of absolute freedom? A drama that is by design a closet drama,

---

33. The power of the law to obliterate free agency appears in *The Borderers* as it would be described in Charles Maturin's *Melmoth the Wanderer*: "one of its most admirable triumphs is in that ingenuity by which it contrives to convert a difficulty into an impossibility, and punish a man for not doing what it has rendered impracticable for him to do" (*Melmoth the Wanderer,* ed. Douglas Grant [New York: Oxford University Press, 1989] 306). The epigram's original context is imprisonment for debt.

34. Mortimer's faceoff with Robert might be seen as figuring the precarious balance between the two sides of William Empson's "realistic pastoral": "So far as the person described is outside society because too poor for its benefits he is independent, as the artist claims to be, and can be a critic of society; so far as he is forced by this into crime he is the judge of the society that judges him" (*Some Versions of Pastoral* [New York: New Directions, 1974] 16).

The Borderers

a text meant to provide a critical perspective on the ways in which theater allows free agency to be read off appearances. Mortimer's apparently haunted line about something appearing in "the shape of man" marks the moment at which Wordsworth's characters step out of their roles to reflect on how those roles were constituted: Robert's by his poverty, Mortimer's by a misrecognition of himself in an abstract moral discourse that claimed to make the shape of man appear. In this passage, Wordsworth's closet drama begins to advance a critique of staged or imitated action as an appearance that *cannot* serve as a reliable ground for a spectator's recognition of his own freedom to act. The momentary alienation effect implicit in the role-playing, dressing-up sense of "putting on the shape of man" hints at a proto-Brechtian critique of sympathetic spectatorship, a convention already called into question by earlier scenes of possibly unreliable sympathetic identification, particularly Rivers's mirror speech.[35]

Yet Mortimer's misrecognition of his own agency—first in the mirror held up by Rivers's moral discourse, now while gazing at Robert "for some time"—results from the same movement of identification that members of an audience must undergo if a play is to hold up a mirror to nature. In *The Borderers,* the mirror of mimetic theater thus appears to shatter in its collision with history, the human things that, in Mortimer's words, "press so hard on" him. Mortimer's confused identification allows us to see that a free man who wants to stand outside history can easily—too easily—recognize his moral or psychological bondage in the compulsory legal bondage of an unfree man. In the same way, an audience of sympathetic spectators can easily—too easily—recognize *its* free agency in actors or characters who are bound by their roles. We normally understand the latter problem to be defined by an ontological difference between characters and spectators, but *The Borderers* shows how theatricality can lead to a misrecognition that denies historical differences. By identifying theatricality with a pervasive pattern of misrecognition—turning theater against theater—this scene offers a powerful rejoinder to Yeats's complaint that Wordsworth's moral sense "has no theatrical element."[36]

---

35. One odd example is the scene in which the blind Herbert envisions his wife seeing his blindness: "She saw my blasted face" (1.1.153).

36. W. B. Yeats, *Memoirs: Autobiography—First Draft, Journal,* ed. Denis Donaghue (London: Macmillan, 1972) 151; quoted from Timothy Webb, "The Romantic Poet and the Stage," in *The Romantic Theatre,* ed. Richard Allen Cave (Totowa, NJ: Barnes and Noble Books, 1986) 9.

The Borderers, then, like many plays written in the aftermath of the French Revolution, comments on the power of theater.[37] Like many others, Wordsworth conceived the theater of the Revolution as a metaphor designating the broader political arena in which a didactic rhetoric of action could be acted out. Yet Wordsworth gives a precise meaning to the cliché of "theatricalized" political action: *The Borderers* exposes a theatrical mechanism by which a discourse teaching radical action can make action contagious, capable of replicating itself unimpeded by historical consciousness. Its final scenes, however, track the emergence of an awareness that might keep that contagion in check.

2.

Before examining those final scenes, I must return briefly to the problem with which I began. Wordsworth's motive for having a man speak on stage—for making scenes, as distinct from telling tales—has begun to emerge as a double wish: to verify the presence of a restricted moral agency that cannot otherwise be known, and to show the political hazards of uses of language that allow one to avoid that agency either by exaggerating it (as freedom) or denying it (as compulsion). The scenes with Robert show how the historical conditioning of agency can occasion confused moral and social judgments. But they also begin to show how the sense of making discoveries about the nature of agency can be morally impoverishing. In taking that further step, they begin to move Wordsworth toward the political quietism whose canonical voice is Burke's *Reflections:* "We know that we have made no discoveries; and we think that no discoveries are to be made, in morality; nor many in the great principles of government, nor in the ideas of liberty, which were understood long before we were born, altogether as well as they will be after the grave has heaped its mould upon our presumption, and the silent tomb shall have imposed its law on our pert loquacity."[38] Mortimer's impoverishment will be signalled most clearly in the delusion of his final speech, a delusion we seem to be invited to

37. See David Marshall, "The Eye-Witnesses of *The Borderers,*" *Studies in Romanticism* 27 (1988): 391–98.
38. Edmund Burke, *Reflections on the Revolution in France,* ed. Conor Cruise O'Brien (New York: Penguin, 1981) 182.

share, in which solipsism is sought out as though it were a sublime and distinguishing achievement: "I will wander on," Mortimer imagines, "Living by mere intensity of thought" (5.3.272). By sentencing himself to a more extreme exile, Mortimer usurps the judicial authority invested in his community of exiles, passing beyond the law to which he means to submit and asserting—as though he were going beyond suicide—the infinite autonomy with which he vindicates, anachronistically, his precarious claim to the status of liberal subject.[39]

In drawing distinctions between Rivers and Robert in the motives that make them claim compulsion, I have implicitly questioned the legitimacy of such claims, even while recognizing that there are circumstances in which liberals like the Wordsworth of 1797 can argue convincingly in their defense. It is, however, affectively impossible to read *The Borderers* without feeling the power of the *idea* of compulsion—without, that is, taking compulsion seriously. Readers are normally inclined to take compulsion as seriously as they take anything, as Wittgenstein noted in explaining the allure of Freudian determinism.[40] It would be presumptuous to try to weigh Mortimer's intellectual gain and moral loss without taking into account, and attempting to explain, the *frisson* Wordsworth uses to link Mortimer's fate to the emotional power carried by the psychoanalytic postulate of a compulsion to repeat.

Marlon Ross has proposed a theoretical explanation of anxieties about repetition among the male Romantic poets:

> The fear of repetition is so overwhelming to the romantics because repetition stresses the disorderliness of desire, the static nature of ideology.... Romantic ideology, in order to assert the purposeful nature of self-possessing desire, attempts to reject the repetitious nature of desire.... The romantic poet fears most that his destiny may come to be controlled by another, that he will be forced to *repeat* another's desire, that his desire will not be the source of its own influence and progression.[41]

---

39. On suicide and liberal autonomy in English tragedy, see Catherine Belsey, *The Subject of Tragedy: Identity and Difference in Renaissance Drama* (New York: Methuen, 1985) 124–25.

40. See Laura Quinney, *Literary Power and the Criteria of Truth* (Gainesville: University Press of Florida, 1995) 3–5.

41. Marlon Ross, *The Contours of Masculine Desire: Romanticism and the Rise of Women's Poetry* (New York: Oxford University Press, 1989) 11.

Ross argues that the canonical Romantics wrote poems "in order to reconfirm their capacity to influence the world in ways sociohistorically determined as masculine" (3), and that they could ensure their productivity only by enlisting ideology to control the "disorderliness" of a desire that (in the terms Ross borrows from Deleuze and Guattari) has no origin, no end, and no direction. If desire and ideology are opposites, then Ross's claim that "repetition stresses the disorderliness of desire, the static nature of ideology" can only mean that the fear of repetition expresses a fear of desire, *but also* a fear of what is powerful enough to stop desire. To assert that this double fear is, however, the peculiar feature of the male Romantic poets is only to recognize that they saw and reflected upon the "machinery" of desire. Although Ross aims to give a historical account of desire ("desire itself is defined by historical process," 7), he succeeds mainly in telling us where to find such an account: in the ambivalent fears of the male romantics.

The Borderers dramatizes the fear of repeating another's desire, and it does this for a specific purpose: to trace the development of a postrevolutionary moral disease Wordsworth terms "after-vacancy." To stop short at enjoying the effects of the ambivalence thematized in the play—the fear of desire being shadowed by a fear of what controls desire—would be to dodge Wordsworth's historical project. For his master plot of "strange repetition" makes us ask: How can we reconcile the motives, judgments, and desires of apparently autonomous characters with the more impersonal mechanism of repetition that appears to govern the replication of action? In blunter terms, is Mortimer (or Rivers, or Wordsworth) active or passive, and how can we tell the difference? The plot's attraction for Wordsworth lay in the ways in which such ambiguities capture a historically specific anxiety he was eager to put to rest.

I call the anxiety historically specific not because its cause can be readily identified but only because it was limited. For within three years Wordsworth would take the ability to tell the difference between active and passive as a criterion for poetic success and, implicitly, moral autonomy. That is the implication of his 1800 "Note on The Ancient Mariner," where he criticizes the man who blesses unaware in terms he would later apply to Coleridge himself: "he does not act, but is continually acted upon."[42] It is easy to admit this as a criticism of Coleridge's

---

42. In *Lyrical Ballads* (1800). On *The Borderers* and *Rime of the Ancient Mariner,* see esp. Geoffrey Hartman, *Wordsworth's Poetry, 1787–1814* (New Haven: Yale University Press, 1977) 131–35; and, more recently, Bromwich, "Revolutionary Justice," 15

narrative technique; but given the force of Wordsworth's anxieties in *The Borderers,* the phrasing seems to express a newfound urge to confine the "wide, wide sea" of Coleridge's moral universe within the alternative: active *or* passive. If Wordsworth's remark seems reductive it is not because we ourselves readily conceive the moral world in some more subtly shaded terms—having no middle voice in English, we have few conventions for what falls between active and passive—but because what we tend to appreciate in Wordsworth and Coleridge is their refusal to rest content with a moral logic structured by the principle of the excluded middle. "What fascinates Coleridge," Mary Jacobus proposes in her reading of "The Eolian Harp," "is the coexistence of action and passivity."[43] That is also what continues to fascinate us in texts that speak out of a moral universe we know is unlike ours. It would be quixotic to try to argue that this fascination is in every instance historically determined; but Wordsworth's impulse to root it out in the second edition of *Lyrical Ballads,* instead of cultivating it as he had in *The Borderers,* suggests that he had come to think of it as having historical determinants at least in his own work.

Wordsworth attempted to resolve his anxiety about telling the difference between active and passive by conceiving action as the outward expression of passive feelings (or passion). His insistence on this orderly relation between passive and active often surfaces when he is looking back at the postrevolutionary disillusionment he recounts in the "Imagination, How Impaired" portions of *The Prelude.* It is the Solitary, *The Excursion*'s reincarnation of Mortimer as a soured radical, who takes it upon himself "not to feel, / And, therefore, not to act." His need to match feeling neatly to action, even by denying both, is easier to state than to fulfill; for the decision "not to act" is undermined as the imperative "not to feel" is betrayed by the speech's pathos. The Solitary seems inadver-

---

and 22–24. Simpson sees Wordsworth himself as "a good example of the way in which the more general debate about freedom and determination, whether carried on by literary critics or by social scientists, is not much furthered by recourse to ungainly extremes. Subjectivity is neither a 'historically' created automaton, passively reproducing its imprinted culture, nor an exclusively individual entity governing itself by choice and free will" (5).

43. Mary Jacobus, *Tradition and Experiment in Wordsworth's "Lyrical Ballads" (1798)* (Oxford: Clarendon Press, 1976) 70. Some critics would make this moral fascination a special case of Coleridge's desire, as Thomas McFarland puts it, "to encompass both black and white" ("Coleridge and the Charge of Political Apostasy," in *Coleridge's Biographia Literaria: Text and Meaning,* ed. Frederick Burwick [Columbus: Ohio State University Press, 1989] 194). I would place it rather at the root of his sense of the urgency of affirming personal autonomy.

tently to speak for Wordsworth himself, who claims elsewhere to avoid action in favor of feeling as a matter of aesthetic principle. Wordsworth speaks in "Hart-Leap Well" of his lack of talent for "the moving accident," and he confessed in the 1800 preface that, because the poet—like Mortimer, perhaps—only identifies with and imitates the passions of others, his work "is in some degree mechanical compared with the freedom and power of real and substantial action and suffering."[44]

Coleridge put Wordsworth's finger on a way of describing the relation between action and feeling shortly after the composition of *The Borderers*. He gave that relation a striking formulation in a letter dictated to Dorothy Wordsworth over William's signature, to be sent to Wilberforce with a copy of the 1800 *Lyrical Ballads*. The opening sentence has Wordsworth speak in anticipation of the Solitary's echo of Hamlet: "I composed the accompanying poems under the persuasion that all which is usually included under the name of action bears the same pro[por]tion (in respect of worth) to the affections, as a language to the thing signified."[45] While the hierarchical, proportional formula may be pure Coleridge, the claim that the grounding of action bears a homologous relation to the grounding of language resembles moments in which Wordsworth himself writes of the relation between action and the affections. In Book 9 of *The Prelude*, for instance, the sympathetic portrait of the good revolutionary Michel Beaupuy provides an occasion for formulating the structure whereby action can be regarded as "signif[ying]" the affections: Beaupuy is described as "one whom circumstance / Hath call'd upon to embody his deep sense / In action, give it outwardly a shape" (9:407–409).[46] Action gives shape to sense, as a body gives shape to the soul—just as "words," in the third of Wordsworth's *Essays upon Epitaphs,* are said to be "an incarnation of thought."[47]

Such formulaic attempts to draw a clean line between active and

---

44. Wordsworth, *Prose* 1:138.
45. Coleridge, *Letters* 2:666.
46. The use of "shape" here joins the portrait of Beaupuy to the passage in which Wordsworth addresses to Coleridge his wish, already fulfilled, to write a play: "Share with me, Friend! the wish / That some dramatic tale, endued with *shapes* / Livelier, and flinging out less guarded words / Than suit the work we fashion, might set forth / What then I learned, or think I learned, of truth, / And the errors into which I fell" (*Prelude* 11:282–87, emphasis added).
47. Wordsworth, *Prose* 2:85. Empson, taking his cue from the adjective "deep," explains the "higher claims" he sees Wordsworth making here for sense: "Good judgment here becomes practically the Creative Imagination applied to politics"; see "Sense in *The Prelude*," *The Structure of Complex Words* (London: Chatto and Windus, 1977) 292.

The Borderers

passive by tracing action (one thing) to its origin in passion (a very different thing) are, however, routinely plagued by uncertainties about the origins of the formulas themselves. Is the *Prelude*'s conception of the political imagination Wordsworth's or Beaupuy's? Is the proportional formula balancing actions and affections Wordsworth's or Coleridge's? Such worries over the ownership of an idea or its expression—over whether one has actively produced it or only passively felt it—can produce a further worry about who owns the worry. Coleridge's later anxiety about critics who "derive every rill they behold flowing, from a perforation made in some other man's tank" (preface to *Christabel*) might be merely a development of Wordsworth's figure in the *Prelude:*

> Who knows the individual hour in which
> His habits were first sown even as a seed,
> Who that shall point as with a wand, and say
> 'This portion of the river of my mind
> Came from yon fountain'?
>
> (1805 2:211–15)

The formulas I have quoted attempt to put a stop to the infinite regress that would follow upon any attempt to point in this way. *The Borderers,* however, seeks to convey the affective intensity of the problem those formulas claim so glibly to resolve. It does so by showing how the belief that individual actions give shape to our very own affections is threatened and finally undermined by a plot in which actions turn out to replicate prior patterns of action, and by making that plot more gripping than any belief.

After exposing the mechanical reproduction of projected agency in the scene between Mortimer and Robert, Wordsworth must arrange for *The Borderers* to shut the process down. But how? An answer to that question must depend upon a more exact sense of how Wordsworth regards the machinery of desire. Readers of *The Borderers* speak routinely of the plot as instancing a compulsion to repeat. The classic formulation is Geoffrey Hartman's: "One needs little psychology to see how deeply compulsive [Rivers] is: the crime he instigates is practically identical to his own, and in an unpublished preface to the play Wordsworth came close to formulating the principle of 'repetition compulsion.' "[48] Hartman may be thinking of Wordsworth's psychological account of the process that leads criminals deeper into crime:

---

48. Hartman, "Wordsworth's *The Borderers*" 767.

"Uneasiness must be driven away by fresh uneasiness," Wordsworth writes in his prefatory essay on Rivers, emphasizing how every new crime helps to make compulsion pass for freedom by seeming "to bring back again the moment of liberty and choice" (67). Or he may be thinking of the superstitious compulsions Wordsworth traces to pride.[49] Such observations hold, however, only for the single compulsive and for his accounts of himself. They may faithfully reflect Wordsworth's sketch of Rivers—or that sketch may strikingly foreshadow psychoanalysis—but they cannot explain the uncanny power of the play. For the perception of a "repetition compulsion" in *The Borderers* extends to the plot in which several characters take part; the crime Rivers instigates may be identical to his own, but it is no longer merely his own. The plot of *The Borderers,* then, follows out not a personal but a social neurosis.

I do not know that Freud touched on the exact effect Wordworth creates. It can be described, however, by considering the eery magical thinking, not unrelated to the idea of tragedy, of which Freud speaks under the rubric of "fate compulsion." It does not require a full-blown neurosis, Freud assures us in *Beyond the Pleasure Principle,* to have the impression "of being pursued by a malignant fate or possessed by some 'daemonic' power." Psychoanalysis will explain to those who feel this way that "their fate is for the most part arranged by themselves." Freud gives a number of examples that make it easy to see how the victims of fate actively arrange their victimization; in such cases, one can readily acknowledge the explanatory power of "repetition compulsion" to enlighten and to liberate. Freud then pushes on to see how far we will accept the power of that explanation: "We are much more impressed by cases where the subject appears to have a *passive* experience, over which he has no influence, but in which he meets with a repetition of the same fatality. There is the case, for instance, of the woman who married three successive husbands each of whom fell ill soon afterwards and had to be nursed by her on their death-beds."[50] There are two ways

---

49. Wordsworth on Rivers: "his pride impels him to superstition and shapes out the nature of his belief: his creed is his own: it is made and not adopted" (*The Borderers* 66). Compare Stekel's description of the compulsive as being "proud of his affliction which he alone has created and he alone fully comprehends," so that the compulsion becomes "both law and punishment at the same time," or something like an "individual religion" (*Compulsion and Doubt* 41–40, 43).

50. Freud, *Standard Edition* 18:22.

to understand such a case, Freud implies. Perhaps the woman's relation to her fate only appears to be passive, but is really an active matter, say, of having chosen only husbands likely to fall ill. In that case, psychoanalysis will be justified in extending the range of the compulsion to repeat. Alternatively, perhaps the similarity among her three marriages is purely a chance matter. In that case, psychoanalysis can explain the woman's sense of fatality as the result not of her suffering under, but merely of her being reminded about, a universal compulsion to repeat of which everyone is vaguely aware. What makes psychoanalysis itself seem uncanny here is its apparent complicity with the undecidabilities it examines. A fate that is felt as passively suffered is either actively courted, or merely random; the compulsion to repeat is either operating secretly, or merely suspected to be operating, but it is equally compulsory in both accounts. Psychoanalysis can give us no certainty about this alternative, only the certainty that the sense of fatality always bears one or the other relation to something within us that can act without our knowledge or consent.

The example of the baffled widow bears a troubling relation to psychoanalytic theory in much the same way as *The Borderers* bears a troubling relation to tragic convention. Freud would have us think of the poor woman who cannot know whether she is unknowingly determined to marry dying husbands, or whether she is only a target randomly selected to be haunted by the idea of a compulsion to repeat. But one cannot help wondering whether he is also making a joke about the plots of criminal literature. The woman has a more active role in her fate than she will admit: Is she—he didn't say it, but he didn't deny it—a poisoner? Is the uncanny indeterminacy of fate merely her cover story? *The Borderers* is, as I have suggested, preoccupied with the indeterminacy of fate, particularly in the multiplicity of frameworks through which the causal power called compulsion may be understood. That indeterminacy plays a part in the superstition Wordsworth's preface makes central to the character of Rivers, more central than it seems in the play itself. But *The Borderers* is also about cover stories, and when the play shifts to foreground the fate of Mortimer, Wordsworth seems to want to look past the indeterminacy of fate to seek a better account than the mysterious one that Rivers (or Freud) might supply.

Like *The Borderers*, Freud's example invites speculations that claim no theoretical justification. What would it feel like, one might wonder, to be the poor woman's third husband? As he lies on his deathbed, he may wonder: has my wife been paying unexplained visits to the apothecary? A less radical version of that poisonous fear might retain its quasi-biological power: Was it *me* that my wife chose, or is my marriage nothing but the punch line in a Freudian joke? Or, if the husband has read "The Uncanny," he may ask himself: is the death I seem to be passively suffering merely random and only seemingly fated, or has my object choice played an active part in arranging it? If he decides that he has, after all, willed his fate, he may be falling deeper into the magical thinking to which he was subject when he merely lamented that he was fated to die. He might well ask himself: Is my thinking now that of an obsessive neurotic? Is it paranoid?

Wordsworth answers that it is tragic. He does so by showing us the ruinous effects of such inevitable thoughts within circumstances that are both like and utterly unlike our own. Mortimer's suffering allows us to experience what it might feel like to have one's actions revealed as the working-through not of one's own, but of another's repetition compulsion. In that way, he brings us to an awareness of what we are doing as we position our reading chairs in Wordsworth's darkened theater, thinking that it is someone else (up on that imaginary stage) who is disowning his desires. By situating Mortimer's fate in relation to others, Wordsworth traces the consequences of that evasion. *The Borderers* shows how the firsthand experience of a secondhand compulsion might alter one's thinking about moral agency, and how one's intellectual discoveries in that realm might themselves gain a daemonic sway over one's actions.

3.

The entrance of historical conditions onto the stage of *The Borderers*, in the person of the tortured (or self-tormenting) cottager Robert, brings Wordsworth to rework his earlier testings of free agency in the closing scene. The final scene is devoted to an elaboration of questions about agency posed not in the discourse of criminal psychology but in the tradition of Shakespearean tragedy. *Hamlet*, *Macbeth*, and *Julius Caesar* all feature moments at which a movement toward action is made vexingly circuitous or discontinuous by discoveries about the nature of action. Shakespeare's tragic heroes meet their difficulties in talking to themselves about action before entering into action. The end of *The Borderers,* by contrast, shows the difficulty of matching talk about action with events that have already occurred, addressing the problem of what makes an event, after the fact, come to count as an action.

One challenge in reading this final scene is to find a continuity between successive stages in Mortimer's revelation of his crime to Matilda. It is hard to see dramatic development except by taking Matilda as somehow personifying Mortimer's repression, acting out his inability to recognize that he has acted in Herbert's death. Their encounters draw the play toward psychomachia, with Matilda figuring a resistance within a mind split between sentimental piety and anomie. The play approaches resolution as Mortimer strives aggressively to overcome that resistance by asserting, as Rivers had hoped to assert, that he has not, like Robert, merely slipped into passive complicity with an accidental death but has indeed acted.

Wordsworth stages Mortimer's ambivalence in three encounters. The final scene opens with Robert, convinced that someone (not himself) has committed a crime, leading in Mortimer as Herbert's murderer. But Matilda fails to identify her lover with the murderer to whom Robert refers, and she embraces Mortimer as her best consoler. The failed confrontation is repeated in the middle of the scene. Mortimer tells Matilda point-blank: "I am the murderer of thy father" (5.1.99). But Matilda runs off in search of the usual suspect. In a final encounter, Matilda prepares herself for a recognition of Mortimer's act, but it never comes; Mortimer denies having committed murder and attributes Herbert's death to culpable negligence. Matilda faints, and with his internal resistance thus disabled, Mortimer relapses into madness, echoing Rivers's retrospective wish to have murdered the old man in a prospective wish that his agency (or anyone's) might be verified with ocular proof: "I'll prove it that I murdered him—I'll prove it / Before the dullest court in Christendom" (5.3.180–81). The court of conscience pulls the play's philosophical conflict toward offstage institutions as Mortimer literally drags his witness toward the court of the Baron of St. Clair. This final movement toward society, with Mortimer surrendering his intellectual struggle, is required for the play's resolution, which must include a judgment on the hero's guilt. But a shift away from the interior casuistry allegorized in the struggle to face Matilda cannot, by itself, resolve the question that was posed: Has Mortimer acted?

One of Coleridge's lectures on *Hamlet* speaks of Hamlet's "great enormous intellectual activity, and a consequent proportionate aversion to real action." Next to that remark, in the righthand margin, Coleridge scribbled: "Action is transitory, a step, a Blow, etc."[51] Coleridge's famous insight, with its not-so-famous marginalium, is more compelling as a reading of *The Borderers* than as a reading of *Hamlet*. Mortimer's intellectual "aversion to real action," which determines his fixation on what cannot be proven to be "real action," might be taken (following Wordsworth's prefatory analysis of Rivers) as a standard problem in criminal psychology. Theodor Reik imagines the criminal mind this way: "To apply Freud's beautiful allegory—the rider has relinquished himself to the bolting horse. Does he know where it is running to and why it takes just this path? Perhaps we should say more correctly that the act occurred through him. Did he do it? Was it not rather done to him by id, by something in him?"[52]

To judge from the prominence of *Hamlet* in its dénouement, however, *The Borderers* is ultimately less concerned with criminal psychology than with the analysis of motive in Shakespearean tragedy. The last act of *Hamlet* returns obsessively to a new version of the problem of knowing whether Claudius really did murder Hamlet's father, as we have heard the Ghost claim. This new problem is not directly related to Hamlet's somewhat overrated difficulty in turning intentions into deeds; yet like that problem it arises, as the Coleridgean psychology of character maintains, from too much thinking about action. The problem of Hamlet appears at the end of the play as the difficulty, first posed by the death of Ophelia and by her family's ensuing struggle with the niceties of canon law, of deciding whether something that has happened has also been done.[53]

Is Ophelia responsible for her own death? Hamlet takes the question

---

51. Lecture 3 of the series "Shakespeare and Education," delivered 4 November 1813, in *Lectures 1808–1819 on Literature, Collected Works*, vol. 5, ed. R. A. Foakes (Princeton: Princeton University Press, 1987) 1:539. The heir of Romantic psychological criticism, A. C. Bradley, continued the quotation from *The Borderers* in discussing Lady Macbeth's "want of imagination": "she hardly imagines the act, or at most imagines its outward show, 'the motion of a muscle this way or that' " (*Shakespearean Tragedy* [New York: Fawcett, 1986] 310).

52. Theodore Reik, *The Compulsion to Confess: On the Psychoanalysis of Crime and Punishment* (New York: Farrar, Straus and Cudahy, 1959) 265.

53. Lars Engle's exceptional essay "Discourse, Agency, and Therapy in *Hamlet*" (*Exemplaria* 4 [1992]: 441–53) provides a different framework for such problems.

The Borderers

very seriously, in part because it allows him to revisit his epistemological difficulties with the Ghost, to act over again the drama of skepticism that Stanley Cavell describes as the challenge of accepting the burden of knowledge.[54] More immediately, Hamlet's interest in the questions surrounding Ophelia's death prepares him to offer an insanity plea to appease Laertes, whose father he has (or has he?) murdered. His attempt at a reconciliation restates the question about Ophelia's responsibility for her own death as a question of obvious pertinence to Mortimer's dilemma in *The Borderers:* Is the hero responsible for the death of his beloved's father?

> Was it Hamlet wronged Laertes? Never Hamlet.
> If Hamlet from himself be ta'en away,
> And when he's not himself does wrong Laertes,
> Then Hamlet does it not, Hamlet denies it.
> Who does it then? His madness.
>
> (5.2.234–38)

"His madness" (not "my madness") is an agent as the Apothecary's poverty was an agent: allegorically.[55] But if agency can thus be maintained without a human subject, then the allegory can be said to acquire its own agency as it exculpates the once distracted but now reunified subject named Hamlet. What light does this overly neat narrative cast on the problem of Ophelia?

First mad and now dead, Ophelia has no chance to reflect on the problem of accepting or denying an active part in her own death; that impossible reflection is therefore voiced by Hamlet. The scholastic gravediggers who open act 5 prepare us to replace both "Hamlet" and "Laertes" in Hamlet's insanity plea with "Ophelia," as subject and object of her own death. When Ophelia from herself was taken away, Ophelia did it not; who did it then? *Hamlet* makes such detective work dependent on the interpretation of narrative. According to Gertrude's report, Ophelia was killed by her garments: "Her clothes spread wide, / And mermaidlike awhile they bore her up. . . . / But long it could not

---

54. See Stanley Cavell, "Hamlet's Burden of Proof," in *Disowning Knowledge* 179–91.
55. A line Catherine Belsey cites from *A Woman Killed with Kindness* (1603) makes a more striking parallel: "It was not I, but rage, did this vile murder" (*Subject of Tragedy* 48).

be / Till her garments, heavy with their drink, / Pulled the poor wretch from her melodious lay / To muddy death" (4.7.175–76 and 180–83). Gertrude's story must be mapped onto Hamlet's insanity plea if we are to see the significance of Ophelia's death for the end of the play. Like Hamlet, Ophelia covered herself in the cloak of madness; unable to strip it from herself, as Hamlet claims to do, she wore it to her grave.[56]

So, did Ophelia act? Gertrude refuses to say, and act 5 ridicules the tools we might use to assemble an answer. "It must be *se offendendo*," the gravedigger pronounces, "it cannot be else. For here lies the point: if I drown myself wittingly, it argues an act, and an act hath three branches—it is to act, to do, to perform. Argal, she drowned herself wittingly" (5.1.9–13). The clown's scholastic spectrum of action does not rescue his argument from tautology: if she killed herself, then she killed herself.[57] Shakespeare takes the analytic breakdown of action as a joke; no analysis can sufficiently verify the adverb "wittingly," as the presence of Ophelia's wits (the *mens rea* of jurisprudence) can only be concluded by first being posited.[58] "To act, to do, to perform": the sequence covers the complete action Aristotle wanted to find at the basis of all plots, but it does not help to decide whether Ophelia's death counts as an action. The event has been replaced by Gertrude's narrative, which offers a plot that lacks a human agent and therefore refuses to be mapped onto a spectrum of action. The analytic breakdown of action cannot locate the moment when a narrated occurrence becomes, at once, legible as a plotted action and inaccessible as occurrence. What cannot be plotted, what exceeds narration, is the passage from the moment of occurrence to the moment of owning up to, accounting for, one's actions.

The final scene of *The Borderers* presents the same problem in the speeches in which Mortimer reflects on Herbert's death. To borrow Nietzsche's terms: Mortimer seeks to add the fiction of a "doer" to what he knows of the "deed," but he must also learn to believe in the fiction. Mortimer's struggle to imagine this doer produces a *Doppelgänger* ef-

---

56. My thinking about Gertrude's account was spurred by a spontaneous remark made many years ago by Ed Schiffer.

57. The term "spectrum," taken from J. L. Austin, is developed by Michael Goldman in *Acting and Action in Shakespearean Tragedy* (Princeton: Princeton University Press, 1985) 17–45, esp. 20.

58. On the positing of *mens rea* in cases of insanity, see Hart, "Ascription of Responsibility."

fect like that of *Frankenstein,* which resembles *The Borderers* in its acute awareness of the difficulties of identifying an ultimate agent for unowned acts. Mortimer's doubling acts out the duplicity he once perceived in Herbert, and which he now denies in an almost impenetrable line: "The dead have but one face" (5.3.46). Like Victor Frankenstein, Mortimer gives himself two faces, the face of the benevolent lover and the face of the "monster" that has exterminated his beloved's family:

> Matilda.   Thy limbs are torn, thy face is pale and haggard—
> Hast thou pursued the monster?
> Mortimer.   Aye, and found him,
> And he must perish.
> Matilda.   Leave him to the pangs
> Of his own breast.
> Mortimer.   He must be put to death,
> And for thy sake, for he will haunt thy bed.
>   (5.3.78–82)

Mortimer's doubling sets up the play's climactic identification. Knowing that Matilda has cursed the "monster," Mortimer now redeems his odd line about Herbert's "one face":

> Mortimer.   Look on my face.
> Matilda.   Oh! when has this affliction visited thee?
> Mortimer.   I am the murderer of thy father.
>   (5.2.97–99)

Wordsworth's drafts of this last line reveal a gradual movement away from the idea of having Mortimer identify himself directly with the murderous "monster." The line had begun slightly closer to an all-out assault on Matilda: "I am thy father's murderer."[59] The 1842 text makes the same identification in a fussy, stuttering circumlocution that makes Mortimer sound like Reik's Freudian criminal: "Through me, through me / Thy Father perished" (2182–83). All three versions hint that Mortimer does not possess his agency: in the first two, the genitive can make him appear as Herbert's possession, while in the last he appears as a means or instrument employed by another person or force. It is as though the direct assertion of agency, as originally written, was

---

59. See the drafts in the Cornell edition (686), and Osborn's note on the lines (276n.).

judged an overly hasty admission on Mortimer's part; the later versions have Wordsworth correcting Mortimer's mistake.

The judgment of overhastiness could be supported by the soliloquy that follows in the early version. Mortimer reflects that having abandoned Herbert without his scrip to sustain him might not, after all, make him a murderer:

> Three words have such a power! This mighty burden
> All off at once! 'Tis done, and so done too,
> That I have cased her heart in adamant.
> This little scrip when first I found it here—
> I sunk ten thousand fathoms into hell.
> I was a coward then—but now am schooled
> To firmer purposes. There doth not lie
> Within the compass of a mortal thought
> A deed that I would shrink from—and I can endure.
> If I had done it with a mind resolved,
> There had been something in the deed
> To give me strength to bear the recollection,
> But as it is, this scrip which would not cause
> The little finger of a child to ache
> Doth lie upon my bosom with a load
> A mountain could not equal.
>
> (5.3.100–15)

Mortimer hesitantly reverts to the rhetoric in which he has been schooled by Rivers. But his reflection on his "deed," cast like Rivers's earlier reflections in the decisive phrasing of *Macbeth* (" 'Tis done"), leaves him wishing he had done this deed more decisively (" 'Twere well 'twere done quickly," *Macbeth* 1.7.2). His vexation seems to arise from a suspicion that he may never have acted. Who is to say? He may have as yet no act to serve as the first term in the series of future acts he envisions, and he is haunted by the idea that he may never be able to recall any well-formed act to repent.

The discourse of motive, "the name of action" Mortimer continues to utter in the borrowed voice of Rivers, is inadequate to name what he did. Naming an act an act does, however, seem to have a "power" of its own: the power to make something that has happened count as an action. It also has a more immediate power to turn the violence of

The Borderers

the act it names upon the interlocutor.[60] The final, climactic encounter between Matilda and Mortimer brings out this "power":

> Matilda. —Did you murder him?
> Mortimer. No, no, not murder him.—But knowest thou this?
> Matilda. That belt—the first gift of my love.
> —It is the scrip that held my father's food.
> Mortimer. I led him to the middle of the heath.
> I left him without food and so he died.
> [*Matilda sinks senseless on the ground*]
> Why may we speak these things and do no more?
> Why should a thrust of the arm have such a power
> And things like these be heard in vain?
> —She is not dead.
>
> (5.3.165–74)

"*And so* he died": Mortimer's anticlimax refuses the linkage of cause and effect that would firmly establish his agency; he cannot be Herbert's murderer because Herbert has no murderer. This negative version of the discourse of motive, however, has the same powers as its positive counterpart: both the power to determine whether an occurrence counts as an action, and the power to work violent effects. Mortimer has to reassure himself that his words have not taken on the power to kill—"*She* is not dead"—because he knows that words do have that power.

Mortimer's decision, after this confession, to call himself a murderer and to prove it, not just in the court of conscience but in the court of the Baron of St. Clair, follows from his recognition that the language of motive, unlike "a thrust of the arm," will act on its own, whether it is intended to establish or to deny agency. Any confession Mortimer can make, he realizes, will confer a false meaning on Herbert's meaningless death. He sees that his language will work upon his actions to produce a coherent account that must be at odds with experience. For what acts upon Mortimer in this final scene appears to him, after all his efforts to assert his personal agency, as a free-floating agency of language that cannot be reduced to the intentions of the character through which it performs.

60. For details on the Schillerian and Parisian antecedents of Mortimer's violent *coup*, see Parker's " 'In some sort seeing with my proper eyes.' "

4.

That discovery—it might also be called an attitude—reduces the urge for accountability that drives Mortimer toward the Baron of St. Clair from a social to a psychological impulse. For Mortimer's movement toward an external seat of judgment is suspended when he lapses briefly into madness. The return of Rivers, a few moments later, brings Mortimer back to himself so completely that he forgets the rest of his world, as he had in the intensity of Rivers's act 4 confession. The world quickly returns with a vengeance; Mortimer's band of outlaws enters to drag Rivers, who "smiles exultingly," to his death. Rivers has indeed won his victory, for Mortimer will never carry through on the social insight that struck him dumb in his scene with the peasant, will never emerge from the psychological discourse that drives all crime and all punishment back into the depths of private subjectivity. Mortimer has been offered a choice: either confront his agency in its social and political aspects, or muse upon it in the privacy of a self-imposed exile like that which Rivers had embraced. His final claim to an unconditioned tragic subjectivity should not, however, be glorified as an active moral choice, for by the time he makes it he seems to have forgotten the alternative. It is the seductive power of the language of tragedy that has allowed him to forget.

I do not mean to lament that power, for it lends the play much of the moral interest so evidently lacking in plays like *The Fall of Robespierre* and *Wat Tyler*. I mean only to point to the costs that are incurred. Consider how Mortimer responds to Matilda's fainting spell (in the wording of the revised text) with a reflection on the futility of trying to master the power of words: "Why should a thrust of the arm have such a power, / And words that tell these things be heard in vain?" It is a peculiarly cold and abstract response; it seems less a meditation on the play's thematic concerns than a defensive flinching from the reality of others' suffering. Yet Wordsworth seems to stand behind the lines; they are his means of turning the play away from actions, such as the lynching of Rivers, back to words, such as deliver the claim to selfknowledge with which Mortimer brings down the curtain. Mortimer's words about words thus seem to represent Wordsworth's perspective, as he reflected on the contagion of action he claims to have witnessed in the French Revolution. They ask: How does language make us replicate actions we do not intend? And in asking a question so inappropriate to the dramatic context, the words act out the problem they name.

Mortimer's words seem inappropriate because they so openly voice Wordsworth's own reflection on the things he has declined to tell by writing a play rather than, say, a history or a confession. A narrative telling what had happened in the course of the Revolution, he feels at this point in his career, would necessarily be heard in vain. For narrative language, capable only of speaking in the terms of *Hamlet*'s Clown— "to act, to do, to perform"—necessarily misses the crucial indeterminacies in the replication of action that Wordsworth appears to have recognized in the Revolution as it was "rapidly advancing to its extreme of wickedness" (813). What Wordsworth wants to dramatize, but not to tell, is the "critical moment" where, as that late Romantic Thomas Mann put it in *Felix Krull,* "something somnambulistic occurs, halfway between action and accident, doing and being dealt with."[61] Wordsworth constructs *The Borderers* upon such moments, deliberately embracing what Drury Lane judged to be "metaphysical obscurity" in order to show the inaccessibility of such moments to ordinary moral explanation. The moment of passage between "doing" and "being dealt with," the "transition in character" Wordsworth speaks of in his late note on the play, appears in the final scene to resist capture within the rationalist discourse of motive shared by Rivers and Mortimer. This recognition would help to shape the complex moral agenda of Wordsworth's best poetry; but it would also help to delimit the social and political scope of that agenda.

In deliberate contrast to the political language it frames, *The Borderers* is resolutely determined to avoid determining history either as "action" or as "accident." That is to its credit, for its *Hamlet*-like irresolution is what gives it its impressive powers of historical diagnosis. *The Borderers* exposes the mechanisms by which a discourse of motive necessarily falsifies history—both what actually happens, and the ways in which people experience what happens—and, by concealing the falsification, leads to its literal reenactment. In working through this critical project, Wordsworth's play thus avoids the ideological pitfalls of the heroic and the daemonic accounts of recent history that were current

---

61. Thomas Mann, *Confessions of Felix Krull, Confidence Man (The Early Years),* trans. Denver Lindley (New York: Vintage-Random House, 1969) 87.

when he wrote *The Borderers*. But at what cost? The play may please modern readers by seeming to commemorate what Paul de Man identifies as an influential Wordsworthian theme, "the gap that separates the completion of an action from its understanding," exemplifying de Man's conclusion that "the poet finally distinguishes himself from the hero through his care for preserving memory, even the memory of the heroic act that throws itself into the future and destroys itself in this project."[62] But to take this as the moral of the play is to believe that Mortimer can, as he dubiously promises, live on as nothing more than an incarnated memory. It is to forget that Wordsworth has been pointing toward the life that lies beyond the magic circle illuminated by what even Mortimer calls *"mere* intensity of thought" (5.3.272, emphasis added).

The critical discourse of agency in *The Borderers* underwrites the recurrent theme of historical change in Wordsworth's later poems, a theme that figures not just as a backdrop for the *Lyrical Ballads* but as a central concern in the revolution books of *The Prelude*, in *The Excursion*, and in less commonly read later works such as *The White Doe of Rylstone*. But the moral vortex generated out of the surrender of agency dictated by the circumstances of historical change can be brought before our eyes only in the genre that shows why living by mere intensity of thought is not living.

62. Paul de Man, "Wordsworth and Hölderlin," *The Rhetoric of Romanticism* (New York: Columbia University Press, 1984) 64–65.

3

Fancy and the Spell of Enlightenment: *Osorio*

> Till Superstition with unconscious hand
> Seat Reason on her throne.
> —*Joan of Arc*

Coleridge's 1797 tragedy *Osorio* and *Remorse,* its highly successful 1813 revision for the stage, are both dominated, in different ways, by the planning, staging, and unfolding of a piece of absurdly bad drama. The author was the first to acknowledge this. "The scene is not wholly without *poetical* merit," he wrote in the margin of one draft, "but it is miserably undramatic, or rather untragic. A scene of magic is introduced in which no single person on the stage has the least faith—all, though in different ways, think or know it to be a *trick*."[1] One might ask what specifically poetical merit should be looked for in a scene of magic known, or thought, to be a trick; and one's next question might be how that merit might have led Coleridge to preserve the "miserably undramatic" part of act 3 as the keystone on which the revised play is constructed. The answer should be sought in Coleridge's fascination

---

1. Note to *Osorio,* in *The Poems of Samuel Taylor Coleridge,* ed. Ernest Hartley Coleridge (Oxford: Oxford University Press, 1927) 2:555. All further quotations from *Osorio* and *Remorse* are taken from this edition; lines from *Remorse* are marked *R;* other verse by Coleridge is quoted from vol. 1 of this edition. Reeve Parker explains the ramifying trickery of *Osorio* by arguing that Coleridge is taking on a problem posed by the success of gothic drama, namely "how to 'admit pantomimic tricks' without compromising the 'higher' art of tragedy" ("*Osorio*'s Dark Employments: Tricking Out Coleridgean Tragedy," *Studies in Romanticism* 33 [1994]: 123).

with the "different ways" in which "single person[s]" can be shown to "think or know" the power of illusion. Illusion does not negate power in this scene, but multiplies power by fracturing it into a wide range of motives and effects. Nor does the thought or knowledge of trickery diminish the "magic" power of belief to conjure emotions. Those emotions grow so strong, indeed, that the characters embodying them become almost entirely opaque to one another. What gives this awful scene its power, a power audiences and readers have sensed as differently and as inarticulately as the characters? The answers I will offer should not only expand our awareness of how dramas of dislocated agency contributed to the early development of Romanticism, but also suggest how other, nondramatic writings from this period draw on the power of acknowledged illusion to sustain the suspension of disbelief voiced in one character's verdict on the "untragic" scene: "This was no feat of mortal agency!" (R 3.2.13).

John Beer and Anya Taylor have written superbly about Coleridge's faith that the deep springs of human character can be revealed through the most obviously absurd forms of magic, which Coleridge took to correspond somehow with "the power of life itself in the human being."[2] Magic in Coleridge's poetry signals the difficulty of making *visible* what motivates people. *Osorio* addresses more openly than any Coleridge text I know the complex relations between such powers—for example, the passions that came to dominate the theory of Wordsworthian Romanticism—and the investment in stage appearances which the development of Wordsworthian Romanticism famously repressed. Joanna Baillie, the period's first theorist of those relations, traces the desire to *see* evidence of the passions to our knowledge of their inaccessibility:

> Let us understand, from observation or report, that any person harbours in his breast, concealed from the world's eye, some powerful rankling passion of what kind soever it may be, we shall observe every word, every motion, every look, even the distant gait of such a man, with a constancy and attention bestowed on no other . . . . If invisible, would we not follow

---

2. John Beer, *Coleridge's Poetic Intelligence* (London: Macmillan, 1977) 7; see also Anya Taylor, *Magic and English Romanticism* (Athens: University of Georgia Press, 1979): "magic serves as a metaphor for the irrational powers of language, and of the sources of language in will and willlessness, in energy and indolence, and in imagination and perception" (13).

him into his lonely haunts, into his closet, into the midnight silence of his chamber? There is, perhaps, no employment which the human mind will with so much avidity pursue, as the discovery of concealed passion, as the tracing the varieties and progress of a perturbed soul.[3]

Coleridge banks on our *desire* to see the passions that cannot be seen, but he is also anxious to probe our *faith* that such a sight can be had. Why should we believe we can see what Baillie promises would come to view only if we were invisible? How is an audience's faith in stage appearances connected with its pursuit of invisibility, secrecy, impersonality? And how do more general aspects of faith come to depend, as they do throughout the poetry we call "Romantic," not on an awareness of our own autonomy but on our access to the motives of other subjects? Such questions, readily articulated and tested in the case of stage drama, apply less intuitively to some of the new kinds of writing Wordsworth and Coleridge would develop in the years after 1797. But those later writings carry forward some of the insights into the passions' mode of appearance the two poets found in their early dramatic experiments. The staginess of *Osorio*, properly understood, can allow us to glimpse hidden aspects of Coleridge's major poems.

Two misapprehensions account for the principal ways in which *Osorio* has been misread. The first is the assumption that Coleridge vindicates the moral power of remorse in Albert's efforts to summon it in his brother Osorio.[4] A reviewer for the aptly named *Theatrical Inquisitor* is, as far as I know, the only contemporary to note what a beating remorse takes in this play: "Remorse is only the secondary impulse by which [Osorio] is guided, and . . . even when that sentiment is called

---

3. Joanna Baillie, "Introductory Discourse," *A Series of Plays* (*"Plays on the Passions"*), in Baillie, *Dramatic and Poetical Works* 3. The opacity of the passions is a keynote in Baillie's theory of tragedy, whose purpose, she says, is to unveil "those passions which conceal themselves from the observation of men; which cannot unbosom themselves even to the dearest friend; and can, oftentimes, only give their fulness vent in the lonely desert, or in the darkness of midnight" (8). Catherine B. Burroughs discusses this tendency under the rubric of Eve Sedgwick's "closet epistemology" in her essay "English Romantic Women Writers and Theatre Theory: Joanna Baillie's Prefaces to the *Plays on the Passions*," in *Revisioning Romanticism: British Women Writers, 1776–1837*, ed. Carol Shiner Wilson and Joel Haefner (Philadelphia: University of Pennsylvania Press, 1994) 274–96.

4. Julie A. Carlson, for example, opens her argument with the claim that "no title in the Coleridgean canon characterizes its subject so succinctly as does the 'Remorse' of 1813" (*In the Theatre of Romanticism: Coleridge, Nationalism, Women* [New York: Cambridge University Press, 1994] 94).

into action, it is imperfectly developed."[5] Albert's design, that is, fails; Coleridge knows this perfectly well. "Remorse is as the heart in which it grows," warns Albert's servant Zulimez, formerly Maurice, in the lines that would serve as a motto on the title page of *Remorse*. The maxim warns, with good cause, that Albert cannot succeed in using the remorse he arouses in his brother to "save him from himself"; his plot succeeds only in inciting Osorio to murder Ferdinand, the would-be assassin upon whom remorse *has* had the desired effect. Coleridge's purpose seems to be much rather to show up Albert's highminded moralism as naively impolitic at best, perhaps even (as Reeve Parker argues) vengeful and sadistic.[6] That impression must be reinforced when we clear up the second misapprehension, namely, that the play's historical setting contributes only a vaguely orientalizing local color that fits the action into a schematic theory of historical progress.[7] *Osorio*'s historical setting is, instead, highly detailed, carefully considered in its political ramifications, and closely woven into the intrigue. Any consideration of what is done in the play—what it shows playing to be capable of doing—must begin from these historical details.

When those misapprehensions are corrected, it will be possible to see both the motives and the consequences of the theatrical means by which

---

5. *Romantics Reviewed* A:2:873.
6. Parker takes Albert's quest "to torture Osorio's conscience" as "a vicious agenda" that is "as damning as Osorio's original crime" ("Osorio's Dark Employments," 134, 138). Coleridge did provide an account of the relation between his revised plot and the workings of remorse in a letter to Southey (9 February 1813): "By REMORSE I mean the Anguish & Disquietude arising from the Self-contradiction introduced into the Soul by Guilt—a feeling which is good or bad according as the Will makes use of it. This is exprest in the lines chosen as the Motto—& Remorse is every where distinguished from virtuous Penitence.—To excite a sanative Remorse Alvar returns—the Passion is put in motion at Ordonio's first entrance by the appearance of Isidore's Wife &c—it is carried still higher by the narration of Isidore, 1 S. 2 A: higher still by the Interview with the supposed Wizard: & to its [acme] by the Incantation Scene & Picture—. Now then we are to see it's effects & to exemplify the second part of the Motto—'but if proud & gloomy, It [is a] poison-tree' &c. Ordonio too proud to look steadily into hi[msel]f catches a false scent, plans the murder of Isidore & the Poisoning of the Sorcerer, perpetrates the one, & attempting the other is driven by Remorse & the discovery of Alvar to a temporary Distraction, & finally falling a victim to the only crime, that had been realized, by the hand of Alhadra, breathes his last in a Pang of Pride—'O could'st thou forget me!' " (*Letters* 3:433–34).
7. See Daniel P. Watkins, " 'In That New World': The Deep Historical Structure of Coleridge's *Osorio*," *Philological Quarterly* 69 (1990): 495–515, reprinted as chap. 2 in *A Materialist Critique of English Romantic Drama* (Gainesville: University Press of Florida, 1993).

Osorio defends the faith of Albert, the exiled good brother, and of Maria, his faithful beloved, as politically empowering, and to see what it means that Coleridge condemns the habit of reasoning on appearances—in the person of Osorio, the murderous usurping brother—for its power to rob agents of their freedom and to make them into instruments of oppression. Coleridge seeks to communicate a politically effective faith that can be placed beyond demystification, and what he finds, I will claim, is what ultimately became known as the Wordsworthian credo. *Osorio*'s linkages between faith and agency, then, point toward two important components of early Romanticism that have been neglected in accounts of its origins: an anxiety about the power of images and appearances to command belief—a stage fright, that is—and a desire to conceive such beliefs as operative within historically specific political conflicts. Because my focus is the year 1797, I will be using primarily the text of *Osorio,* and as with *The Borderers,* I will use the names of the early version even when, for the sake of clarity, I quote the later text of *Remorse*.[8]

I.

Readers have not done well in recovering the meaning of *Osorio*'s setting. Carl Woodring finds an "opposition to the established regime" being expressed only "by indirection and implication." He sees that indirection as broadly generic, attributing Coleridge's sketch of Inquisitorial bloodlust, for instance, to the "routine anti-Catholicism" of gothic convention and identifying a genuine "anti-Ministerial" import only in the Inquisitor's violations of the sacred domestic hearth.[9] Daniel Watkins goes to the other extreme, expanding these few hints into a full-blown, if ambiguous, historical allegory. On the one hand, Watkins argues, "In writing about sixteenth-century Spain, Coleridge was describing a familiar and exotic past world that his audience could com-

---

8. Parker pits the two versions against one another and, without denying the later version's increased clarity, argues persuasively against it: "It's precisely such an ideology of clarity—in its own way a repetition of the enlightenment positivism Coleridge was calling into question in *Osorio*—that, paradoxically, obscures what is dramatically at stake in the play" ("Osorio's Dark Employments," 120n). For a full treatment of the changes between the two versions, see Carlson, *Theatre of Romanticism.*

9. Woodring, *Politics in the Poetry of Coleridge* 204–5.

fortably condemn, while at the same time taking pride in the successes of their own nation against an imperialist and religiously dogmatic enemy." On the other hand, Coleridge is found to believe that the Spain of *Osorio* "strikingly resembles the England of his own day, which was marked by a repressive and often violent government that sought to crush all resistance." Watkins resolves the disparity between these views with a master narrative that converts historical details into episodes of class conflict, the cumulative effect being "to situate Albert, despite his aristocratic birth, among an emergent bourgeoisie and to establish him as a carrier of modern attitudes and values."[10] Such readings typify a tendency in Romantic studies to seek out the general lineaments of historical allegory before attending to historical verisimilitude. Watkins is not wrong to assert that "the imperialist exploits of Spain in the sixteenth century were not radically different from those of England in the eighteenth," but he fails to see that the parallel's interpretive force does not reach very far beyond the propaganda theater of, say, *Pizarro*, which Sheridan wrote shortly after rejecting Coleridge's *Osorio* for its supposed "obscurity."[11]

Osorio's concern for historical detail begins with the setting, which Coleridge specifies as "The reign of Philip II., just at the close of the civil wars against the Moors, and during the heat of the persecution which raged against them, shortly after the edict which forbad the wearing of Moresco apparel under pain of death." For Watkins, this boils down to "the world" of the later sixteenth century: Sir Francis Drake, Bloody Mary, and the Spanish Armada, none of which is even mentioned in the play. For Coleridge, however, it means a specific date, 1570, at the end of the two-year rebellion of the Moors that followed the 1568 edicts, and a specific place, named in the opening scene of *Remorse* as "Alpujarras," where the rebellion originated. Albert's ser-

---

10. Watkins, *Materialist Critique* 24, 31. Watkins's "materialist" account of *Osorio*'s "historical dimensions" starts from the elision of detail because "the explanatory authority of empirical data" is found to leave "larger historical considerations unexamined." When Watkins does interpret details, he bends them to repeat his master narrative: he identifies Albert with "an emergent bourgeoisie" by alleging that he has been kidnapped "by a merchant ship," though Osorio's story is that his brother has been taken by pirates *from* a merchant ship; and he summarizes Albert's service to "the heroic Prince of Orange" by identifying the Netherlands as "a strong trading nation" (31).

11. Donahue gives abundant attention to *Pizarro* in *Dramatic Character* 125–56; Sara Suleri gives a briefer but more politically pointed reading of the play in *The Rhetoric of English India* (Chicago: University of Chicago Press, 1992) 68–74.

vice to the Prince of Orange, mentioned several times in the early scenes, can be dated at 1568, the year of the first, failed campaign of resistance against the tyrannic rule of Philip's henchman the Duke of Alva, and the beginning of the revolution that established in the Netherlands a model for modern republics. This is the milieu of the events that had recently been dramatized in Goethe's *Egmont* and Schiller's *Don Carlos*, not to mention Schiller's 1788 history of the revolt of the Netherlands.[12] The revolutionary significance of these events—both for the sixteenth century and for the 1790s—constituted their whole importance for some British reviewers of the German dramatists.[13]

To neglect the specificity of the setting is to overlook one of the plot's main motives. It is not enough to recognize, with Watkins, that "the drama contains strong anti-Catholic, antimilitary, and antiaristocratic sentiments"; to say that a drama *contains* such sentiments is to say little if the protagonist's ideal of heroism is the Prince of Orange—an aristocratic military leader raised Catholic. From the historical details scattered throughout *Osorio,* Coleridge assembled a new opening scene for *Remorse* so that his plot would follow from a focused historical conflict: the conflict, namely, between a Catholic absolutism and the Protestant liberty of conscience that would overthrow it in the Netherlands. Albert tells exactly how he has spent the three years since his brother's failed plot to have him assassinated: "I sought / The Belgic states: there joined the better cause; / And there too fought as one that courted death! / Wounded, I fell among the dead and dying, / In death-like trance: a long imprisonment followed" (*R* 1.1.74–78). Two more references to Albert's "long imprisonment" frame the action like bookends (*R* 1.1.102 and 5.1.199), contrasting his service to that of his brother, who has stayed in Spain to torment rebel Moors on behalf of the Inquisition. Early in the play the Inquisitor Francesco congratulates Osorio on his "zeal" as the Holy Church's "faithful soldier" in the suppression of the Moors (*R* 1.2.172, 122, 130–31); later we learn that Osorio once imprisoned the children of Alhadra, the play's alternately sympathetic and vengeful Moorish matron, and that he spared her husband Ferdinand on the battlefield only to win him as an instrument for his plot against Albert. While Osorio "march'd / With fire and deso-

---

12. Schiller's history appeared in English, however, only in 1807.
13. See the review of the two 1798 translations of *Don Carlos* in the *Monthly Review,* n.s. 29 (1799): 143–48.

lation through their villages," Albert "ne'er fought against the Moors, —say rather, / He was their advocate" (R 3.2.151–53). The same concern for the oppressed led him to serve the Prince of Orange, as we learn when Maria remembers how, "with swelling tears, / Flash'd through by indignation, he bewail'd / The wrongs of Belgium's martyr'd patriots" (R 4.2.59–61).

Maria's characterization of the patriots as "martyr'd" confirms what the other details might have led us to suspect: that Albert has become a Protestant. That seemingly hyperbolic conclusion gives way to an even more radical view when we learn about Albert's early relation with Maria. Her disgust at the Inquisition, one of the first things we learn of her (1.2.104), is later traced to Albert's teaching: "These were my Albert's lessons," she says, "and whene'er / I bend me o'er his portrait, I repeat them, / As if to give a voice to the mute image" (4.2.36–38). Osorio has already spoken of Albert's having taught Maria: "She hath no faith in Holy Church, 'tis true: / Her lover schooled her in some newer nonsense!" (2.1.35–36). One might call that "newer nonsense" Protestantism, but that would be to elide the details Coleridge supplies in allowing Maria to deliver a specimen of the faith she has shared with Albert:

> O Albert! Albert! that they could return,
> Those blessed days that imitated heaven,
> When we two wont to walk at eventide;
> When we saw nought but beauty; when we heard
> The voice of that Almighty One who loved us
> In every gale that breathed, and wave that murmur'd!
> O we have listen'd, even till high-wrought pleasure
> Hath half assumed the countenance of grief,
> And the deep sigh seemed to heave up a weight
> Of bliss, that pressed too heavy on the heart.
> (R 4.2.98–107)

Her rhapsody bears an unmistakable resemblance to the "sentiment of being" that makes the "one life" sensible to Wordsworth's Pedlar and to the Coleridge of "The Eolian Harp."[14] Albert's nonsense is not just a

---

14. Compare *Prelude* 1805 2:420–34:

> I felt the sentiment of being spread
> O'er all that moves, and all that seemeth still,
> O'er all that, lost beyond the reach of thought
> And human knowledge, to the human eye

vague Protestantism, it is the faith promulgated by the early Wordsworth and Coleridge: a pantheism that verges on what Kenneth Gross speaks of as "the displaced, diffused, demystified, ironic, and hyperbolized Protestantism we have learned to call Romanticism."[15] Watkins seems to grasp this in an inchoate way when he locates Maria's attacks on the Inquisition within "a larger ideological shift involving the subversion of church authority and its replacement by a more personal religious sensibility," so that "Maria appears as the new Mary, a secularized and personalized version of the feminine principle idealized by Francesco's Catholicism" (33). But he fails to register Coleridge's effort to locate the origins of a modern poetic faith at the same place where he locates the origins of modern revolutionary politics.

Coleridge's historical details give that faith a precise political location, and its political meaning in turn informs the most basic plot developments. *Osorio*'s main historical allusions—to Philip's oppression of the Moors in Spain and of Calvinists in the Netherlands—concern the freedom of religious conscience. Coleridge's primary source, Robert Watson's *History of the Reign of Philip the Second*, links the two episodes thus: "While Philip's bigotry, joined to his despotic and arbitrary conduct, had engaged him in war with his subjects in the Netherlands, the same causes produced a similar effect in the province of Granada; where the Moors, who had long yielded a tame submission to the crown of Spain, were provoked, by the tyranny of the present government, to throw off their allegiance, and have recourse to arms."[16] Philip's troubles with the rebellious Netherlands figure in *Oso-*

        Invisible, yet liveth to the heart,
        O'er all that leaps, and runs, and shouts, and sings,
        Or beats the gladsome air, o'er all that glides
        Beneath the wave, yea, in the wave itself
        And mighty depth of waters. Wonder not
        If such my transports were, for in all things
        I saw one life, and felt that it was joy;
        One song they sang, and it was audible—
        Most audible then when the fleshly ear,
        O'ercome by grosser prelude of that strain,
        Forgot its functions and slept undisturbed.

Parker speaks not of pantheism but of "the subversive animism pervading the action and rhetoric of the play" ("Osorio's Dark Employments" 142).

    15. Kenneth Gross, *Spenserian Poetics: Idolatry, Iconoclasm, and Magic* (Ithaca: Cornell University Press, 1985) 10.

    16. Robert Watson, *The History of the Reign of Philip the Second, King of Spain*, 6th ed. (London, 1803) 1:341.

rio mainly to fill in the years of Albert's absence and to associate him with suffering under tyranny: "Well, to the Netherlands / We will return," Albert comforts his servant Maurice; "the heroic Prince of Orange / Will grant us asylum, in remembrance of our past service" (2.1.184–87). A few lines later, when Albert explains why he is unlikely to be recognized even by his brother—"Manhood has swell'd my breast, and taught my voice / A hoarser note"—Coleridge emphasizes the bodily investments that political commitment shares with the theater. Maurice's response explains to us where Albert has come by his manhood: "Most true! And Alva's Duke / Did not improve it by the unwholesome viands / He gave so scantily in that foul dungeon, / During our long imprisonment" (2.1.196–200).

Coleridge underscores Watson's link between struggle against the Duke of Alva and the struggle of the Moors most clearly in a scene written for *Remorse* in which Alhadra, wavering between formal and familiar modes of address, quizzes Albert about his Moorish costume: "If what you seem'st thou art, / The oppressed brethren of thy blood have need / Of such a leader." He responds in a sustained double-entendre that allows her to hear him championing the Moors, while we hear him summarizing his frustrated plot to avenge his brother's usurpation:

> Long time against oppression have I fought,
> And for the native liberty of faith
> Have bled and suffered bonds. Of this be certain:
> Time, as he courses onward, still unrolls
> The volume of concealment. In the future,
> As in the optician's glassy cylinder,
> The indistinguishable blots and colours
> Of the dim past collect and shape themselves,
> Upstarting in their own completed image
> To scare or to reward. I sought the guilty,
> And what I sought I found: but ere the spear
> Flew from my hand, there rose an angel form
> Betwixt me and my aim. With baffled purpose
> To the Avenger I leave vengeance, and depart!
> (R 2.2.3–19)

Alhadra hears the unknown Moor proclaim his struggle against the Inquisition, his pledge that its crimes shall not go unavenged, the frustration of his own vengeance, and his wish to leave justice to Allah. In

Osorio

the same speech, *we* hear that Albert has stood for a lover's "faith" against his brother's "oppression," but that Maria—whose angelic "form" he still thinks disguises a perfidious betrayal—has caused him to abandon that struggle to the Christian God. After Alhadra leaves the stage, however, a third interpretation gains ascendency: "Yes, to the Belgic states / We will return. These robes, this stained complexion, / Akin to falsehood, weigh upon my spirit. / Whate'er befall us, the heroic Maurice / Will grant us an asylum, in remembrance / Of our past services" (R 2.2.23–28). We now see that Albert has recognized himself in Alhadra's wish for a hero to lead "the oppressed brethren of thy blood": his speech was telling us about his struggle on behalf of the Lowlanders' "native liberty of faith" against the oppressions of the imperial rulers, the cause in which Albert was wounded and imprisoned. In narrating the domestic plot we have been watching, Albert's prophecy about the brother of his blood was actually forecasting the future liberation of his brethren in the Netherlands and the triumph of the Reformed faith. In offering one plot as the other's allegorical screen, Albert's speech teaches us how to read Coleridge's play.

2.

Coleridge has Albert present his plotting of remorse as an extension of his fight for freedom; the domestic plot follows from political motivations, carries them home, so to speak. But what does the plot of the two brothers add to Coleridge's political genealogy of the enthusiasm that would become familiar to the nineteenth century as "Romantic"? An answer to that question should be the burden of any political reading of the play, but no answer can be given until the question is fully understood. What, then, do we know of *enthusiasm* in *Osorio*? We know that it is among the first things Coleridge wanted to put before our eyes, and that he wanted to attach to it a skeptical irony that endows it with a power to resist authority.

Maria's first speech develops her claim to be "faithful" to Albert, whether he is dead or alive, by sketching both an enthusiasm and a stance toward enthusiasm. Velez, the brothers' father and Maria's guardian, has urged her to marry Osorio, exclaiming "I must not see thee wretched!" She answers his misapprehension with an astounding flight of fancy:

> There are woes
> Ill-barter'd for the garishness of joy!
> If it be wretched with an untired eye
> To watch those skiey tints, and this green ocean;
> Or in the sultry hour beneath some rock,
> My hair dishevell'd by the pleasant sea-breeze,
> To shape sweet visions, and live o'er again
> All past hours of delight; if it be wretched
> To watch some bark, and fancy Albert there;
> To go through each minutest circumstance
> Of the bless'd meeting, and to frame adventures
> Most terrible and strange, and hear *him* tell them....

Remorse appends a note at this point, attempting halfway through Maria's speech to supply the correct nuances: "Here [Velez] bends back, and smiles at her wildness, which [Maria] noticing, checks her enthusiasm, and in a soothing half-playful tone and manner, apologizes for her fancy, by the little tale in parenthesis." The speech continues with that parenthetical apology:

> (As once I knew a crazy Moorish maid,
> Who dress'd her in her buried lover's cloaths,
> And o'er the smooth spring in the mountain cleft
> Hung with her lute, and play'd the selfsame tune
> He used to play, and listen'd to the shadow
> Herself had made)....

In her fanciful act of faith, Maria is playing Albert's tune; but her awareness that Velez is listening brings a self-consciousness that registers in her account of watching herself play Albert. The tale of the crazy Moorish maid, whose faith is both laughed off and subtly vindicated in her reflection, leads Maria to renew her flight of fancy:

> ... if this be wretchedness,
> And if indeed it be a wretched thing
> To trick out mine own death-bed, and imagine
> That I had died—died, just ere his return;
> Then see him listening to my constancy;
> And hover round, as he at midnight ever
> Sits on my grave and gazes at the moon;
> Or haply in some more fantastic mood
> To be in Paradise, and with choice flowers

> Build up a bower where he and I might dwell,
> And there to wait his coming! O my sire!
> My Albert's sire! if this be wretchedness
> That eats away the life, what were it, think you,
> If in a most assur'd reality
> He should return, and see a brother's infant
> Smile at him from *my* arms?
>
> (1.1.18–50)

The staging Coleridge later imagined for Drury Lane shows, as the script alone cannot, how the power of enthusiasm is both suffered and self-perpetuated, like what the *Biographia Literaria* would famously call (in reference to the *Lyrical Ballads*) "that willing suspension of disbelief for the moment, which constitutes poetic faith."[17]

A shaping power that can also make one hear voices, Coleridge's "poetic faith" is as "crazy" but also as "willing" as the solipsistic mourner who communes with herself. When embraced in full awareness, it is as central to Coleridge's conception of poetic activity as is his fanciful interchange with the "stranger" in "Frost at Midnight." There, as also in "Kubla Khan," "The Eolian Harp," and here in the opening scene of *Osorio,* Coleridge can own his enthusiasm only by pretending to disown it. The play makes clear, however, as the lyrics cannot, how this gesture originates in a defensive response to the demands of authority—here, Velez's authority to dispose of Maria's hand. Her fanciful critique of fancy clears for her a limited space of autonomy; "Frost at

---

17. Coleridge, *Biographia Literaria,* chap. 14, in *Collected Works,* 7.2:6. Frederick Burwick sees this speech as dramatizing "the problem of imaginatively informed vs. pathologically perverted perception," and as vindicating Maria's "volitional control of the imagination" as "the power that sustains [her] love" (*Illusion and the Drama: Critical Theory of the Enlightenment and Romantic Era* [University Park: Pennsylvania State University Press, 1991] 269–70). He reads the parenthesis as "an example contrasting to her visions, a tale of actual delusion" (270), overlooking the likeness Maria asserts between her fancy and that of the crazy Moorish maid. Burwick's distinction between (volitional) illusion and (suffered) delusion is cognate with Coleridge's distinction between imagination and fancy, in Thomas McFarland's rendering: "It is the existence of the unbidden mental phantoms of the first order [viz. the monsters a child fears] that sanctions Coleridge's 'fancy', and it is the unified, consciously willed, creative control of the potential ramifications of a situation . . . that sanctions Coleridge's 'imagination' " (*Coleridge and the Pantheist Tradition* [Oxford: Clarendon Press, 1969] 310). For a further account of "willing illusion" in Coleridge, see Patricia M. Ball, "The Waking Dream: Coleridge and the Drama," in *The Morality of Art,* ed. D. W. Jefferson (New York: Barnes & Noble, 1969) 165–74.

Midnight" will do much the same for Coleridge himself, though without signalling, as *Osorio* must, the institutional determinants of the needs met by fancy. *Osorio,* then, *places* the ambivalence with which Maria laughs off her own fancy as though it were someone else's, showing its causes and its effects. It allows one to see the *social* situatedness of the imagination in terms of pragmatic functions that the conversation poems typically mask with their intense focus on their speakers' *physical* situations. As the verbal resemblance to "Kubla Khan" might suggest—Coleridge would write that poem shortly after submitting *Osorio* to Sheridan—Maria's parenthetical aside moves us from what seems mere fancy toward the heart of the Coleridgean imagination. For the reflexive and self-consuming gesture by which fancy is disavowed, made an *other* agency, is central to the politics of the Coleridgean imagination, and it is here, not in any of Coleridge's later theoretical writings, that we discover why.

Maria's enthusiasm belongs among the earliest developments in Coleridge's careerlong quest to join imagination to faith. Her speech about how Albert taught her to perceive God in nature is hardly Coleridge's first venture into pantheism. It draws on his 1795 contribution to Southey's *Joan of Arc,* the beginning of book 2 (subtitled "Preternatural Agency"), which Coleridge later excerpted and published as "The Destiny of Nations."[18] Coleridge began by deriving freedom from the perception of God:

> For what is Freedom, but the unfettered use
> Of all the powers which God for use had given?
> But chiefly this, him First, him Last to view
> Through meaner powers and secondary things
> Effulgent, as through clouds that veil his blaze.
> For all that meets the bodily sense I deem
> Symbolical, one mighty alphabet
> For infant minds . . .
> ("Destiny of Nations," 13–20)

Jonathan Wordsworth believes these lines were written in the weeks before "The Eolian Harp" (August, 1795); he calls them "Coleridge's

---

18. Coleridge later dismissed *Joan of Arc* as a "transmogrification of the fanatic Virago into a modern novel-pawing Proselyte of the Age of Reason, a Tom Paine in Petticoats" (11 June 1814; *Letters* 3:510).

Osorio

first great poetic statement on the theme of perception."[19] They are both more explicit than later statements, in offering a theory of God's immanence, and more openly political, in using that theory to plumb the origins of human agency. Coleridge first offers a theory of God's agency in nature:

> But Properties are God: the naked mass
> (If mass there be, fantastic guess or ghost)
> Acts only by its inactivity.
> Here we pause humbly. Others boldlier think
> That as one body seems the aggregate
> Of atoms numberless, each organized;
> So by a strange and dim similitude
> Infinite myriads of self-conscious minds
> Are one all-conscious Spirit, which informs
> With absolute ubiquity of thought
> (His one eternal self-affirming act!)
> All his involved Monads, that yet seem
> With various province and apt agency
> Each to pursue its own self-centering end.
> ("Destiny," 36–49)

Beer sees this passage—a theoretical account of *Wat Tyler*'s problem of the individual and the collective—as a source for Albert's conjuring speech in act 3 of *Osorio*, where the obviously fake magic helps to reveal Albert's natural piety as obviously genuine.[20] That scene dwells upon the powers of nature in order to exhibit the power of the passions (in Osorio's case) and of the moral intelligence (in Albert's case); but in this too it resembles the sequence written for *Joan of Arc*. Among the forms of "preternatural agency" Coleridge had depicted acting on human agents, he gave priority to the power that educates natural man toward supernatural reason:

> Fancy is the power
> That first unsensualizes the dark mind,
> Giving it new delights; and bids it swell
> With wild activity; and peopling air,
> By obscure fears of Beings invisible,

---

19. Jonathan Wordsworth, "Introduction," *Joan of Arc* (New York: Woodstock, 1993) no p.
20. Beer, *Coleridge's Poetic Intelligence* 111.

> Emancipates it from the grosser thrall
> Of the present impulse, teaching self-control,
> Till Superstition with unconscious hand
> Seat Reason on her throne.
> ("Destiny," 80–88)

That "unconscious hand" leads Coleridge to the "Beings invisible" with which Joan's fancy, with wild activity, peoples the air. He explains why those Beings come to her:

> I deem no nobler province they possess,
> Than by disposal of apt circumstance
> To rear up kingdoms: and the deeds they prompt,
> Distinguishing from mortal agency,
> They choose their human ministers from such states
> As still the Epic song half fears to name,
> Repelled from all the minstrelsies that strike
> The palace-roof and soothe the monarch's pride.
> ("Destiny," 128–35)

In "unsensualizing" the mind, superstition leads it not only toward the reason that unseats superstition, but also toward an unacknowledged constructive power. The lesson of this sequence might be summarized with Leslie Brisman's argument about Coleridgean faith: that "Coleridge 'believes in' the sublime as he believes in miracles," yet that what counts most for Coleridge is "the historicity of the narrative movement from miracle to moral."[21] Maria's enthusiasm, like Joan of Arc's fancy, does not count for anything, cannot be turned toward moral significance, until it draws her from her static melancholy into the movement of a plot.

We cannot see the place of enthusiasm in *Osorio* until we distinguish it from superstition. Although others may see a contest between fancy and imagination or, as in Frederick Burwick's reading, between illusion and delusion, I insist on the opposition between enthusiasm and superstition because it structures an important and related passage in Coleridge's "Religious Musings" (1796), which begins with a tribute to the faith that has allowed Maria and Albert to perceive the One Life:

---

21. Leslie Brisman, "Coleridge and the Supernatural," *Studies in Romanticism* 21 (1982): 147.

> 'Tis the sublime of man,
> Our noontide majesty, to know ourselves
> Parts and proportions of one wondrous whole!
> This fraternises man, this constitutes
> Our charities and bearings. But 'tis God
> Diffused through all, that doth make all one whole;
> This the worst superstition, him except
> Aught to desire, Supreme Reality!
> The plenitude and permanence of bliss!
> (126–34)

This faith contrasts with the shortsighted "desire" that characterizes superstition, the account of which might be read with Osorio in mind:

> O Fiends of Superstition! not that oft
> The erring priest hath stained with brother's blood
> Your grisly idols, not for this may wrath
> Thunder against you from the Holy One!
> But o'er some plain that steameth to the sun,
> Peopled with death; or where more hideous Trade
> Loud-laughing packs his bales of human anguish;
> I will raise up a mourning, O ye Fiends!
> And curse your spells, that film the eye of Faith.
> (135–47)

Druids, slave traders, Inquisitors—all historical wielders of the spell that is cursed here for political rather than religious reasons—are so many prototypes of the fiend of superstition *Osorio* incarnates in its title figure. Jonathan Wordsworth expresses bafflement that Sheridan should have solicited a political play from the author of "Religious Musings"; this passage shows why he might have done so.[22]

Maria's enthusiasm enters the plot with Osorio's account of it to his remorseful Moorish sidekick, Ferdinand, in the scene where he first mentions the conjuring plot. *Remorse* gives the fuller version:

> [*Osorio*]. In blunt terms, you can play the sorcerer.
> She hath no faith in Holy Church, 'tis true:
> Her lover schooled her in some newer nonsense!
> Yet still a tale of spirits works upon her.

---

22. Jonathan Wordsworth, "Introduction," *Remorse* (Oxford: Woodstock, 1989), no p.

> She is a lone enthusiast, sensitive,
> Shivers, and can not keep the tears in her eye:
> And such do love the marvellous too well
> Not to believe it. We will wind up her fancy
> With a strange music, that she knows not of—
> With fumes of frankincense, and mummery,
> Then leave, as one sure token of his death,
> That portrait, which from off the dead man's neck
> I bade thee take, the trophy of thy conquest.
> [*Ferdinand*]. Will that be a sure sign?
> [*Osorio*].   Beyond suspicion.
> Fondly caressing him, her favour'd lover,
> (By some base spell he had bewitched her senses)
> She whispered such dark fears of me forsooth,
> As made this heart pour gall into my veins.
>   (R 2.1.34–51)

Osorio seems to think of the "newer nonsense" Albert has taught Maria alternately as a taste for the occult and as its opposite, a Voltairean enlightenment that disdains whatever the "Holy Church" might have in common with a "sorcerer." Coleridge is concerned to distinguish Maria's fancy from both. Her enthusiasm for secular tales, however, does sustain in her a susceptibility to just those influences—music, incense, mummery—which Coleridge expects his British audience both to pay good money to see, and to despise as popish. If Maria is moving toward a Protestantism still rolled up in the volume of concealment, Osorio himself seems unconsciously poised on its cusp: though he is aware that Roman rites can look like sorcery and that sorcerers, like Inquisitors, may turn out to be stage players, he also retains a habit of suspecting "some base spell" by which his brother has "bewitched her senses." He sees his brother's enlightenment as a spell, a form of witchcraft, differing from the sorcery of Catholic rite only in having a more profound effect on Maria. Osorio is not wrong about the spell of enlightenment; he is wrong only in wagering that secular stagecraft wields a greater power.

3.

The elaborate staging of the conjuring scene is all the more remarkable in light of the dispatch with which Schiller treats it in *Der Geist-*

erseher, which (along with *Die Räuber*) has long been recognized as one of Coleridge's main sources.[23] Coleridge's interest in this source lies in its striking parallels to religious politics under Philip II, whom *Osorio*'s headnote associates with a politicized Catholicism whose edicts are devoted to the regimenting of costume. *Der Geisterseher,* too, examines the politics of what Schiller treats as Jesuitical stagecraft, narrating a struggle between Catholics and Protestants that turns on the aesthetic deployment of true and false sorcery.

Coleridge's use of Schiller in *Osorio* has been much discussed, most recently by Julie Carlson, who emphasizes the revision's indebtedness to Coleridge's translation of *Wallenstein*.[24] But the most important debt has not been examined in many years. Coleridge's 1796 "Effusion XX," which addresses Schiller as "Bard tremendous in sublimity," encapsulates its argument in a note: "Schiller introduces no Supernatural Beings." The sonnet connects the "mute awe" and "wild ecstasy" Schiller induces in his reader with his enlightened overcoming, or surpassing, of the supernatural: "A triumphant shout / Black Horror scream'd, and all her goblin rout / Diminish'd shrunk from the more withering scene!"[25] If we look in Schiller for an enthusiasm predicated on an overcoming of the supernatural, we would do well to look past *Die Räuber,* to which this sonnet (and most criticism on *Osorio*) refers, and take a fresh look at *Der Geisterseher*.

Schiller's unfinished novel catalogues a series of ways to exploit the spell of enlightenment that Coleridge praises for its power, in Schiller's hands, to rout goblins. The plot traces the stratagems that allow an enlightened skepticism, with its persuasion of rational self-sufficiency, to tip a balanced mind from faith to superstition, and explores how a discourse of demystification can thereby be made to serve a politically useful irrationalism. Only at the very end of Schiller's fragment, dominated by quack sorcerers and their dupes, is "faith" revealed to be a religious matter, the contest between Protestantism and Catholicism.

---

23. "I omit the description of the farce itself," says Schiller's apparitionist, "as it would lead me to too great a length" (*The Ghost-Seer,* trans. Henry G. Bohn [Columbia, S.C.: Camden House, 1992] 33). Alois Brandl seems to have been the first to identify this text as Coleridge's source; John Livingston Lowes explored the connection in a long footnote to *The Road to Xanadu: A Study in the Ways of the Imagination* (New York: Houghton Mifflin, 1930) 540–41.
24. See Carlson, *Theatre of Romanticism* 102.
25. Coleridge, *Poems* 1:73.

But at this point religion quickly becomes a screen for politics, as we suddenly understand that we have watched a Lutheran prince forfeit his fathers' faith in favor of one that the Inquisition has chosen for him. The prince can be converted to Catholicism only after the rational disposition of his faith—his belief in free choice—has been undermined. Skepticism works in the service of superstition here, almost as, in *The Borderers*, Rivers is able to make Mortimer lend credence to whatever he himself approaches with skepticism. In posing as impersonal knowledge devoid of personal agency, demystification acquires the power to command faith.

The Jesuit plot, a perennial staple of the paranoid gothic, is important in the context of *Osorio* for the same reason Catholicism is important to Coleridge's contribution to *Joan of Arc*. There Coleridge had defended the power of fancy with evidence of God's immanent agency, and had used that argument to claim that fancy brings on an enlightenment that allows the "disposal of apt circumstance / To rear up kingdoms." Political power, as Burke would have agreed, follows from faith, not from demystification, which is liable rather to rob its victims of their moral bearings. Coleridge's interest in *Der Geisterseher* can be understood in terms of Schiller's motive in putting the powers of demystification into the hands of Jesuits: to make it clear that enlightenment, far from being inherently liberating, can facilitate repressive political control. Coleridge's treatment of Schiller's material in *Osorio* is designed to offer an alternative faith whose progressive political power lies beyond demystification.

There is much to be gained by considering how Coleridge might have thought through the politics of faith using the materials provided by *Der Geisterseher*. Schiller shows how the prince's skepticism is stirred by his interview with the jailed apparitionist who confesses to him the tricks of the trade by which the prince had been duped: "The confessions of the Sicilian left a deeper impression upon his mind than they ought, considering the circumstances; and the small victory which his reason had thence gained over this weak imposture, remarkably increased his reliance upon his own powers." His victory over faith in its minor mode—over his credulous belief in the powers of a stage magician—makes him think he has identified a delusion inherent in all faith. "The unmasking of a deception made even truth suspicious to him," Schiller writes; "From this instant there arose in his mind a scepticism which did not spare even the most sacred objects." The prince's skepticism is displayed in a long philosophical dialogue maintaining "the relativity of morality, immorality as a delusion, the self as externally determined, the greatness of evil, and the identification of good with energy and effort." This sequence of positions, which are portrayed as working together to undermine the prince's autonomy, marks the endpoint of a disillusionment that begins with the prince seeing through a cheap sorcerer's stage performance, a victory he attributes to his knowledge of the stage. ("I have seen Richard the Third performed by Garrick," he says.) Having effected this demystification—with his own intellectual powers, he believes—the prince falls under the sway of a passion not unknown to Coleridge himself, a passion Schiller describes as "a propensity which rendered everything irresistible which was incomprehensible." That the mysterious "Armenian" cleric who seems to stage-manage every event in the novel is known to locals "by the name of the Incomprehensible" lends an allegorical dimension to the novel's demonstration that the most powerful means of demystification can amount to merely so many tools wielded by the "invisible hand" of conspirators.[26]

It is in his interview with the Sicilian fraud that the prince hears the tale that provided Coleridge with the rudiments of *Osorio*'s conjuring scene; as Frederic Ewen notes, the plot of this inset tale is virtually identical to that of *Osorio*.[27] In Schiller, the missing brother actually has been murdered by the man who employs a conjurer to prove that he will not return; no magician is needed in *Osorio*, as the lost brother remains alive—or is, as Parker suggests, reanimated—to play the part himself. Schiller provides a complex political context for the desire for certainty which both Schiller's and Coleridge's fake conjurings are supposed to satisfy. In the Sicilian's tale, the conjurer fakes the appearance of the dead brother by producing his ring, and the surviving brother is allowed to marry his brother's lover; but on their wedding night the spirit of the dead brother appears—at the bidding of the man known as the Incomprehensible—to accuse his murderer, bringing on him a remorseful death. The tale's effect on the prince is curious: when

---

26. Schiller, *The Ghost-Seer* 47–48, 44, 25, 51. The summary of the philosophical dialogue is from the introduction by Jeffrey Sammons, ix; Sammons quotes a letter in which Schiller confesses that "composing the dialogue 'had almost made my Christianity waver' " (x).

27. Frederic Ewen, *The Prestige of Schiller in England, 1788–1859* (New York: Columbia University Press, 1932) 60–62.

the Sicilian conjurer cannot say where he got the dead brother's ring, the prince realizes that the tale indicts its teller; even the second apparition of the dead brother becomes suspect, although as a mysterious manifestation of the Incomprehensible, it continues to command an inchoate belief.

The Sicilian's feeble gothic tale builds the prince's confidence in his power to see through such mummery, even the mummery of enlightenment to which he is, as his confidence suggests, more than ever in thrall. A friend expresses doubt whether the Incomprehensible would "destroy the illusion he has himself created, and disclose the mysteries of his science to the eyes of the uninitiated." The prince replies just as we might wish to reply, with a seemingly unassailable, because totally enlightened, theory of persuasion:

> What mysteries does he disclose? None, surely, which he intends to practice on me. He therefore loses nothing by the discovery. But, on the other hand, what an advantage will he gain, if this pretended victory over juggling and deception should render me secure and unsuspecting; if he succeeds in diverting my attention from the right quarter, and in fixing my wavering suspicions on an object the most remote from the real one! He could naturally expect that, sooner or later, either from my own doubts, or at the suggestion of another, I should be tempted to seek a key to his mysterious wonders, in the mere art of a juggler; how could he better provide against such an inquiry than by contrasting his prodigies with juggling tricks. By confining the latter within artificial limits, and by delivering, as it were, into my hands a scale by which to appreciate them, he naturally exalts and perplexes my ideas of the former. How many suspicions he precludes by this single contrivance! How many methods of accounting for his miracles, which might afterwards have occurred to me, does he refute before-hand![28]

The prince catalogues so completely the range of means by which the spell of enlightenment can be used to charm the enlightened that this reads like an abstract of the remainder of the novel, in which he falls victim to the techniques he outlines here. The charm is not rendered any less potent by its demystification. The problem is not that the prince does not know this, but that the charm cannot be deactivated by any amount of knowledge.

Osorio's historical conception of its characters' religious backgrounds can be clarified by answering a question about a plot detail:

---

28. Schiller, *The Ghost-Seer* 42–43.

Why does Coleridge put an *image* in the place of Schiller's ring? One answer might be extrapolated from Watson's account of the first popular rebellion among the Calvinist Lowlanders, which itself focuses on images: "In Antwerp the reformers indulged themselves in the most unjustifiable extravagancies. They insulted the Catholics when employed in the functions of their religion. They broke furiously into the great church, which was one of the richest edifices in Europe, overturned the altars, defaced the paintings, and destroyed all the images of the saints" (1:267–68). There is a striking parallel in Watson's account of the Moresco revolt, which begins with their "destroying the altars and images in the churches [of Alpuxara], which they converted into mosques" (1:355). If *Osorio*'s act 3 stagecraft tests the powers of sorcery to command a belief that will overcome doubt, then its centerpiece —a smoking picture on an altar—establishes a link between the power of the stage and the politics of image-worship. In this light it would be doubly correct to speak of Coleridge attempting a *reformation* of the stage: his powerful unmasking of religious mummery and his wrapping it in a plot of oppression and emancipation are designed to reveal the political power of a theatrical spectacle that can both liberate and enthrall.

The power of demystification to command faith is what allows Coleridge to turn the conjuring scene against its instigator. But Coleridge also facilitates that twist by substituting a series of images for Schiller's ring and by deploying those images as punctuation for a sustained *verbal* conjuring. Maria's fancy, which she later says works "as if to give a voice to the mute image" (4.2.38), may serve as a paradigm for Albert's conjuring. His ceremony before the altar picks up the most important aspect of English iconoclasm, which Ronald Paulson defines as "the replacement of visual images with words."[29] Albert delivers long soliloquies that draw visible signs of guilt from his brother long before anyone sees the painting that is the ostensible sign of that guilt, and Coleridge gives those words a priority and an authority which the

---

29. Ronald Paulson, *Breaking and Remaking: Aesthetic Practice in England, 1700–1820* (New Brunswick: Rutgers University Press, 1989) 17. This form of iconoclasm was alive and well in Romantic antitheatricalism, for example in Lamb's reason for lamenting any staging of Shakespeare: "the sight actually destroys the faith" ("On the Tragedies of Shakespeare," *Complete Works and Letters of Charles Lamb* [New York: Modern Library, 1935] 300). On Romantic antitheatricalism, see Jonas Barish, *The Antitheatrical Prejudice* (Berkeley: University of California Press, 1982) 295–349.

painting cannot claim. (Burwick notes that "neither of the two paintings, the props which command so much attention on the stage, can be seen by the audience."[30]) Yet the unexpected effect of the painting, when it does appear, bears out an ambivalence Paulson glimpses beneath the iconoclast's self-assurance. The iconoclastic sensibility, he argues, "was that of the Protestant who had been an idolator and probably in his heart feared that he remained one—and so joined a strong inner attaction to an even stronger public manifestation of rejection."[31] What better account could we have of Coleridge's ambivalent deployment, in act 3, of the artifice of stagecraft?

Albert opens his conjuring with an aside to Maria: "Doubt, but decide not" (3.1.10). His skeptical imperative is not only to doubt, that is, to decide not, but also to keep doubt from deciding the matter one way or the other. Maria's moment of crisis arrives when the altar bursts into flames, and she follows Albert's advice as though instinctively: "This is some trick—I know, it is a trick. / Yet my weak fancy, and these bodily creepings, / Would fain give substance to the shadow!" (3.1.113–15). She doubts, but, thanks to the "bodily creepings" she shares with the audience she addresses, she decides not. Yet as her body creeps toward unconsciousness ("She swoons"), the scales tip toward decision.[32] Awakened from her fit by Albert's voice, she thinks that voice a mere dream, one from which she has often awakened. Persuaded by her body that she is dreaming, and knowing from sore experience that such dreams do not come true, she reasons that Albert cannot be present, and if he is not present, then he must at last be acknowledged to be dead, "Murder'd perhaps!" "Believe it not, sweet maid!" the disguised Albert responds, "believe it not, / Beloved woman! 'Twas a low imposture / Framed by a guilty wretch" (3.1.128–32). He succeeds in talking her out of her certainty, but the unbearable uncertainty puts her again at the mercy of her body: "Nay—nay—but tell

---

30. Burwick, *Illusion and the Drama* 303.

31. Paulson, *Breaking and Remaking* 17. Ann Kibbey makes a similar argument in *The Interpretation of Material Shapes in Puritanism: A Study of Rhetoric, Prejudice, and Violence* (New York: Cambridge University Press, 1986): "Simultaneously adoring and destroying, they both rejected visual shapes and endowed them with sacred meaning" (42).

32. Burwick calls attention to Maria's embodiment in taking her opening speech as refuting Albert's formula, "what the mind believes impossible, / The bodily sense is slow to recognize": "the false report of [Albert's] death is what her 'mind believes impossible,' yet her 'bodily sense' is very much alert" (*Illusion and the Drama* 270).

me! [*A pause—then presses her forehead.*] Ah! 'tis lost again! / This dead confused pain! [*A pause—she gazes at Albert.*] Mysterious man!" (3.1.144–54). Her fancy that Albert is present gains support from her physical responses, but the involvement of her body, which she takes to be her weakness, makes her underestimate fancy, count it as mere dreamwork. Yet her body speaks the truth, above all by suspending her denials in the repeated silences of these last lines. Albert's stagecraft carries Maria from an intellectual doubt, through a creepy experience of bodily recognition, toward what she knows but cannot acknowledge that she knows.

How does Albert's stagecraft act upon the other members of the onstage audience? In Velez it induces a smug knowingness about the artifice he takes to be Osorio's. In Osorio it induces what a stage direction calls "a state of stupor" in which he cannot even hear his brother calling to the insensible Maria: "My love! my wife! Maria!" (3.1.119). The confusion of responses, indeed, became too much for even Coleridge to bear. Osorio meets his father's "mirth and raillery" with a disdain whose source is unclear: "I am content to be more serious," he says in one draft, but it comes out "I am content to be more superstitious" in another; in the first, "serious" is cancelled and replaced by "superstitious," while the second has "superstitious" cancelled and replaced by "serious." Coleridge's ambivalence is interesting not because it is improbable that a superstitious person would take his superstition seriously, but because it shows Coleridge unable to convince himself that he knows what such a person would say. The opacity of superstition dictates the pacing of what follows. While Velez is full of assurances, Osorio stumbles blindly from darkness to darkness:

> I was benumb'd, and stagger'd up and down
> Thro' darkness without light—dark—dark—dark—
> And every inch of this my flesh did feel
> As if a cold toad touch'd it! Now 'tis sunshine,
> And the blood dances freely thro' its channels!
> (3.1.195–99)

Like Maria, Osorio responds to Albert's stagecraft with his body. Unlike her, he believes only what he wants his body to tell him. The consequence will be a madness, in the final scene of the play, that has him acknowledging the power of the beings with which his fancy has peopled the air.

Perhaps the most striking aspect of Osorio's scene with Velez is the way in which his stupor fractures the dialogue into what Burwick calls "dual monologues."[33] What does it mean that each character speaks to no one, hears no one? Some critics have judged this to be the general condition of Romantic drama.[34] But Coleridge devises for *Remorse* an effective means of helping us (in spite of the common perception that Wordsworth's dialogues are similarly monological) to judge it as an aberration *from* the main line of Romanticism, one that can be exposed only in drama. *Remorse* clarifies what had been confusing in *Osorio* by adding an onstage audience to respond to these dual monologues, which make up a spectacle which that onstage audience helps us to see as even stranger than the conjuring scene that preceded it. For Maria, who acts out our own wish for invisibility when she "retires out of sight," has overheard the entire exchange we too have overheard. During Osorio's rantings she "reappears and advances slowly," as though to dramatize the limits of the invisibility which, Baillie argued, we embrace as we search out others' passions. When Osorio has finished and Velez has dismissed his confession of murder as "mere madness," Maria "moves hastily forwards, and places herself directly before" Osorio, as though compelling him to acknowledge what he has confessed. But he cannot acknowledge even her reality:

> [*Osorio.*] [Maria]? or the phantom of [Maria]?
> [*Maria.*] Alas! the phantom only, if in truth
>   The substance of her being, her life's life,
>   Have ta'en its flight through [Albert's] death-wound.
>   (R 3.2.115–18)

Osorio continues to voice his guilt, and his father continues to attribute it to the spell of the "magic imagery" that has led his passions to "give reality / To the creatures of his fancy" (R 3.2.142–43). Velez hopes Maria might "disenchant his spirit," but she quickly departs, seeking "A better, surer light / To guide me" (R 3.2.137, 157–58).

What is clarified in *Remorse*'s staging of an audience's response, particularly in the striking line in which Osorio—his mocking tone covering a genuine terror—takes Maria for a phantom? The point of

---

33. Burwick, *Illusion and the Drama* 276.
34. See, for example, Robert Langbaum, *The Poetry of Experience: The Dramatic Monologue in Modern Literary Tradition* (New York: Norton, 1963).

having the failed dialogue climax in that strange moment is to suggest that Osorio's malcontent rantings, which serve to defend against his unconscious confession, reject dialogue by denying the substance of others. The persistent presence of others—of an audience for his soliloquies, of society, of us—pulls Osorio toward a recognition that solipsism, in any social context, engenders superstition. Osorio's lines also show that he glimpses—tragically, only in passing—the quickest way out of that trap: to ask the other to confirm her presence, and to take her word for it.

4.

What should be our response to Coleridge's stagecraft? The conjuring scene, as it openly fails to unite its audience, suggests that our responses might be not one but many: some will be transfixed by the spectacle, others will not. The *British Review* found act 3 "very unfitted to the grave and lofty genius of tragedy"; the *Theatrical Inquisitor* accused it, in good inquisitorial form, of "absurd profaneness."[35] Hazlitt, by contrast, called the scene "one of the most novel and picturesque we remember to have witnessed," placing an invisible irony-mark, perhaps, over "picturesque" (18:465). The variety of possible reactions follows, I believe, from the presence, at the center of the scene, of a picture—or more than one picture—open to a wide range of interpretations.

Social critics have argued that multiple interpretability works in the service of the liberal state, which requires that its citizens either tolerate or remain blind to their essential differences. Among Romanticists the touchstone for this argument is the painting at the end of *Waverley*, which allows each of its viewers to embrace a different interpretation of the events Scott has narrated, holding those viewers together in a mutual respect that suspends further inquiry. The multiplication of responses in *Osorio*, however, focuses attention not on liberal tolerance but on the power of art to command faith. The conjuring scene may seem to unmask that power, to demystify faith as superstition—a madness, an avoidance. In context, however, it works also to exhibit the political power of one *kind* of faith, and the corresponding weakness of another. That distinction is not a matter of the gravity of one's belief

35. *Romantics Reviewed* A:1:225; A:2:874.

—fancy is as serviceable as what Coleridge would later call imagination, as he affirms in lines he eventually cut from "Frost at Midnight":

> But still the living spirit in our frame,
> That loves not to behold a lifeless thing,
> Transfuses into all its own delights
> Its own volition, sometimes with deep faith,
> And sometimes with fantastic playfulness.
> (*Poems*, 240)

For the Coleridge of *Osorio*, the difference between "deep faith" and "fantastic playfulness" is nothing in the face of the difference between love, which prompts both, and hate, which can disturb neither. Those distinctions, before they assume their canonical form in the conversation poems, emerge from the political context detailed in *Osorio*. Coleridge is interested not so much in diagnosing or defending the function of stagecraft in the liberal state as in using it to show his readers how they dispose of their own living spirits, and by that means to guide them to a more discerning understanding of faith and of those who would either attack or manipulate it.

If, as Coleridge learns from Schiller, the unmasking of faith can serve political repression, what, in Coleridge's view, can guarantee the survival of a progressive political agency? Only a faith that cannot be demystified by any amount of knowledge. For Coleridge, in 1797, that faith is the faith in the "one life within us and abroad," and *Osorio* is the first text to recognize its political power. Its resistance to demystification is only partly a matter of its avowing the apparent craziness of its mournful enthusiasts, an avowal that only enhances its power, as we see in Maria's first speech. It is also a matter of its "natural" conception of faith as an acknowledgment, rather than a knowledge, that God's hand is everywhere. What opposes this faith appears in *Osorio* not as a lack of knowledge, but as an inability to achieve acknowledgment.

This inability, I believe, is the key to the emotion Coleridge names "remorse." A good place to look for the origins of Coleridge's conception of that emotion is again book 2 of *Joan of Arc,* in the vision that follows immediately upon Coleridge's defense of fancy. Southey followed Coleridge's theory of "preternatural agency" with an allegorical vision of the Palace of Ambition, to which come flocks of allegorical agents such as Superstition, Hypocrisy, Revenge, and Slaughter, all of which displace human agency in the best tradition of sublime personification.[36] At the gate of the Palace of Ambition, they meet Southey's final personification:

> REMORSE for ever his sad vigils kept,
> His heart the viper's feast: worn down his face,
> If face it were when scarce the shrivell'd skin
> Wrap'd o'er the bone, proclaim'd the gnawing pang:
> Inly he groan'd, or starting wildly, shriek'd,
> Aye as the fabric tottering from its base
> Threaten'd destruction, tho' oft announc'd withheld,
> Tho' still withheld, expected.
>
> (198–205)

A personification with no face, Remorse holds a liminal place in Southey's allegory, its voice—perhaps inward, perhaps outward—ever about to bring down the entire edifice. This self-consuming allegory of self-consumption—the very image of iconoclasm—is a peculiarly Protestant allegory, directed against the idolatrous displacement of human agency that allows it to assume its shape. Its self-deconstructing evasion of human agency, in which the fabric of the building threatens (by imaging) its own destruction without being able to enact it, is calculated to elicit the reader's awareness of his or her own place among what had seemed remote agencies. This is the very awareness that leads Joan toward heroic action: "These the Maid / Mark'd as they steer'd their dusky flight along; / And lo! she was amidst them" (205–7).

Remorse first works on Osorio to elicit from him a wish to deny all moral distinctions, in a Rivers-like parody of the One Life:

> I kill a man and lay him in the sun
> And in a month there swarm from his dead body
> A thousand—nay, ten thousand sentient beings
> In place of that one man whom I had kill'd.

---

36. Knapp studies this displacement in *Personification and the Sublime*. Coleridge says that he himself "despised" "these images imageless, these *Small-Capitals* constituting themselves Personifications" (Coleridge, *Poems* 1:145, editorial apparatus). Robert Sternbach helps to explain why, when he notes that "the secondary powers have achieved an autonomy that seems to put them out of control of the human mind," and that Southey both "attributes to these passions substantial personal existence, and at the same time denies the centrality of the self as the author of its own code of behavior" ("Coleridge, Joan of Arc, and the Idea of Progress," *ELH* 46 [1979]: 252, 255).

> Now who shall tell me, that each one and all,
> Of these ten thousand lives, is not as happy
> As that one life, which being shov'd aside
> Made room for these ten thousand?
> (3.1.224–31)

"Wild as madness!" his father exclaims; and when Osorio continues to rave about the assassination plot depicted in his brother's fraudulent history-painting, he is warned against the power of passions which "Unsettle you, and give reality / To these your own contrivings" (3.1.240–41). Osorio, who does not know who contrived the picture, holds that diagnosis in contempt, but he cannot invent a better explanation for the evidence that his plot against his brother has become known. Nor, indeed, can he deny his belief that the plot he contrived has become a reality: he has, after all, the evidence of the painting. By exposing as objective reality what had merely been internally contrived, the artwork stirs in Osorio the passion that makes him believe in the reality of what it contrives to show, and he can only take that reality as his own contrivance. In disowning the agency responsible for the artwork that makes him own the agency responsible for what it depicts, Osorio does not offer a psychological portrayal of remorse. If that were Coleridge's object, the *British Review* would be correct in judging that he "sinks very much in a comparison with Miss Joanna Baillie, as a delineator of the passions."[37] Without wishing to deny that Coleridge might have meant the title *Remorse* to take advantage of Baillie's reputation, I can only assert that the villain of the early version serves an entirely different purpose. Osorio acts out not the psychology of "remorse," but Southey's self-consuming *allegory* of Remorse.

The result is what would be the strangest scene in the play, if we were not already familiar with such complexities from *The Borderers*, from which, critics have suggested, Coleridge borrowed much of his dénouement.[38] A review in *The Satirist* hit on what is most strange in Osorio's scene with Ferdinand in the cave: "He goes to commit murder, and spends half an hour in allegorical ratiocination with the person he is about to kill, in order, as it were, to persuade him to be killed in a

---

37. *Romantics Reviewed* A:1:225.
38. See Stephen Maxfield Parrish, *The Art of the Lyrical Ballads* (Cambridge: Harvard University Press, 1973) 70–79, and Paul Magnuson, *Coleridge and Wordsworth: A Lyrical Dialogue* (Princeton: Princeton University Press, 1988) 61–64.

peaceable and becoming manner."[39] It is, indeed, the entirely unmotivated, *allegorical* cast of Osorio's actions that seems so unaccountable here. Coleridge's marginal explanation for the scene reads like an account of Rivers' behavior in act 4 of *The Borderers*: "Under the mask of the third person Osorio relates his own story, as in the delusion of self-justification and pride, it appeared to himself—at least as he wished it to appear to himself." Osorio's rhetoric, indeed, seems almost wholly cribbed from Rivers; almost, but not quite. The difference lies in Coleridge's attention to the telling of his tale as a means by which contrivance becomes reality. The gap between thought and action is the central mystery that occupies Osorio, who speaks of it in reverent tones, as though closing it were a miracle that might scarcely command belief: "With his human hand / He gave a being and reality / To that wild fancy of a possible thing" (4.1.105–7). That is not the end of the tale, however; for Osorio must now, on stage, again give "being and reality" to his "wild fancy." Ferdinand, who Osorio thinks has served him as "his human hand," asks what "he" did with the villain whom Osorio calls "some over-ready agent." Osorio brings the tale up to the present: "He made the traitor meet him in this cavern, / And here he kill'd the traitor" (4.1.132–33). As he proceeds to do, but not without allowing Ferdinand a moment to draw his sword; for Osorio claims that, in listening to his own tale, "My heart was drawing back, drawing me back" (4.1.143). The tale meant to bridge the gap between conception and execution had, he claims, actually widened that gap, suspended his hand "with womanish pulls of pity" (4.1.144). The reason is evident in the allegorical cast of the tale: as long as he is speaking of himself as an other, Osorio cannot act that other's part. Yet if Ferdinand had not drawn his sword, would Osorio have carried his tale forward to narrate the villain's funeral, the murderer's remorse, his future life? The fruitlessness of such speculation reminds us that Ferdinand *must* draw his sword, that Osorio's narrative *must* be brought back to the stage on which it is told so that it may be acted out. But when we realize this, we see that Osorio's fall into narrative has been a fall away from agency. It is as though the "contrivance" of paintings and mummery in act 3 had absorbed Osorio into a realm in which—as in a painting of an assassin, his blade poised to enter the flesh of his victim—intentions are permanently suspended on the verge of action. Osorio's faith in the

39. *Romantics Reviewed* A:2:849.

scene he has been shown has withdrawn him from the world of flesh and blood—the flesh and blood we acknowledge when we enter the theater—into a life of allegory that freezes action into emblematic poses. Even his rousing himself to kill Ferdinand cannot bring him back to the realm of the living, if we are to judge from his "pointing at vacancy" in the depths of his madness in the play's final scene. That Osorio's agency has become almost somnambulistic is underscored by a small change in *Remorse*, in the line where Osorio speaks of how the murderer in his tale "gave a substance and reality / To that wild fancy of a possible thing." In *Osorio* it was "with his hand"; in *Remorse* it is "with *this* hand." Osorio's acknowledgment of his own agency, apparently as self-evident to him as his own body, escapes him unawares. His own body has become a phantom to him; the slip in which he acknowledges its instrumentality seals his delusion.

When *Remorse* was reviewed in the *Quarterly*, the reviewer—Coleridge's nephew John Taylor Coleridge—suggested that Osorio, in his madness, resembled John Bellingham, "the murderer of the lamented Perceval," the prime minister who had been cut down outside the House of Commons in 1812. The play, it is suggested, depicts just such a monster of autonomy, "in his moral madness framing a new code of action, in which he is self-constituted judge and executioner, and by which the most dreadful acts of vengeance stand justified of guilt; feeling indeed at times the tortures of unperverted conscience, yet neither terrified nor subdued and angry, at the weakness of a nature, which he deems unworthy of him."[40] Coleridge's play shows how to confront those monsters who cannot see their autonomy as relative—the subhuman machines of destruction Coleridge imagined, in his meditation on Michelangelo's Brutus, confusing regicide with tyrannicide and so demonstrating their incapacity to do anything that might properly count as an action. One confronts such non-agents not with elaborate efforts to stir their moral sensibilities—for remorse is likely to push such machines to yet greater isolation and yet greater crimes—but by working to elicit from them an acknowledgment of what the Wordsworthian faith would teach them, their bond to nature. Wordsworth's remarks on Bellingham—whose execution, as Parker notes, he was eager to attend—suggest that the great spokesman for that faith had himself learned a somewhat different lesson:

40. Ibid. A:2:823.

Osorio

> Would it not be a horrible thing, that the extreme of a Man's guilt, should be pleaded as a reason, why he should be exempted from punishment; because, forsooth, his crime was so atrocious that no Man in his senses could have committed it? All guilt is a deviation from reason. And had such an Assassin as this been acquitted upon the ground of insanity, the verdict would have been held out an encouragement to all wicked Men, to transcend the known bounds of Wickedness, with a hope of finding security from every law in the very enormity of their crimes.[41]

Parker hears the voice of Rivers echoing on in Wordsworth's indignation, as his suspicion of preternatural agency undermines the compassion we might have expected from the author of the *Lyrical Ballads*. What is still more noteworthy is that Coleridge had already decisively answered that voice in *Osorio* by tracing the disintegration of the villain from a man into an allegory. His answer, which supplies his hero with a faith on which to ground his politically progressive agency, also helped to make Wordsworth the poet he was—the poet whose lost faith was fondly remembered on January 23, 1813, on the stage of Drury Lane, to "unexampled Applause."[42]

---

41. *The Love Letters of William and Mary Wordsworth*, ed. Beth Darlington (Ithaca: Cornell University Press, 1981) 162; quoted from Parker, " 'Oh Could You Hear His Voice!' " 141–42.

42. Coleridge to Sara Coleridge, 27 January 1813, in Coleridge, *Letters* 3:429.

Part Two

SHELLEY, BYRON, AND
THE BODY POLITIC,
1819–1822

4

Performing Skepticism: *The Cenci*

> We cannot kill and not kill in the same moment; but a moment is room wide enough for the loyal and mean desire, for the outlash of a murderous thought and the sharp backward stroke of repentance.
>
> —GEORGE ELIOT, *Daniel Deronda*

In September 1819, when news of the Peterloo Massacre reached Shelley in Leghorn, he vented his rage in a letter to his publisher that has become familiar to every Shelley scholar. "The torrent of my indignation has not yet done boiling in my veins," he wrote; "I wait anxiously to hear how the Country will express its sense of this bloody murderous oppression of its destroyers." Having roused his emotions to the point where they overheat his body, Shelley then steps out of that body and into the words of his recently completed tragedy *The Cenci*. He traces the boiling torrent back to his heroine, who is herself quoting King Lear: " 'Something must be done,' " he quotes; "What yet I know not.' "[1] Publicly, in the play, Beatrice's imperative could be referred only to remote literary contexts that might seem to lie almost beyond

---

1. 6 September 1819, quoting *The Cenci* 3.1.86–87; *The Letters of Percy Bysshe Shelley* ed. Frederick L. Jones (Oxford: Clarendon, 1964) 2:513. The Peterloo passage has become a touchstone for "political" interpretations of *The Cenci*, but the line quoted from the play is more elusive than critics have noticed. Richard Lansdown may be correct in suggesting that, "where Shelley is unwilling to face the implications of what Cenci or Beatrice have to say, he prefers to have them borrow from Lear, or Troilus, or Claudio" (*Byron's Historical Dramas* [Oxford: Clarendon Press, 1992] 209). But here Shelley exhibits Lear's unwillingness to face implications by having Beatrice's passive voice qualify and complicate his fantasy of intact agency: "I will do such things— / What they are, yet I know not" (*King Lear* 2.4.279–81).

history; privately, in the letter, Shelley took advantage of his own earlier decontextualization to apply that imperative to the present moment. What is Shelley doing with Beatrice here, or what is she doing with him? In quoting Beatrice, does Shelley act out a scenario from the *Defense of Poetry*, in which he grants drama the power to construct agents by dissolving the boundaries of identity? Or do the quotation marks signal Shelley's effort to distance himself from a temptation *The Cenci* warns against?

The choice between these alternatives will depend on assumptions about the potential spillover of literary language into the violent action it purports merely to represent. Shelley himself was usually more comfortable posing questions about the political efficacy of his writing than answering them, opting characteristically to suspend himself between a commitment to direct action and a critique of its seductions. In circumstances urgently demanding decisive action, however, his resistance to partisan dogmatisms could not have been sustained without a trust that the skeptical suspension of judgment might itself act to clear the way for further consolidations of political agency. In marking the limits of such dialogic irresolution with the materiality of the body, *The Cenci* dramatizes Shelley's quest for a literary mode capable not just of arguing but of embodying skepticism, in the hope of allowing that skepticism to perform what mere writing cannot.[2]

Contemporary reviewers were certain that plays could do things to audiences, that a work like *The Cenci* was capable of inciting violence. The *New Monthly Magazine* declared that "there can be little doubt that the horrible details of murder, which are too minutely given in our public journals, lead men to dwell on horrors till they cease to petrify, and gradually prepare them for that which once they trembled to think on."[3] This moralization of Macbeth's anxiety about the Weird Sisters can hardly serve to condemn *The Cenci*, as it draws on Giacomo's climactic lament over the representation of evil that "made me look / Upon the monster of my thought, until / It grew familiar to desire," a line of rationalizing immediately dismissed as evasive

---

2. Merle R. Rubin has argued on different and more general grounds that skepticism "is for Shelley (as it was in a way for Hume) a double-edged weapon that can free him to act" ("Shelley's Skepticism: A Detachment Beyond Despair," *Philological Quarterly* 59 [1980]: 356).

3. *New Monthly Magazine* 13 (1820): 551: *Romantics Reviewed* C:2:735.

(5.1.19–32).[4] *The Cenci* does, however, aspire to have an effect off the stage. That aspiration can be formulated as a faith in the power of imagining an agency that cannot be asserted but that is, by that imaginative act, effectually performed. Shelley's profession of scorn for "the extreme depravity and disgusting nature"[5] of the Regency stage differs from the *New Monthly*'s expression of dread; he likely thought the stage did not do enough to prepare audiences for that which once they trembled to think on. But Shelley had his own anxieties about the power of the theater, and he used them to advantage in working out the moral and political arguments embodied in *The Cenci*. And it was *The Cenci* that enabled him to articulate a workable conception of the relation between his identity as a poet and his agency in the world of political consequences.

Shelley uses dramatic character as a laboratory for studying the agencies of social change as they might develop in isolation from the social constraints that would otherwise bind them. His use of generic convention reveals this exploratory motive. Tragedy requires that change be swift and inexorable for any particular person, but glacial, almost unimaginable, for the larger social world. Any tragedy can be located on a spectrum between those poles, on the basis of its tactics for grappling with their irreconcilability. Shelley positions *The Cenci* by isolating, within a broadly sketched society of immutable oppression, moments at which unpredictable shiftings in the language of its characters signal the larger changes that structure his plot. *The Cenci* might be said to position itself within tragic convention by working out the problem of "lyrical drama" that Shelley had posed, but hardly resolved, in *Prometheus Unbound;* but while that titanic psychomachia seems calculated to distract attention from the difficulty of establishing a relation between personal and social change, *The Cenci* pursues Shelley's concern with the agencies of historical progress by giving sustained attention to just those jagged seams where personal (or lyric) agencies of change run up against social (or dramatic) constraints.

The center of the play, a moment of apparently suspended development joining the halting exposition of acts 1 and 2 to the suspenseful

4. Passages from Shelley will be quoted, whenever possible, from *Shelley's Poetry and Prose*, ed. Donald H. Reiman and Sharon B. Powers (New York: Norton, 1977).
5. Mary Shelley, *Mary Shelley's Journal* (13 October 1814), ed. Frederick L. Jones (Norman: University of Oklahoma Press, 1947) 20, commenting on Kean's Hamlet.

murder plot of acts 3 and 4, is built upon the most unstable of these fault lines, a passage in which something happens—personal agency is conceived—not in spite of, but on the basis of a recognition that nothing can be done. Act 3 begins with a mad lyric soliloquy in which Beatrice manifests for the audience (but not for herself) that her father has raped her. Beatrice cannot reach out of her solitude far enough to grasp the dramatic context in which she is speaking; her attempt to describe the disposition of characters on the stage refers to nothing beyond her own language: "I see a woman weeping there, / And standing calm and motionless, whilst I / Slide giddily as the world reels . . ." (3.1.10–12). Her broken lyric, itself sliding giddily from one figure to the next, prepares a crucial exchange between the distraught Beatrice and her bewildered stepmother Lucretia. In this exchange, the scene turns from an assertion of loss toward a performance of agency that remedies that loss:

> *Lucretia.* What ails thee, my poor child? She answers not:
> Her spirit apprehends the sense of pain,
> But not its cause; suffering has dried away
> The source from which it sprung . . .
> *Beatrice (franticly).* Like Parricide . . .
> Misery has killed its father: yet its father
> Never like mine . . . O, God! What thing am I?
> (3.1.33–38)

Lucretia's diagnosis of Beatrice's unresponsiveness does not occasion a fuller understanding of her incoherence, but seems to cure (or obliterate) that incoherence by drawing from her a coherent response. Beatrice's apparent recovery then seems to lead to a restoration of what may, or may not, be free agency. The shift here from an isolated lyric soliloquy to a collaborative dramatic dialogue seems to supply the precondition for the action that will soon unfold: a practical trust in moral agency, underwritten by a stable personal identity disclosed through interpersonal understanding. Yet Shelley stages Beatrice's movement away from suffering and toward action not to stake for his heroine a morally admirable claim to autonomy, something he is not ready to take for granted, but to prompt the question: How do we come to *believe* we are actors rather than sufferers? For *The Cenci*, unlike many of the more overtly political lyrics of 1819, solicits and means to answer the question of how such a change takes place, so that we may learn to think about the circumstances under which it can be considered empowering. Hearing Shelley's answer is not a matter of venturing generalities about the "world" of *The Cenci* but of attending to the elaboration of beliefs about personal agency that Shelley formulates within the conventions of stage tragedy. How Beatrice's language allows her to assume agency, even while forfeiting personal identity, should be regarded, in the political context of late 1819, as *the* central issue addressed in *The Cenci*.

I will be running this crucial segment of the play in slow motion in order to assist Shelley in his effort to make visible the process by which a suspension of certainty can condition a recovery of agency. Such a possibility was of obvious importance to Shelley as a politically active skeptic. Links between skeptical arguments and moral imperatives can be gathered, for example, from *A Philosophical View of Reform*, which does not, however, attend as *The Cenci* does to the problematic details of the genesis of agency.[6] To move from the drama's experiments with character toward the referential claims of Shelley's political prose is, however, to play out the movement of the tragedy itself from the suspension of law in the middle acts to the return of social institutions that conditions the dénouement. What can that shift *within* the play tell us about Shelley's understanding of the relation *between* his dramatic experiments with agency and the world beyond the stage in which any agent is bound to act?

I.

The outward movement at the end of the play can be seen as the final phase of a shift that is found in every play, but that is studied with peculiar intensity in *The Cenci:* the movement from language to action,

---

6. The political force of skepticism in Shelley's prose is given full consideration in Terence Hoagwood, *Skepticism and Ideology: Shelley's Political Prose and Its Philosophical Context from Bacon to Marx* (Iowa City: University of Iowa Press, 1988). Hoagwood gives special attention to Shelley's skeptical vindication of political action in the face of his refusal to affirm or deny that writing causes social change (see 4, 29, and 144). He extends the line of argument in his more recent study *Byron's Dialectic: Skepticism and the Critique of Culture* (Lewisburg: Bucknell University Press, 1993). For background on Shelley's skepticism, it is still worthwhile to consult C. E. Pulos, *The Deep Truth: A Study of Shelley's Scepticism* (Lincoln: University of Nebraska Press, 1962).

effected by embodying discourse in human agents. Shelley calls attention to this movement by bringing his heroine's language up against the barrier of her body. Beatrice's relation to language is usually understood in terms of Shelley's wish to maintain a decorous silence on the most shocking element of the Cenci story, his heroine's rape by her father. Yet Beatrice is surprisingly voluble in explaining that she can "feign no image in my mind / Of that which has transformed me" (3.1.108–9).[7] Unlike Shelley, who works with Mary's translation of the Cenci family history at hand, Beatrice lacks the means to construct a survivor's story. Yet she articulates in rich, if circumlocutory, detail what it is like to live on, unable to conceive herself as a survivor: "There is none to tell / My misery: if another ever knew / Aught like it, she died as I will die, / And left it, as I must, without a name" (3.1.113–16). Beatrice's accounts of her silence feature so prominently in so many scenes that preterition becomes a basic structuring device. Its importance lies not in Shelley's wish to defer to (or restore) early-nineteenth-century standards of propriety, regularly violated in popular melodramas, but in the defensive show of arms with which Beatrice's language patrols a zone of silence in which Shelley can focus on her body apart from the social contexts assumed in any drama.[8]

Beatrice's question "What *thing* am I?" signals her troubling awareness of what it feels like for a moral ideal to be stuck in a body.

---

7. Generalizations about language and action in *The Cenci* often begin with Beatrice's supposed inability to express herself. Michael Worton locates the play's "fundamental modernity" in "its analysis of the efficacy of language," reading *The Cenci* as though it were a precursor of *Billy Budd:* "A character incapable of full self-expression will thus become, almost inevitably, a rebel, will be forced to find expression in a non-verbal way —in action" ("Speech and Silence in *The Cenci*," in *Essays on Shelley*, ed. Miriam Allott [Totowa, N.J.: Barnes and Noble, 1982] 105, 108). This idea of character as a spontaneous overflow of psychology into action may articulate anxieties underlying Shelley's social thought; but while *we* may wish to agree with Martin Luther King that "a riot is at bottom the language of the unheard," *The Mask of Anarchy* shows that it was not so easy for Shelley to accept violence as a supplement to language.

8. Marilyn Gaull persuasively dismantles the critical emphasis on Shelley's decorum: "While Shelley and most of his advocates believed that the play was rejected by Covent Garden because it was written by an atheist (although it was submitted anonymously), it is, in fact, the constant invocation of God that made it inappropriate for the stage. Similarly, while Shelley, and his followers as well, believed that the incest theme was too offensive for the stage, it was, in fact, among the repertoire of horrors to which audiences of the period had become acclimated through gothic melodrama and even found especially appealing" (*English Romanticism* 103). Among stage dramas featuring such plot elements, Walpole's *The Mad Mother* was probably the most notorious.

The prominence and particularity of her bodily awareness show how explicitly *The Cenci* addresses the general problem of embodying ideas. Outside the text, that problem seems to cross Shelley's mind whenever he thinks of his play reaching the stage, as when he declares to Peacock that "the principal character Beatrice is precisely fitted for Miss O Neil, & it might even seem to have been written for her—(God forbid that I shd. see her play it—it wd. tear my nerves to pieces)."[9] In expressing a fear that seeing Beatrice embodied by Eliza O'Neill would "tear [his] nerves to pieces," Shelley imagines his own embodiment in a way that can tell us a great deal about how he imagines his heroine. He figures his emotions as bodily, but just barely: "nerves" can be either physiological or emotional, and Shelley seems to want to touch on that precarious balance of literal and figurative to claim for his emotions the peculiar vulnerability with which delicate body parts are invested. Even more striking is the match between what he imagines seeing and how he imagines the consequence of that seeing. As a way of imagining O'Neill embodying emotions he himself *has* felt while writing Beatrice's lines, Shelley imagines as embodied the emotions he *will* feel and imagines that embodiment torn apart. The fear expressed in the image of torn nerves surfaces in a similar image in the text of the play, where the malcontent Orsino imagines the workings of Beatrice's mind as an interchange of bodily effects:

> I fear
> Her subtle mind, her awe-inspiring gaze,
> Whose beams anatomize me nerve by nerve
> And lay me bare, and make me blush to see
> My hidden thoughts.
>
> (1.2.83–87)

Orsino expresses the shame of exposure not as a stripping off of clothes to reveal his body, but as a stripping off of skin to reveal something composed of nerves called "me." His shame is not at having a body, but rather at his "nerve" (gumption) in using that body as a mask or mantle to cover over something he would prefer not to face. He thinks that her nerve exposes his.

Orsino's shame is the shame of an impersonator, which, to judge from the Preface to *The Cenci*, is a shame that Shelley knows from

---

9. 20 July 1819; Shelley, *Letters* 2:102.

experience. While Shelley denies "converting names and actions of the sixteenth century into cold *impersonations* of my own mind," he can find no other term for the heroine he has plucked from the ideal realm of the "Guido" portrait and placed in the historical world he recreates in his drama: "The crimes and miseries in which she was an actor and a sufferer are as the mask and the mantle in which circumstances clothed her for her *impersonation* on the scene of the world" (240, 242, emphasis added). Shelley's use of "impersonation" splits the word into two opposed aspects, as he uses it to indicate both the idealizing abstraction of allegory and the anti-idealizing embodiment of historical literality. His understanding of the "Guido" portrait as presenting an ideal which the historical Beatrice and his own character can only imperfectly approximate matches the reputation of Eliza O'Neill, who was described by a contemporary in terms remarkably similar to Shelley's description of the "Guido" Beatrice: "In her it was only the pure abstract human mind and soul that spoke;—nation, time, and external appearance, vanished from the thoughts in an ecstacy which carried all before it."[10]

The paradox of a pure, abstract human mind that nonetheless speaks unfolds Shelley's double use of "impersonation," which can signal either ideality or degradation, postlapsarian personhood or its transcendence. The impersonation named Beatrice is "torn to pieces" by her rape, split irreconcilably between the two vectors. Freud would have us see her doubleness as the exhibit of repression requisite for psychopathic characters on the stage, but one might simply see each Beatrice as the "outlaw" of the other's "dark mind," to borrow Byron's phrase from *Childe Harold*. That doubleness can also be given a political sense if we think of it as a transposed representation of the irreconcilability between Shelley's imageless deep truths of moral justice and the indignation that boiled in his veins in the aftermath of Peterloo. But is there a way to understand the anxious doubleness of Shelleyan impersonation before slotting it into a psychological or a political interpretation?

As an ideal of moral justice, Beatrice can be seen as playing out a scenario of displaced agency, of remote control, that Shelley first imagined in *Queen Mab*, where good does not kill evil but occasions its suicide. *Queen Mab* uses the metaphor of the scorpion ringed by fire,

---

10. Prince Hermann von Pückler-Muskau, *A Regency Visitor* (New York: Dutton, 1958) 303.

which Byron borrowed in *The Giaour* (422–38) and which Shelley reclaimed for *The Cenci* (2.2.70):

> Some eminent in virtue shall start up,
>   Even in perversest time:
> The truths of their pure lips, that never die,
> Shall bind the scorpion falsehood with a wreath
>   Of ever-living flame,
> Until the monster sting itself to death.
>   (6:33–38)

Beatrice should, according to the idealizations of Shelley's preface, provide the ethereal *verbal* flame that would make her father's evil turn on itself; that is her aspiration in acts 1 and 2. The problem that comes clear as Shelley moves the scorpion figure from the narrative of *Queen Mab* to a drama to be performed on stage is that Beatrice must also take herself (starting in act 3) as the monstrous *body* that allows evil to turn back and sting itself, as it does in act 4. Beatrice's double role, which may be regarded as expressing Shelley's awareness of having given his moral ideal a stage embodiment, also allows Shelley to see the consequences of that allegorical impersonation. The sufferings of Beatrice Cenci show what happens to ideals when they undergo their transmigration into persons, or personages.

However much Shelley may wish to imagine himself as innocently embodied, as Beatrice wishes her language to be, he must also—intolerably—imagine himself to be responsible for inflicting embodiment, as Count Cenci is in taking on the role of God the Father.[11] The anxiety arising from Beatrice's fraught relation to her body is inextricable from the anxiety about embodiment that Shelley expresses when he imagines seeing O'Neill in the theater. To witness his own impersonations impersonated is an emotional threat Shelley must state as though it were a bodily threat, because it originates in his ability to cover his feelings with bodily forms that will be taken to express those feelings. Shelley's stage fright expresses a fear that Eliza O'Neill will expose his wish to

---

11. The criminality of writing a play like *The Cenci* is a recurrent theme in the reviews, as in this sample from the *Edinburgh Monthly Review* (May, 1820): "Mr. Shelley should consider . . . that the perpetration of actual guilt, may possibly be to some natures a pastime of scarcely a different essence from that which is afforded to himself, and some others of his less-gifted contemporaries, by the scrutinizing and anatomizing discovery of things so monstrous" (*Romantics Reviewed* C:1:347).

hide behind her, as though his body were not him, but other to him, that is to say, her. Even though no one in the audience may discover that evasion, surely O'Neill will know it, as Orsino thinks Beatrice must know his hidden thoughts. When Shelley imagines his feelings embodied, he imagines his embodied feelings torn apart, dispersed, made other; and that tearing, which he both fears and, as a dramatist, *desires,* will (he fears) be inflicted upon him by O'Neill's gazing back at him from the stage: she will "anatomize [him] nerve by nerve / And lay [him] bare, and make [him] blush to see / [His] hidden thoughts."

It might be said that Shelley feels this anxiety and believes in its power because he wrote the lines O'Neill would speak. But his idea of drama stipulates that everyone in the audience must feel singled out by Beatrice's gaze, that everyone will be forced to confront his or her own feelings about embodiment being embodied, and that everyone must risk having those embodied feelings torn to pieces. In other words, Shelley understands the price of admission to his tragedy literally as the risk of admitting something. By convention, he asks his audience to address his characters as he addresses the West Wind: "Be thou me!" But far from forgetting the facts of embodiment—*we* sit passively in the audience, while *they* act and suffer on stage—that sympathetic surrender of identity depends on admitting one's embodiment. This admission seems, in Shelley, to justify recourse to the "depravity" of the theater; for his efforts to confront his own mortal body, elsewhere, often seem to be made theatrically. When he writes, for example, in "Ode to the West Wind," "I fall upon the thorns of life! I bleed!" one's first impulse may be to say: no, you do not. But that response would replicate Lucretia's evasion when Beatrice says, at the opening of act 3, "My brain is hurt; / My eyes are full of blood; just wipe them for me." Instead of wiping her stepdaughter's eyes, Lucretia responds, "My sweet child, / You have no wound" (3.1.1–4). Lucretia cannot see the wound we see because she is not, as we are, in the theater; she does not know, as we know, that ocular proof always demands the act of imagination by which, suspending our disbelief, we admit our embodiment and that of others.

If the moral imperative illustrated in that sad exchange is the necessity of imagining embodiment, what seems most shocking in *The Cenci* is the bodily disgust with which Count Cenci has foreclosed Beatrice's imagination. After claiming to be wounded at the beginning of act 3, she claims to be mad, but corrects herself immediately: "No, I am dead!

The Cenci

These putrefying limbs / Shut round and sepulchre the panting soul / Which would burst forth into the wandering air!" (3.1.26–28). Beatrice meets the unwelcome knowledge that she has (or is) a body with the wish to take her mortality as meaning that she is already dead. But why must she rush to *claim* that she is dead? Because thinking that this is what being embodied means is easier than lingering in the inhuman degradation her father inflicts when he refers to her as a "mass of flesh" and a "monstrous lump of ruin" (4.1.115, 95). Yet dehumanization will remain a threat as long as she maintains her wish to be disembodied, and she does maintain it at least to the point of her father's death, where she says: "I am as universal as the light; / Free as the earth-surrounding air; as firm / As the world's centre" (4.4.48–50). In killing her father, Beatrice thinks she sloughs off her body, to return to what she, in fact, never was: as though her body were not her, but other to her, that is to say, him. We are not to congratulate her on this, but to see it as the most unreachable depth of the suffering her father has inflicted on her. When Camillo judges her in the trial scene to be "as pure as speechless infancy" (5.2.69), we see how pervasive that suffering has become. Speech, like embodiment, is an impurity we all share, even when we are silent, when we feel like nothing more than bodies in pain. The desire to be pure, as an infant is pure, is the desire not to share in that impurity, and it is this impossible longing—or solipsistic horror—that Count Cenci has managed to instill in Beatrice. To witness it is to confront one's own denials, as they tear at one's nerves: to confront one's nerves *as* one's body.

2.

The Cenci attempts to confront such matters not only by projecting and meditating upon the embodiment of characters, but also, more problematically, by putting pressure on its characters' language, which must be our main concern in reading the play. The suffering of embodiment is inextricable in *The Cenci* from the relational term "father," a term loaded, in Shelley's framing of patriarchal discourse, with skeptical connotations. For Shelley's characters consistently see the genealogical relation between Count Cenci and his children as a cause–effect relation. That habit of mind is clear when Giacomo characterizes his father, in a quick chain of quasi-physical metonyms, as "the life that kindled mine," "the blood / Which fed these veins," and "the form that moulded mine" (3.2.16, 18–19, 20). Such figures interpret the succession of generations as the metonymic link between a genetic cause and the contiguous genetic effect that also (metaphorically) resembles that cause. In a play set "During the Pontificate of Clement VIII," it is easy to understand this rhetorical pattern within the theological framework provided by Earl Wasserman:

> Like God, [Count Cenci] is the fatherless father, the uncaused cause.... The relation of Beatrice to her father, then, is not only filial but also temporal and causal. Given a necessitarian world in which events must act out their invariable causal succession but from which the ultimate cause is inaccessibly remote, there must be a point at which ultimate cause, which is outside time, is allowed to enter the finite as the first event of a temporal sequence. That point is the "father."[12]

Shelley may indeed see patriarchal rhetoric as a way of patching over difficulties arising in the discourse of theodicy. Wasserman's grasping after the origin of evil cannot, however, exhaust Shelley's purpose in having the Cenci family bind itself with its patriarchal discourse.

The broader scope of Shelley's strategy appears in his use of the figure of causality in *A Refutation of Deism,* where he derives it in Humean fashion "from the constant conjunction of objects, and the constant inference from one to the other."[13] Shelley represents the consequence of such patterns of thought in *The Cenci* by having his characters speak in a language severely constrained by his understanding of Catholicism in sixteenth-century Rome: "They are represented as Catholics," he writes in his preface, "and as Catholics deeply tinged with religion." Shelley's dramatization of how, in such a culture, "the most atrocious villain may be rigidly devout, and without any shock to established faith, confess himself to be so" (240), should be recognized as a dramatic application of identical arguments Hume had made in extending the epistemological critique of his *Treatise* to moral and cultural problems, here summarized by C. E. Pulos: "the superstitious man does not

---

12. Earl Wasserman, *Shelley: A Critical Reading* (Baltimore: Johns Hopkins University Press, 1971) 87. Wasserman's reading of *The Cenci* concludes his section on "Skepticism," but does not say precisely what the play does with the skeptical tradition.

13. Quoted from *Shelley's Prose, or The Trumpet of a Prophecy,* ed. David Lee Clark (Albuquerque: University of New Mexico Press, 1954) 136.

recognize that the best way to serve God is by serving mankind; he is liable, therefore, not only to fall into some useless way of expressing his devotion—such as fasting a day or giving himself a whipping, but also to view such piety as compatible with the greatest crimes."[14] Against this Humean background, the religious discourse that generates and authorizes such figures as "a father's holy name" (2.2.73) appears merely as a particular, culturally determined instance of the mind's habitual grasping after cause–effect relations, among which Hume had counted family relations.[15] But *The Cenci* will not affirm (or deny) the necessity of a *causal* link between its characters' patriarchal discourse and a more general misapprehension of causality, any more than Shelley would affirm (or deny) the certainty of an effect's link to its cause or of a child's link to its father. For to explain "a father's holy name" as the effect of a cause identified by Hume would mean assenting to the misapprehension the explanation means to correct. Shelley's staging of such unaffirmable (but undeniable) connections involves deploying "a father's holy name" only in circumstances that will remind his audience of the Humean claim that "cause is only a word expressing a certain state of the human mind with regard to the manner in which two thoughts are apprehended to be related to one another," as Shelley puts it in his essay "On Life" (478). Shelley's own habitual association between causality and filial relation—habitual, as Hume observes the "constant conjunction" of ideas to yield a habitual notion of causality—is at once confirmed and disavowed in his review of *Frankenstein*, which maintains a scrupulous refusal to present the relation between causality and genealogy as anything other than figurative: "Nor are the crimes and malevolences of the single Being, though indeed withering and tremendous, the offspring of any unaccountable propensity to evil, but flow irresistibly from certain causes fully adequate to their production. They are the children, as it were, of Necessity and Human Nature." Shelley's "as it were" should be taken as indicating his wish to

14. Pulos, *Deep Truth* 20–21, summarizing Hume.
15. The power of such figures is not exclusively Shelley's concern. Wordsworth closes the first act of *The Borderers* with the despair it occasions in his free-thinking hero Mortimer: "Father! To God himself we cannot give / An holier name, and under such a mask / To lead a spirit spotless as the blessed / To that abhorred den of brutal vice! / The firm foundation of my life appears / To sink from under me" (1.3.177–82). The "parricidal" action of *The Borderers* can presumably be traced to this moment.

protest that the figures he uses to express his Godwinian ethics—begetting, flowing from a source, even causality itself—are all *merely* figures.[16]

Without wishing to affirm that Hume's skepticism causes Shelley's, or that Shelley's causes Beatrice's, I want to argue that Shelley's hints about the rhetoric invalidated by a Humean skepticism help to explain why Lucretia should describe the language of Beatrice's suffering as having forfeited the customary cause–effect structure of dramatic discourse. Count Cenci's incestuous rape of his daughter fathers (occasions, results in, causes) a disruption in the logic that structures meaningful language as the effect fathered upon a speaker's intention. If the enlightened atheist Shelley regards the rape of Beatrice as disrupting the apprehension of relation that structures the figure of genealogy in the same way as it structures the figure of causality, his characters are bound to understand it as a violation, perpetrated by a known genealogical cause upon its proper genealogical effect, of the natural order: "He has cast Nature off, which was his shield, / And Nature casts him off, who is her shame" (3.1.286–87). In the plotting of the play, which necessarily appears to observe a causal pattern, this violation must seem to operate as a hidden cause producing as its open effect the language of Beatrice's suffering.

The complexities that arise from the absenting of cause provide a covert structure for the dense metaphoric exchange I quoted earlier, in which Shelley calls attention to the fundamental preconditions for his tragic action. When Beatrice returns to the stage at the beginning of act 3, Lucretia understands her suffering not from anything Beatrice tells her, but only from the fact that she now speaks a language categorically different from that in which Shelley had, in earlier scenes, constructed the interpersonal relationships required for the play's dramatic exposition. For Beatrice's language, unfolding in a purely private register inaccessible to other characters and to readers alike, impedes rather than facilitates understanding. By blocking her own desire to trace her suf-

---

16. "Review of Mary Shelley's *Frankenstein*," *Shelley's Prose* 307; partially quoted by Wasserman, in *Shelley* 107. Paul Fry notes Shelley's simultaneous rejection of genealogy and causality in "Mont Blanc": "In an ode, the main purpose of expression is to establish kinships, to affirm causality through the convention of the divine genealogy. But the subject of 'Mont Blanc,' which entails the irony of this ode as an ode, cannot be subdued to any cycle of birth and rebirth." See *The Poet's Calling in the English Ode* (New Haven: Yale University Press, 1980) 198.

fering back to its cause, what can only appear as Beatrice's "private language" induces in her a cognitive split between causes and effects, producing in her language a legible sign of the disturbance in the "natural order." Her language cannot *name* the cause of which its inability to name is the effect; but it is bound, as a body might be bound, to *signify* it.

Lucretia's role in this scene is to make Beatrice's splitting of effect from cause comprehensible to herself and perceptible to Shelley's readers. Her explanation proceeds upon religious assumptions cast in a peculiarly Shelleyan light, arguing an epistemological interpretation of the break incest introduces into the belief system structured by genealogical causes and effects. As Beatrice can no longer link herself to her father, so she can no longer trace the language of her suffering back to its cause in her violation. Lucretia sees this effacement of causal links as a characteristic of Beatrice's language, as the basis of her resistance to dialogue. The commonsensical but abstract language of cause and effect supplies what seems to her a suitable metaphor for Beatrice's incomprehensible language: "She answers not: / Her spirit apprehends the sense of pain, / But not its cause; suffering has dried away / The source from which it sprung . . ." (3.1.33–36). Lucretia's figure for her stepdaughter's dispirited language combines an inherited diction with a syntax that observes Shelley's own scruples about ungrounded philosophical assertions. Her abstract use of "spirit" in making an empiricist's observation is doubtless part of Shelley's effort to depict a culture in which, as his preface declares, a religion devoted to mortifying the flesh "is interwoven with the whole fabric of life" (241). (Less obviously, the metaphor of source and stream for speaker and speech can be traced to Dante's *Inferno* 1:79: "Or se' tu quel Virgilio e quella fonte / che spandi di parlar sì largo fiume?"[17]) But Lucretia's metaphoric procedure also resembles that of *Prometheus Unbound,* as Shelley had described it in that poem's Preface: her "imagery" is "drawn from the operations of the human mind, or from those external actions by which they are expressed" (133). The sources of Lucretia's metaphor are less important than the "operations of the mind" it diagnoses in presenting the constitutive element of Beatrice's broken language as a break in consciousness between causal source and suffered effect. One might

---

17. Dante Alighieri, *The Divine Comedy,* bilingual ed., trans. Charles S. Singleton (Princeton: Princeton University Press, 1980) 1:8.

refer to any number of passages in Shelley's prose in which an anxiety about such a breakdown seems to recapitulate Hume's dictum on the relations among memory, causality, and identity: "Had we no memory, we never shou'd have any notion of causation, nor consequently of that chain of causes and effects, which constitute our self or person." But it is not enough to paraphrase Lucretia's lines with a precursor of Shelley's skeptical philosophy; for *The Cenci* shows *what happens* when the mind's habitual or superstitious grasping after cause–effect relations breaks down.[18]

Lucretia's metaphor of a stream drying up its source spills over into Giacomo's figure for parricide in the next scene: "this very hand / Must quench the life that animated it" (3.2.59–60). But the parricide plot has not yet been conceived, except in the suspicions of Count Cenci himself, when Lucretia speaks; her only concern is the solipsistic opacity of Beatrice's language. What should strike us first about Beatrice's response to Lucretia's figure is not that Beatrice utters for the first time the word "parricide" but only that her language is suddenly no longer sliding giddily. If she seems, for the first time after the rape, to understand her interlocutor, that understanding is the result not so much of her stumbling upon "parricide," the word Shelley's audience has been waiting to hear her speak, as of her stumbling upon a perception of *likeness*. Her phrase "Like Parricide," stranded grammatically between two ellipses, both completes her stepmother's sentence in an unexpected way and begins a thought that, while being *like* her stepmother's, can be called her own, or (to put it less prejudicially) has the power to call her back to herself. "Like Parricide," the verbal hinge that both joins and divides the two speeches, does double service in both asserting and establishing a likeness between Beatrice's sentence and Lucretia's. Although it might well be asked why Lucretia is driven to abstraction by her puzzlement, it cannot be denied that her abstraction succeeds in returning Beatrice to the dramatic space of dialogue. For the accord between the lines spoken by two persons overcomes their separation without denying it, as though their having two separate bodies made no difference. (Indeed, Beatrice will soon start to call her stepmother "Mother.") In substituting a simile for Lucretia's metaphor, however,

18. Hume, *Treatise* 309. Critics have often overlooked this problem, as this conclusion shows: "with the exception of *The Cenci,* almost all of Shelley's work after 1815 symbolizes cause and effect" (Curt R. Zimansky, "Cause and Effect: A Symbolism for Shelley's Poetry," *Journal of English and Germanic Philology* 78 [1979]: 214).

The Cenci

Beatrice acknowledges, as Lucretia had not, the purely figurative basis of that accord.

Yet it cannot be certain that Beatrice actually understands, as a reader might understand, what has been said. Her understanding presumably operates according to the disrupted logic that Lucretia identifies in the language of her suffering, a language severed from both intention and referent. If Lucretia is to be believed at all, then we must see that Beatrice responds to her with a figure that has itself "dried away / The source from which it sprung." What we might take as a sign that Beatrice understands Lucretia's figure could just as easily be taken as a mechanical replication of the figure that divorces the exchange of figures from any referential ground. For Beatrice answers her stepmother's metaphor not with an interpretation that brings it back to a referent—her state of mind, say—but with another figure so impenetrably dense that it is far easier to literalize Beatrice's speech, to misunderstand her as plotting her father's death, than to understand her speech as an effort to characterize her suffering. What Beatrice's language does to the cause of which it is the effect, she says, is "Like Parricide . . . / Misery has killed its father: yet its father / Never like mine . . . O God! What thing am I?" (3.1.36–38). Out of its incoherence, Beatrice's language speaks its own truth: it has originated, unfathered, through the same inexplicable process that provides Wordsworth with the figure "unfathered vapour" to name the Imagination in *The Prelude* (6:527). In attempting to characterize the incomprehensibility of her own language from within that language, Beatrice comes upon an "unfathered" figure that converts the violence directed against her into a language that seems itself (as the *New Monthly* had feared) capable of violence. Her language, if we are to believe what it tells us, is devoted to annihilating "that through which I suffer": not just her "expressionless" violation, the "father" of her suffering, but also "the man they call my father" (3.1.214, 138, 144).

Beatrice's figure of ungrounded figurality unexpectedly turns the scene not inward but outward, away from reflection on the language of solipsism and toward the literalistic impurities of the murder plot, for Beatrice commits herself to murdering her father shortly after hearing the figure of "parricide" slip out of her own mouth. But why? Certainly we are to entertain the possibility that her actions originate in a literalistic identification of a "pure" figure as a moral imperative, in a particularly spectacular enactment of what Shelley calls in his notes to *Queen Mab* "the vulgar mistake of a metaphor for a real being, of a word for a thing" (6:198n).[19] Yet that cannot entirely explain the agency of the figure in restoring to Beatrice her sense of moral agency.

Critics have maintained that Beatrice's relation to her father—a similarity and contiguity established either genetically or, as is more usually argued, through the moral corruption imparted either by her father's crime or by her own sense that her loss of virginity is *her* crime—leads her to embrace his violence, to turn it back on him: as in the paternal metaphors of *Prometheus Unbound* "tyranny begets its own downfall," so in *The Cenci* "ill must come of ill" (1.3.151).[20] Yet Beatrice has rejected this resemblance to her father, to whom she regards herself as no longer related. "I have no father," she declares (3.1.40), and I believe it is *this* assertion, which converts her futile wish to deny natality into a successful foreclosure of her "father's holy name," that ultimately enables her to justify the murder of her father as a sacrifice of genealogical relation prompted by Cenci's own violation of the natural order. "I am more innocent of parricide / Than is a child born fatherless," she will assert in her most openly casuistical moment (4.4.112–13), disclaiming not her father's literal paternity but his right to claim protection from the social institutions founded upon patriarchal discourse (that is, from the law). What allows her to do this, the agency that makes parricide conceivable if not imperative, stems not from an experience of self-knowledge—although Beatrice's sudden responsiveness necessarily leaves that impression—but from a new understanding of language's radical freedom, engendered without regard to the consequences for the agent in which it is embodied.

19. Reiman and Powers omit the note; see *The Complete Works of Percy Bysshe Shelley,* ed. Thomas Hutchinson (New York: Oxford University Press, 1965) 812. On this and other issues of language pertinent to my reading, see Anne McWhir, "The Light and the Knife: Ab/Using Language in *The Cenci*," *Keats-Shelley Journal* 38 (1989): 145–61. Beatrice follows a pattern psychiatrists have discerned in psychotics, in which "words and even sentences seem to be substituted according to the law of the signifier rather than to the logic of the signified," a pattern that can result (Lacanians argue) "when the real father himself has a hypocritical relation to the Law [and] the Name-of-the-Father as signifier is foreclosed" (John P. Muller, "Language, Psychosis, and the Subject in Lacan," in *Interpreting Lacan,* ed. Joseph H. Smith and William Kerrigan [New Haven: Yale University Press, 1983] 28, 23).

20. The maxim on *Prometheus Unbound* is Carl Woodring's; see *Politics in English Romantic Poetry* (Cambridge: Harvard University Press, 1970) 292.

3.

Yet *The Cenci* is, after all, a tragedy, as *Prometheus Unbound* is not; and Beatrice cannot maintain her conscious denial of genealogical relation once the play falls back into the social context that is conventional in drama. With the death of her father, the figure of genealogical relation passes into the more persistent symbolic form of the law, which dominates act 5 not only in external events but in internal states as well. Should it then be understood that Shelley, in choosing to build a tragedy from this agency problem, wished to contain or defuse Beatrice's experience of radical freedom, to undo the illusion of agency produced in her exchange with her stepmother, and to condemn his readers and himself to the quietist wisdom that action against oppression is radically irresponsible? To draw that conclusion would, I think, be to decline Shelley's invitation to experience the intellectually liberating thrill of the performance that converts Beatrice's mad skepticism into cold violence. Shelley warns his audience to avoid such final conclusions, if they would forestall more terrible avoidances. The development of Beatrice's mad scene shows why.

A contemporary review of *The Cenci* in the *Theatrical Inquisitor* (April 1820) quotes this scene at length, judging it "perhaps a fairer specimen of the present drama than any other extract could afford."[21] The speeches that open the scene may sound, to modern ears, like exercises in melodramatic excess, pandering to the jaded taste of a bygone era in an idiom that illustrates the subliterary tendency F. R. Leavis found in Shelley, above all in the ravings of Beatrice.[22] Beatrice's mad scene, regarded as typical of Romantic drama's failings, seems to distance us from the sympathetic identification that drama supposedly facilitates by presenting us with all that is dated and dispensable in Shelley, all that need no longer concern us. To this perhaps crude perception of failure, I add one modification: that the collapse of the dramatic, as we see it here, is a central component in the design of Shelley's play.

---

21. *Romantics Reviewed* C:2:846. The reviews count Beatrice's opening speech among "the admired passages" so consistently that *The British Review* (1821) can claim to controvert popular opinion in calling her madness unnatural (ibid. C:1:254).

22. See F. R. Leavis, *Revaluation: Tradition and Development in English Poetry* (New York: George W. Stewart, 1947). Peter Brooks considers more carefully the idea of melodrama as a break in literary language in *Melodramatic Imagination* 65.

If Beatrice's mad scene is judged to be undramatic in a manner characteristic of the period, the judgment must be due to a perception that the scene fails to exploit the sine qua non of drama, dialogue. Yet it is more precise to say that the scene does not simply lack dialogue, but rather, like the exchange between Prometheus and his mother Earth in act 1 of *Prometheus Unbound,* it declines to presuppose the possibility of dialogue.[23] Beatrice's frantic opening soliloquy reaches for extremes of solipsism ("I am dead!") from which the rest of the scene, if it is to be compatible with the conventions of drama, can only fall away. Even as she enters "to" Lucretia, Beatrice stands alone on stage—speaking, to be sure, but speaking to no one, including herself. The ability to speak *to another* has already, at the opening of the second act, been presented as a criterion for judging sanity: *"Lucretia:* Are you gone mad? If not, pray speak to me. / *Beatrice:* You see I am not mad, I speak to you" (2.1.33–34).[24] In the opening of the third act, Beatrice's language is expressive rather than communicative, yet it is not self-expressive, since what it expresses is a fragmentation of self that results in a fragmenting of relationship, rendering communication impossible.

Throughout her mad speeches Beatrice attempts to keep the full extent of her suffering at bay by refusing to recognize her identity with the Beatrice who has been raped by her father. Alan Richardson describes Beatrice's peculiar lack of identity as an "inability either to image or obliterate the deed, to remember or forget it."[25] This hovering between remembrance and forgetting is the only condition under which identity *must* be performed, since it can be neither accepted nor rejected. But the suspension of identity swerves precipitously toward a denial that ironically restores identity at the very moment when Beatrice performs her inability to conceive it as hers:

---

23. In his reading of *Prometheus Unbound,* Wasserman notes the imposition of dramatic dialogue upon a situation that is not dialogic: "The coherent dialogue in Act I between Earth and Prometheus takes place, paradoxically, despite a total absence of communication between the speakers" (*Shelley* 266).

24. The circumstance of Beatrice's *other* being played by her (step-) *mother* can be understood here, and in the opening of act 3, in terms of the Lacanian psycholinguistics ingeniously applied to Shelley by Barbara Charlesworth Gelpi in *Shelley's Goddess: Maternity, Language, Subjectivity* (New York: Oxford University Press, 1992). For Hume's argument about mothers and stepmothers, see *Treatise* 2.2.4, "Of the Love of Relations."

25. Richardson, *A Mental Theater: Poetic Drama and Consciousness in the Romantic Age* (University Park: Pennsylvania State University Press, 1988) 112.

> Do you know
> I thought I was that wretched Beatrice
> Men speak of, whom her father sometimes hales
> From hall to hall by the entangled hair;
> At others, pens up naked in damp cells
> Where scaly reptiles crawl, and starves her there,
> Till she will eat strange flesh. This woeful story
> So did I overact in my sick dreams,
> That I imagined . . . no, it cannot be!
>
> (3.1.42–50)

The story's lurid imagery tells us something, as we jump to fill in the ellipsis: "I imagined that he raped me." But that augmented story tells us less than the speech as printed, which attempts to *avoid* the hard fact of estranged flesh by tracing a potentially infinite (or self-consuming) circle from "I thought" to "I imagined." Having imagined that she was Beatrice, she mentally acted the part until she imagined that she was that wretched Beatrice men speak of, and so on. Without the anxiety prompted by the tautology looming on the narrative horizon, Beatrice might never talk herself beyond a merely formal assertion of identity to the substantial self-recognition she has so far successfully avoided. To put it in more theoretical terms: while the narratorial "I" can be merely formal, its audience cannot. Beatrice can maintain the soothing skeptical suspension of identity as long as she is merely telling her circular story of nonidentity, but as soon she feels compelled to stop and listen, she will have to occupy some identity.

But *how* is the assertion of nonidentity trumped by the performance of identity? One way of answering the question can be drawn from Hume's skeptical treatment of personal identity, in the *Treatise*, as "fictitious": as both actively produced by the imagination (particularly the memory) and passively maintained by force of habit. In this respect, identity resembles causality in being based in the habit of uniting the various perceptions that slide giddily through our minds. Hume's "Of Personal Identity" offers a striking pair of figures for the mind without the fiction of identity, and with it. First: "The mind is a kind of theatre, where several perceptions successively make their appearance; pass, re-pass, glide away, and mingle in an infinite variety of postures and situations." The fiction of a unified identity must be imposed on this chaotic theater of disparate perceptions. But once it has been imposed, "the same person may vary his character and disposition, as well as his impressions and ideas, without losing his identity": may, that is, perform his or her identity at will, without, however, being able to shake it off. This ineluctable sense of identity prompts a second figure: "I cannot compare the soul more properly to any thing than to a republic or commonwealth, in which the several members are united by the reciprocal ties of government and subordination, and give rise to other persons, who propagate the same republic in the incessant changes of its parts."[26] That the identity of a state, or of a soul, must be "feigned" has no bearing on its efficacy in uniting "the several members" who "pass, re-pass, glide away, and mingle in an infinite variety of postures and situations." But the choice to regard oneself either as a mere bundle of perceptions—as being like a theater—or as an unalterable soul uniting those perceptions—as being like a state—makes all the difference. For my purposes the crucial difference is that while the theater demands a confrontation with disaggregated mortal bodies, the state dissolves that demand in the idea of an immortal body politic. Beatrice, who has suffered that incessant exchangeability, cannot help performing her infinite variety as though her mind were a Humean theater. And her performance must bring her back to her body.

Beatrice attempts to forestall that eventuality, however, by striking a theatrical posture toward her identity, one based on the assumption that identity is always feigned, or feigning: a performance. In looking back at herself, Beatrice plays the part of an enlightened spectator in relation to her former role. She says that she was once a naively *sympathetic* spectator who identified with a representation that was offered to her, with "that wretched Beatrice / Men speak of." Now, however, in recounting that past episode, Beatrice figures herself as a *disinterested* spectator who does not sympathize even with that former role, except in recognizing it as a role no longer her own. The sympathizing self lacked the knowledge of the wiser spectator who speaks; what is now known is the deceptive allure of sympathetic identification. The supposed gain in knowledge allows Beatrice to analyze the process of sympathetic identification, and she does so by using theatrical terms: "This woeful story / So did I *overact* in my sick dreams, / That I imagined...." The sympathizing spectator moves toward this "imag-

---

26. Hume, *Treatise* 306, 301, 309. Andrew M. Cooper compares Hume's figure of the mind as a theater to Shelley's imaging of the poet's mind in *Alastor;* see *Doubt and Identity in Romantic Poetry* (New Haven: Yale University Press, 1988) 170–71.

ined" identification through an intermediary stage, the process of mentally acting out the story that is represented to her. Her recognition of a shift from passively suffering to actively perpetrating this delusion brings with it a moralizing tone, audible in her condemnation of mental participation as *over*acting."[27] She seems to realize that the mental act required to overcome sympathetic delusion—the act of recollecting that "I am I"—can take place only in the language in which she performs her internal pantomime, not in the visible stage-world its assertions purport to represent. Just as Kant, revising Hume, argues in the *Paralogisms of Pure Reason* that "the identity of the consciousness of myself at different times" is "only a formal condition of my thoughts and their coherence, and in no way proves the numerical identity of my subject," so in Shelley's staging of Beatrice's struggle with personal identity, "I am I" is not a conclusion of the story but a precondition for its telling.[28] All that the story can add is that "I am I" is true under various conditions, including the delusion of being someone else. That is the knowledge that Beatrice would, but cannot, avoid. Beatrice must forfeit the merely formal identity provided by her experience of mental theater because that identity can have no substance. Her experience of Hume's theater, like Shelley's imagination of O'Neill's theater and my argument about Shelley's theater, leads beyond the trap of a merely formal identity by focusing attention on its denial of embodiment.

The success of Beatrice's plot to murder her father moves the play's focus from the "paternal power" embodied in Count Cenci to the disembodied authority of the pope, who speaks (through Camillo) but never actually appears in the play. That shift away from the domestic and the psychological allegorizes the aspiration to disembodiment in every allegorical impersonation. The overtly allegorical character of Beatrice's inhuman father, something Cenci himself cultivates, received prominent attention in contemporary reviews. *The British Review*

---

27. Shelley may be recalling Dr. Johnson's moralistic condemnations of the idea that actors believe themselves to be the characters they play: "If Garrick really believed himself to be that monster, Richard the Third, he deserved to be hanged every time he performed it" (*Boswell's Life of Johnson*, ed. G. B. Hill and L. F. Powell [Oxford: Clarendon Press, 1934] 4:244).

28. Immanuel Kant, *Critique of Pure Reason*, ed. Norman Kemp Smith (London, 1958) 153, quoted from Henry E. Allison, "Locke's Theory of Personal Identity: A Re-examination," in *Locke on Human Understanding: Selected Essays*, ed. I. C. Tipton (New York: Oxford University Press, 1977) 121.

(1821) exclaims that Cenci expresses only "pure abstract depravity and impiety," concluding that "he is a mere personification of wickedness and insanity" and that "No such being as Cenci ever existed; none such could exist." *Gold's London Magazine* (1820) speaks of Shelley's characters as "daemons in human guise." The *New Monthly* (1820) echoes these judgments at least for Count Cenci, adding an allusion to *Frankenstein:* "With the exception of Cenci, who is half maniac and half fiend, [Shelley's] persons speak and act like creatures of flesh and blood, not like the problems of strange philosophy set in motion by galvanic art."[29] Count Cenci aspires to be just such a problem set in motion—an impersonation—as inhuman as the pope appears in Camillo's description:

> He looked as calm and keen as is the engine
> Which tortures and which kills, exempt itself
> From aught that it inflicts; a marble form,
> A rite, a law, a custom: not a man.
> He frowned, as if to frown had been the trick
> Of his machinery. . . .
>
> (5.4.2–7)

Clarifying this aspiration toward disembodied agency, which is as pervasive in the play as the dismantling of patriarchal and divine justice, might open the way for a more specific historical interpretation than has been given in any of the attempts to decode *The Cenci* as an allegory of the French Revolution.[30] In decreeing the death of the king, the National Assembly attempted to replace what Foucault saw as the spectacular judicial "cratylism" of ancien régime punishments with the swift and impersonal justice of the people, in which sentences were no longer grounded in anything beyond the law's mechanical self-expression. That "parricidal" act seemed to lead by necessity to the legally sanctioned violence of the Terror, which, far from embracing the symbolic punishments inflicted in the name of the king, adopted decapitation as

---

29. *Romantics Reviewed* C:1:251, 253; C:2:607; C:2:736.
30. See Wasserman, *Shelley* 128 and passim. This theme has become routine in interpretations of *The Cenci,* most recently in Michael Rossington's "Shelley, *The Cenci,* and the French Revolution," in *Revolution in Writing: British Literary Responses to the French Revolution,* ed. Kelvin Everest (Philadelphia: Open University Press, 1991) 138–57, and Suzanne Ferriss's "Reflection in a 'Many-Sided Mirror': Shelley's *The Cenci* Through the Post-Revolutionary Prism," *The Wordsworth Circle* 23 (1992): 134–44.

a new form of punishment that, according to the Foucauldian analysis of Marie-Hélène Huet, "would function as a sign." This shift in the conception of legal authority might be recognized in *The Cenci*'s passage from the magical cratylism of Cenci's curses to the pope's use of capital punishment (specifically, beheading) as a sign of his authority.[31]

Such a reading could be elaborated at length. But is this the most serious way to recover Shelley's political aims? The ease with which such historical interpretation refers to the world beyond the stage conceals its impoverished view of drama's many resources for intervening in that world and simplifies Shelley's carefully nuanced injunction against separating (stage) performance from (offstage) action. In bypassing the problem of embodiment in favor of a disembodying allegoresis, it scorns the specificity of Beatrice in favor of her father's riotous and insane quest to disperse himself throughout his world. *The Cenci* warns against such evasions. It shows that the act of suspending all one's habitual certainties, the skeptical *epoche*, can never finally be isolated from the social world or the material body in which it is performed. To suspend judgment, to "leave a vacancy" as Shelley defines the task of philosophy in his essay "On Life" (477), is not to suspend the course of history, as certain revolutionaries (including the younger Shelley) might wish, but to perform an action with definite consequences. Embodying the history of Beatrice Cenci helped Shelley see how the empowering freedom of radical skepticism is purchased with denials that can lead to the disempowerment of psychosis.

Skepticism *can* take on a definite subversive power. But those who see only subversion in Shelley's skepticism, or in a performative sense of identity, should attend to the dénouement of *The Cenci*, which teaches that skepticism is as skepticism does. In the speeches of Beatrice that Shelley has taught us to read as the performance of skepticism, Savella, the papal legate who arrives to pronounce upon Count Cenci his now superfluous death sentence, can hear nothing but casuistry. Savella's response is itself, however, a model of the skeptical refusal to

---

31. Marie-Hélène Huet, *Rehearsing the Revolution: The Staging of Marat's Death, 1793–1797*, trans. Robert Hurley (Berkeley: University of California Press, 1982) 52, 55. Count Cenci himself compares the power of his curses (somewhat anachronistically) to that of the ancien régime *lettres de cachet*. For an analysis of this conception of language by a contemporary of Shelley, see Thomas De Quincey, "Modern Superstition," *The English Mail Coach and Other Essays*, ed. John E. Jordan (New York: Dutton, 1970) 210–49.

conclude causality from the contiguities that seem to link together the evidence passing before his eyes. Yet the justice of his skeptical frame of mind can do nothing to stop the Justice he was sent to uphold. "Strange thoughts beget strange deeds," he declares, voicing, in an echo of the Doctor's diagnosis of that earlier sleepwalker Lady Macbeth, the conventional genealogical figure of causality that would hand Shelley's heroine over to the regime she had hoped to annihilate. He finishes the thought with a skeptic's suspension of judgment that leaves room for a sliver of hope on Beatrice's behalf: "Here are both: I judge thee not" (4.4.138–39). Disavowing his action with that verbal shrug of the shoulders, he places the entire family under arrest.

4.

What writing *The Cenci* taught Shelley about his own agency, as a writer working for change within the constraints imposed by particular historical circumstances, might be judged from a sequence of poems about the prospects for political renewal that Shelley composed while finishing the play and shortly afterwards. Just as he was completing *The Cenci,* he was finally able to assemble the pieces of *Julian and Maddalo,* the skeptical debate poem on Byronic fatalism that had grown from his early effort to write a tragedy on Tasso's madness. *Julian and Maddalo* develops Shelley's response to the final canto of *Childe Harold,* which he had described to Peacock as "the most wicked & mischievous insanity that ever was given forth." Byron, he felt, "is heartily & deeply discontented with himself, & contemplating in the distorted mirror of his thoughts, the nature & the destiny of man, what can he behold but objects of contempt & despair?" Shelley followed that scathing condemnation by making a single exception: "But that he is a great poet, I think the address to Ocean proves."[32] Shelley was probably remembering the final stanza of Byron's peroration, which salvages, at the last moment, more than a scrap of free agency from the flood of fatality that has rolled through canto 4:

> And I have loved thee, Ocean! and my joy
> Of youthful sports was on thy breast to be

32. 17 or 18 December 1818; Shelley, *Letters* 2:58.

The Cenci

> Borne, like thy bubbles, onward: from a boy
> I wanton'd with thy breakers—they to me
> Were a delight; and if the freshening sea
> Made them a terror—'twas a pleasing fear,
> For I was as it were a child of thee,
> And trusted to thy billows far and near,
> And laid my hand upon thy mane—as I do here.

In turning to the controlling power of the "hand" that writes, "here," about its own passive subjection, Byron clears the way for Julian's salvaging of agency:

> Much may be conquered, much may be endured
> Of what degrades and crushes us. We know
> That we have power over ourselves to do
> And suffer—what, we know not till we try;
> But something nobler than to live and die.
> (183–87)

In comparison with Maddalo's ringing denunciation of the "mortality" of "our thoughts and our desires" (120, 125), this seems defensive, nearly as fragile as the lines from *King Lear* that echo both here ("we know not") and in *The Cenci*. But it does suggest what *The Cenci* would argue more forcefully, that a skeptical suspension of judgment—skeptical to the point of not distinguishing between the power to do and the power to endure—can clear the way for an agency capable of trumping the fatalistic evacuation attempted in Maddalo's speeches. The awareness that this agency can proceed from an effort to articulate the suffering that threatens to undo it is what Shelley salvages from the end of *Childe Harold*. He turns it into a powerful rhetorical reversal not just in *Julian and Maddalo,* but at the most crucial moments in *The Cenci*.

That turn from suffering to doing also structures the concluding stanzas of "Ode to the West Wind," written in late October 1819. The fourth stanza voices a wish to suspend the agitated competition with the wind that the speaker's alienation from nature has led him to stage, and to turn that poetic activity into a passive surrender: "Oh! lift me as a wave, a leaf, a cloud!" (53). The final stanza expands this request to include a dissolution of personhood that draws on *The Cenci*'s derivation of agency from the surrender of identity:

> Be thou, Spirit fierce,
> My spirit! Be thou me, impetuous one!
>
> Drive my dead thoughts over the universe
> Like withered leaves to quicken a new birth!
> And, by the incantation of this verse,
>
> Scatter, as from an unextinguished hearth
> Ashes and sparks, my words among mankind!
> (61–67)

"I will animate you so that you will animate, or reanimate, me," is how Barbara Johnson paraphrases this passage, emphasizing the acknowledgment that life follows from, rather than precedes, the imperative of metaphoric exchange.[33] But how does that acknowledgment support rather than obliterate the belief in an effective agency of change? Shelley's ability to shore up his sense of personal agency with the fragments of its apparent dissolution can be seen from a striking image in the notebook where these lines were first drafted. Their seed can be found in a notebook draft (Huntington MS. HM 2176, folio *15R) where Shelley struggles with the potentially fatalistic implications of his simile for the reproductive power his dead thoughts envy in the words he wants scattered among mankind: "But as my hopes were fire, so my despair / Shall be as ashes covering them." At this point one can glimpse, peeking out from beneath the canceled scrawls, a comically rendered male face, prompting questions that seem capable only of further dissolving the poet's identity. Is it Shelley's face? Is it even Shelley's sketch? And who, or what, does "Shelley" designate in such questions? An unexpected answer is given in a caption written over the face in a self-deprecating French: *Je suis un homme grave*: "I am a serious man." The last words are canceled and replaced with a phrasing that makes the statement seem at once less and more serious: *un homme gravide*, "a pregnant man."[34] At this moment, when Shelley hopes to rescue for his own poetic voice the power to effect a change that cannot be absorbed in the cycles of natural generation, he confronts the dissolution of his own person not by brooding over the abyss of Byronic

---

33. Barbara Johnson, "Apostrophe, Animation, and Abortion," quoted from *Feminisms: An Anthology of Literary Theory and Criticism*, ed. Robyn R. Warhol and Diane Price Herndl (New Brunswick: Rutgers University Press, 1991) 633.

34. *Shelley's 1819–1821 Huntington Notebook*, vol. 6 in *The Manuscripts of the Younger Romantics*, ed. Mary A. Quinn (New York: Garland, 1994) 322–23.

fatalism but by cracking a joke. That a loss of identity might, instead of drowning one in despair, be articulated in such a way as "to quicken a new birth" is one of the progressive strategies Shelley learned from the dramatic voices he had confined within the "sad reality" of *The Cenci*.

The concluding couplet of Shelley's "Sonnet: England in 1819," written in December of 1819, carries this pattern forward by conjuring a spirit of change from what the body of the poem anatomizes as England's *disjecta membra*. What must have seemed merely emblems of England's deadly torpor, Shelley now asserts, "Are graves from which a glorious Phantom may / Burst, to illumine our tempestuous day." Shelley's uncertainties about authorial agency return in the uncertainties embedded within this sonorous declaration. How, exactly, will the change from darkness to light take place, and who will be bringing it about? The couplet's reticence, far from being a weakness of the sonnet, exemplifies a strength peculiar to a writer so meticulous in his thinking about personal identity, political agency, and social change that he consistently evaded the imperative to assert their interrelation. That strength lies in the couplet's pointed but unmarked conjoining of optative imagining and actual performance. Shelley's sonnet *imagines* the agency of social change as a "Phantom" that "may" appear to carry on the work of enlightenment: the work of making England's deadness appear in order, by that means, to make it disappear. But the sonnet also *performs* that apparition, itself bursting forth to illumine its tempestuous day in the hope that its supernatural brilliance might hasten the close of that day. The words that express a hope for illumination in the world whose coordinates are "England" and "1819" also realize that hope for every reader of "England in 1819."

A final instance of the impact on Shelley's own writing of the recuperation of agency performed in *The Cenci* can be seen in Shelley's "Ode to Liberty," written the following spring. The opening stanza poses the speaker directly against Byronic despair in tracing the ode to a moment when his soul "spurned the chains of its dismay," ascending "in the heaven of fame" and leaving behind a trace that, in being compared to "foam from a ship's swiftness," bears the unmistakable signature of the *Childe Harold* fatalism it means to leave behind. The crux of the ode's argument is stated in a gap that opens in the political history it stages, where Shelley returns to the binding and loosing power of words dramatized in *The Cenci*:

> O, that the free would stamp the impious name
>   Of KING into the dust! or write it there,
> So that this blot upon the page of fame
>   Were as a serpent's path, which the light air
> Erases, and the flat sands close behind!
>   Ye the oracle have heard
>   Lift the victory-flashing sword,
> And cut the snaky knots of this foul gordian word.
>   (211–18)

The argument that our bondage to powers exerted by mere words can be undone by *writing* those words, the better to erase them, would seem to follow directly from Beatrice's deployment of the patriarchal metaphor in her simile "Like Parricide." The "Ode to Liberty" derives from this stanza an argument for the political force of a skeptical critique of political discourse:

> O, that the words which make the thoughts obscure
>   From which they sprung, as clouds of glimmering dew
> From a white lake blot heaven's blue portraiture,
>   Were stript of their thin masks and various hue
> And frowns and smiles and splendours not their own,
>   Till in the nakedness of false and true
> They stand before their Lord, each to receive its due!
>   (234–40)

This vision of a last judgment will be carried forward to the end of Shelley's career, where it forms the basis for the apocalypse of agency in *The Triumph of Life*. But it originates in the violent dramatic literalism of *The Cenci*, where, although it may not "receive its due," the performance of skepticism proves itself capable at least of stripping bare the name of the father.

5
Fatal Autonomy: *Marino Faliero*

> See—how one man acts upon himself and others—or upon multitudes?—The same Agency in a higher and purer degree may act upon the Stars, etc., ad infinitum.
>
> —BYRON, *Journal* (1821)

"If *Marino Faliero* is a drama, *The Cenci* is not." So Shelley declared to Leigh Hunt in August 1821 after hearing Byron's criticism of his play as "essentially undramatic."[1] Shelley may have been thinking of their disagreements about dramatic form; perhaps he saw the lopsided exposition of *Marino Faliero* as vindicating his own Shakespearean models at the expense of Byron's neoclassical unities. But he must have been struck by more significant differences, considering that the two plays treat similar themes: in each, an experimental recovery of individual agency collapses when it can no longer be cordoned off from the power of a ubiquitous authoritarian state. Charles Robinson has argued that Shelley was disappointed to find Byron impersonating, as he had himself denied doing in *The Cenci*, his own "apprehensions of the beautiful and the just" (Dedication, 237). The critique of Byronism in *Julian and Maddalo* supports Robinson's contention that Shelley would have taken Faliero's embrace of fatalism as Byron's own:

> For I would rather yield to Gods than men,
> Or cling to any creed of destiny,
> Rather than deem these mortals, most of whom
> I know to be as worthless as the dust,

---

1. Shelley, *Letters* 2:345.

> And weak as worthless, more than instruments
> Of an o'er-ruling Power.
>
> (5.2.67–72)[2]

Unlike Shelley's characters, who speak like Roman Catholics, Byron's doge speaks like the Calvinist Byron himself was raised to be: even Faliero's recollection of smiting a bishop (5.2.23) seems to place him within the traditions of British Protestantism. With this degree of palpable design, Robinson argues, *Marino Faliero* strikingly failed to confirm the conviction Shelley had expressed in *A Philosophical View of Reform* that poets can produce effects counter to their own creeds. "Whatever systems they may [have] professed by support," Shelley wrote, "they actually advance the interests of Liberty. It is impossible to read the productions of our most celebrated writers, whatever may be their system relating to thought or expression, without being startled by the electric life which there is in their words."[3] However persuasive Robinson's arguments may be, I will be arguing that Byron's first stage play does the opposite of what Shelley seems to have thought. Far from expressing a fatalism that can be attributed to Byron, *Marino Faliero* dramatizes the political implications of the Shelleyan process by which alluringly fatalistic deconstructions of free agency are overridden by what Shelley calls, in a thoroughly Byronic phrase, "the electric life which there is in . . . words."

I.

Judgments on *Marino Faliero* have evolved according to ever more sophisticated conceptions of the relation between Byron's assertive political phrasemaking, first emphasized by Hazlitt, and his self-effacing attunement to history, first discerned by Goethe.[4] The play's political

---

2. Quotations from *Marino Faliero* are keyed to Barry Weller's text in Lord Byron, *The Complete Poetical Works*, ed. Jerome J. McGann (Oxford: Clarendon Press, 1986). Subsequent references provide act, scene, and line numbers; citations for texts other than *Marino Faliero* refer to volume and page number.

3. See Charles E. Robinson, *Shelley and Byron: The Snake and Eagle Wreathed in Fight* (Baltimore: Johns Hopkins University Press, 1976) 143–60; this passage from *A Philosophical View of Reform* is quoted on p. 150. For another sustained comparison between *Marino Faliero* and *The Cenci*, see Carlson, *Theatre of Romanticism* 188–204.

4. *Marino Faliero* confirms Hazlitt's diagnosis of Byron's fundamental egotism: "We know not much about the plot, about the characters, about the motives of the persons introduced, but we know a good deal about their sentiments and opinions on matters in

side was, in spite of Byron's protests, the first to be seen, for it seemed to offer ready confirmation of the view that Byron, confined within what Herbert Butterfield would label "the whig interpretation of history," could only see the past as a commentary on present affairs.[5] Byron knew that his readers would find not a dramatization of *res gestae* but a political manifesto. In a letter to Murray (31 August 1820), contemplating the prospect that his tragedy would be damned, he tried to forestall criticism by pointing away from his own views: "Recollect that it is not a political play—though it may look like it—it is strictly historical, read the history—and judge."[6] The phrase "strictly historical" reformulates Byron's first comment to Murray on the Faliero story:

---

general, and hear some very fine descriptions from their mouths; which would, however, have become the mouth of any other individual in the play equally well, and the mouth of the noble poet better than that of any of his characters" (Hazlitt, *Works* 19:44). Hazlitt's criticism of Byron quickly became a cliché: "Nothing has been more constantly asserted of Byron than his want of variety in character," Bulwer-Lytton wrote in 1833; "Every criticism tells us that he never paints but one person, in whatever costume; that the dress may vary, but the lay figure remains the same. Never was any popular fallacy more absurd! It is true that the dogma holds good with the early poems, but is entirely contradicted in the later plays." Bulwer-Lytton leads with the example of *Marino Faliero*, perhaps to imply that Hazlitt was unable to see the play apart from his idea of the poet, as were contemporary audiences, whose yearning for the Byronic was disappointed by "that very versatility, that very coming out from self, the want of which has been so superficially complained of" (*England and the English*, ed. Standish Meacham [Chicago: University of Chicago Press, 1970] 269–78). Goethe pushed that idea of versatility toward negative capability: "Lord Byron, notwithstanding his predominant personality, has sometimes the power of renouncing himself altogether—as may be seen in some of his dramatic pieces, particularly in his *Marino Faliero*. In this piece we quite forget that Lord Byron, or even an Englishman, wrote it. We live entirely in Venice, and entirely in the time the action takes place. The personages speak from themselves, and from their own condition, without having any of the subjective feelings, thoughts and opinions of the poet" (J. W. von Goethe, *Conversations with Eckermann*, trans. John Oxenford [London, 1930] 357; quoted from Martyn Corbett, *Byron and Tragedy* [London: Macmillan, 1988] 48). It is worth noting that the play was to have been dedicated to Goethe, but that Byron withdrew the dedication before the play was published. See E. M. Butler, *Byron and Goethe: Analysis of a Passion* (London: Bowes and Bowes, 1956) 45–85 and 170–73.

5. See Herbert Butterfield, *The Whig Interpretation of History* (London: G. Bell, 1931). A review in the *Beacon* gives elegant expression to this view of Byron, arguing that the reader or spectator "cannot see, at one instant of time, both the past and the present; yet the concluding scene of the tragedy, to which we allude, is made to do this" (*Romantics Reviewed* B:1:73). The execution scene would have seemed to allude to the execution of the Cato Street conspirators.

6. *Byron's Letters and Journals*, ed. Leslie A. Marchand, 10 vols. (Cambridge: Harvard University Press, 1973–1980) 7:168. Byron also insisted to Murray that "History is closely followed" (17 July 1820), in a letter that resembles the play's Preface (ibid. 7:131).

what made the subject "very dramatic" for Byron was not its potential for allegorizing contemporary politics, but its singularity as "the most remarkable and only fact of the kind in all history of all nations."[7] Whether sincere or merely prudent, Byron's efforts to mute political overtones were unavailing, as reviewers eagerly reported on audience reactions confirming their ideas about Byron's politics.

The tendency was renewed in this century by Samuel Chew, whose idea of Byron as "the poet of revolution" led him to see *Marino Faliero* as unambiguous: "Byron is thoroughly in sympathy with the conspirators."[8] Critics have generally rejected Chew's verdict, even when they share his wish to find unambiguous political allegiances. Byron's claim of kinship with revolutionary heroes among the nobility persuades most to place his sympathies rather with the aristocratic doge than with the plebeian conspirators. "I can understand and enter into the feelings of Mirabeau and La Fayette—but I have no sympathy with Robespierre —and Marat," Byron confessed to Hobhouse, referring implicitly to the Cato Street conspiracy to assassinate the cabinet.[9] That confession

---

7. 25 February 1817; *Byron's Letters and Journals* 5:174. Byron would later qualify this insistence on the singularity of "an old man . . . conspiring against the state of which he was the actual reigning Chief" (25 February 1817) by recalling that the story resembles that of "Agis King of Sparta—a prince *with* the Commons against the aristocracy—& losing his life therefor" (17 July 1820; *Byron's Letters and Journals* 7:132). The single precedent is written into the doge's death speech, where he reflects on the rarity of princes sacrificing themselves for their people: "One sovereign only died, and one is dying" (5.3.19). Here the singularity of the "strictly historical" ("one . . . one") is asserted at the very moment in which history is invoked as a model to be replicated in ever new political contexts.

8. Samuel Chew, *The Dramas of Lord Byron: A Critical Study* (Baltimore: The Johns Hopkins University Press, 1915) 91.

9. *Byron's Letters and Journals* 7:80; Byron had just begun *Marino Faliero*. His next letter to Hobhouse elaborates his views on revolution with an allusion to the Gunpowder Plot: "It is not against the *pure* principle of reform—that I protest, but against low designing dirty levellers who would pioneer their way to a democratical tyranny" (7:99). His awareness of Cato Street can be documented from letters to Hobhouse on 29 March and 22 April 1820. As an outburst of a repressed underclass that led to a shoring up of state repression, Cato Street might have appeared to Byron to follow the pattern established in *The Cenci* and to match *Marino Faliero*'s diagnosis of revolution. He noted that Cato Street would likely help conservatives in the Westminster election—which was, however, won by Hobhouse, somewhat disproving Jerome Christensen's thesis that *Marino Faliero*, in showing how subversion abets containment, both diagnoses and practices the "political homeopathy" operative in contemporary England (*Lord Byron's Strength* [Baltimore: Johns Hopkins University Press, 1993] 266). Few knew the pressures of Cato Street on electoral politics better than Hobhouse, second cousin to Henry Hobhouse, the undersecretary in Sidmouth's Home Office responsible for maintaining the spies who betrayed the conspiracy; see Henry Hobhouse, *Hobhouse Memoirs* (Taunton: Wessex Press, 1927)

leads E. D. H. Johnson to conclude that "Byron himself was just such another patrician rebel as Mirabeau and Lafayette; and Marino Faliero is in this sense really an imaginative projection of the author into circumstances like those which make up the plot of the tragedy."[10] Johnson reverses Chew's verdict by taking the doge as a mouthpiece for Byron's frustrations with the shortsighted Carbonari nationalists, whose meetings he frequented in Ravenna.[11] Both judgments follow Hazlitt's line in taking the play as a vehicle for the poet's well-known "sentiments and opinions on matters in general"; they differ only in finding opposite certainties.

A second strand of criticism takes *Marino Faliero* not as an expression of Byron's political opinions, but as a starkly objective depiction of inexorable historical processes. This view—as much an idea about history as a judgment on the play—might be traced to Byron's chronicle sources, particularly Marino Sanuto's *Vite dei Dogi,* which seems to have contributed an air of fatality to Byron's display of historical causes and effects. Sanuto evacuates his narrative of human agency with almost comical insistence, as in his report on how Faliero's hubris in striking a bishop set in motion the machinery of cosmic justice: "Therefore, heaven allowed Marino Faliero to go out of his right senses, in order that he might bring himself to an evil death. . . . Now it was fated that My Lord Duke Marino was to have his head cut off. And as it is necessary when any effect is to be brought about, that the cause of such an effect must happen, it therefore came to pass."[12] Sanuto's depersonalized causation reappears in the line of criticism that sees in Byron's

---

51. The execution of the Cato Street conspirators was reported in "Galignani's Gazette," which Byron claimed was the only paper he read in Italy (17 July 1820, *Letters* 7:131, in a letter to Murray indicating that *Marino Faliero* was done). Galignani's paper was "neither more nor less than an octavo reprint" of the *Literary Gazette* (as the latter's editor pointed out, *Romanticism Reviewed* B:4:1416), which reported the execution (1 May) in its issue for 6 May 1820, alongside a lengthy report on Byron's doings in Venice.

10. Edward Dudley Hume Johnson, "A Political Interpretation of Byron's *Marino Faliero,*" *Modern Language Quarterly* 3 (1942): 421. A fuller discussion of Byron's admiration for Mirabeau and Lafayette can be found in Malcolm Kelsall, *Byron's Politics* (Totowa, N.J.: Barnes and Noble, 1987) 55, 86–87.

11. Richard Lansdown astutely notes "that *Marino Faliero*—a play about an aristocratic rebel—was written before Byron's direct involvement with the Carbonari, while *Sardanapalus*—a play in which a king is *threatened* with just such a rebellion—was written while Byron's sympathy with the Italian revolutionaries was at its height" (*Byron's Historical Dramas* 6).

12. See Byron, *Poetical Works,* 4:532–33.

Venice not a humanistic recreation of the Whigs' model republic, but a template for the modern authoritarian state.[13] The impersonal mechanisms of Venetian governance, in this argument, receive appropriate aesthetic embodiment in the play's mechanical reflection of objective historical processes consuming human subjectivity as fuel. Paul West faults Byron's plays for presenting characters not as human beings but as "puppets," with the result that Byron captures "nothing of the drama's suggestion of life's movement: the plays are statuesque." He allows that the flatness of Byron's characters may express his contempt for "the futility of the human will in everyday affairs," without noticing that in *Marino Faliero* it is not Byron but his narrowly motivated characters who call the doge a "puppet" of the state (1.2.515, 2.2.32, 3.2.194).[14] Jerome McGann casts the same perception more positively, attributing *Marino Faliero*'s lifeless neoclassicism to an honest effort to depict a society in which there can be no "life," no freedom, no individuated subjectivity: "the whole play suggests that it is humanly impossible to live a completely real life."[15] Malcolm Kelsall comes down on both sides, faulting Byron for his woodenness while praising his depiction of a people silenced by repression: "Shakespeare creates the dramatic illusion that the people can speak for themselves. They do not, and they cannot, in *Marino Faliero*. In this respect, 'the people' in Byron's tragedies are in the same position as the Luddites in the House of Lords debates. The oratory of the leaders of state operates over an immense void of silence."[16] If *Marino Faliero* displays *aesthetic* limitations, according to this view, it does so in a calculated effort to mark objectively verifiable *political* limitations.

Jerome Christensen attempts to reconcile the two viewpoints by ar-

---

13. See Z. S. Fink, *The Classical Republicans: An Essay in the Recovery of a Pattern of Thought in Seventeenth-Century England* (Evanston: Northwestern University Press, 1962).

14. Paul West, *Byron and the Spoiler's Art* (New York: St. Martin's, 1960) 105, 107, 105. West echoes the *British Review*'s judgment that the "agents are only rhetorical puppets" (*Romantics Reviewed* B:1:479) and Hazlitt's description of Angiolina as "a very fair, unsullied piece of marble" (19:46); Hazlitt is in turn echoing Young's criticism of Addison's *Cato* as "an exquisite piece of statuary," a figure Young takes from Addison himself (see Edward Young, *Conjectures on Original Composition*, in *The Great Critics: An Anthology of Literary Criticism*, ed. James Harry Smith and Edd Winfield Parks [New York: Norton, 1967] 434).

15. Jerome J. McGann, *Fiery Dust: Byron's Poetic Development* (Chicago: University of Chicago Press, 1968) 213.

16. Kelsall, *Byron's Politics*, 102.

guing that Byron stumbles on the story of the doge as an allegory of his own subjection to historical (especially economic) forces. It is not just the people who are deprived of voice and of freedom in Byron's Venice; the same holds true for the doge himself and for all whose subjectivity is defined by their subjection to the authoritarian rule of "the Forty." Even in what should be the private life of the doge and his wife, Christensen notes, "nothing that could be called privacy ever subsisted between them, no subjective space in which a theoretical liberty could be exercised." The doge's fatalistic rejections of free will—"I act no more on my free will, / Nor my own feelings—both compel me back" (3.2.517–18)—can thus be taken neither as confessing the opinions of Lord Byron, nor as expressing the correct judgment of a historical personage with whom Byron might or might not sympathize, but as revealing an objectively verifiable social mechanism that happens also to define Byron's subjective position in English politics, one in which "the freedom of his movement was politically insignificant: he ran on a leash that confined him within a well tended consensus." *Marino Faliero* thus offers, without calculating the political consequences, an impartial view of historical reality that turns out to express Byron's personal relation to commercial capital and political power.[17]

The debate about whether *Marino Faliero* is more fundamentally a political or a historical drama has been lively, and any commentator must begin from its terms, which were first Byron's terms. But either position must consider the problem of agency that dominates the play and that emerges from a complicated position toward his own agency that Byron articulates throughout his career in remarkably consistent terms. For what is in dispute is the significance of having historical personages voice fatalistic sentiments; and before deciding whether such sentiments have a primarily political or historical meaning, we must determine the extent to which they work on readers or audiences as Byron's own sentiments.

The most familiar example of fatalistic writing in Byron is found in

17. Jerome Christensen, "*Marino Faliero* and the Fault of Byron's Satire," *Studies in Romanticism* 24 (1985): 325, 319. In revising this essay for *Lord Byron's Strengh*, Christensen deleted the sentence restricting Byron's agency to a "politically insignificant" run on a leash; cf. 263. His arguments are confirmed by the doge's claim that the patricians have left him "no privacy of life," and by his wish to inflict the same on them: "To me, then, these men have no private life, / Nor claim to ties they have cut off from others" (3.2.349, 382–83).

the stanzas that bracket the last two cantos of *Childe Harold's Pilgrimage* with reflections on the mix of activity and passivity in a writer seeking to show how poets "live / A being more intense," "gaining as we give / The life we image" (canto 3, stanza 6). The second stanza of canto 3 arranges those mixed feelings by moving artfully from control to surrender:

> Once more upon the waters! yet once more!
> And the waves bound beneath me as a steed
> That knows its rider. Welcome to their roar!
> Swift be their guidance, wheresoe'er it lead!
> Though the strain'd mast should quiver as a reed,
> And the rent canvas fluttering strew the gale,
> Still must I on; for I am as a weed,
> Flung from the rock on Ocean's foam to sail
> Where'er the surge may sweep, the tempest's breath prevail.

Christensen admires Byron's control of the figure that presents his loss of control: "More impressive than the poles of titanic mastery and Shelleyan passivity is the positioning of the pivot that efficiently transforms existential bewilderment into rhetorical antithesis."[18] That the loss of agency should be recuperated as stylistic mastery is appropriate in a stanza whose subject is not, of course, aquatic travel, but writing. Writing also emerges as the subject of the third-to-last stanza of canto 4, which I quoted at the end of Chapter 4. Here Byron develops the same oceanic figure within a similar antithetical structure:

> And I have loved thee, Ocean! and my joy
> Of youthful sports was on thy breast to be
> Borne, like thy bubbles, onward: from a boy
> I wanton'd with thy breakers—they to me
> Were a delight; and if the freshening sea
> Made them a terror—'twas a pleasing fear,
> For I was as it were a child of thee,
> And trusted to thy billows far and near,
> And laid my hand upon thy mane—as I do here.

The last line recalls the "steed" of 3.2, twisting the maternal imagery of passive surrender back toward the control that is manifested "here," in

---

18. Christensen, *Lord Byron's Strength* 152.

the writing whose reigns Byron holds in his "hand." In the first passage, Byron fixes on the experience of surrendering to his writing as an occasion to demonstrate rhetorical control. In the second, he grasps for that rhetorical control in order to put in the past his sense of being "flung" like a "weed" or "borne" like a "bubble" along the surfaces of his text. Such figures for the loss and recovery of agency are familiar from Wordsworth's metaphors of inundation and from Reik's Freudian allegory of the criminal riding his id, quoted in Chapters 1 and 2. Their function in Byron's work is not so much to develop political or psychological themes, however, as to provide an index of the poet's investment in stylistic control.

Whether the switching between active and passive in these stanzas is seen as rhetorical antithesis, psychological equivocation, skeptical suspension, or dramatic re-enactment, it must be realized that Byron is writing about what it is like to create fictive voices that deliver actual speeches—what it is like, in short, to write dramatic poetry. Critics have sought to place the ambivalent fatalism of Byronic romance within the discourses of theology, psychology, or commercial ideology; I will insist that the ironizing of fatalism from *Marino Faliero* onward is conditioned primarily by his own experience of writing that first historical drama.[19] A. B. England observes in *Marino Faliero* "a spirit that subverts the confining pressures both of the plot and [of] those deterministic structures to which the protagonist from time to time subscribes," and notes astutely that the play was written at a transitional interlude in the composition of *Don Juan*, between cantos 4 and 5, where Juan moves from passive absorption to emotional autonomy.[20] Although it is hazardous to read anything in *Don Juan* as an assurance of emotional development, I will argue that the experience of writing

19. Most modern readers seem to agree with Peter Thorslev's contention that, while Byron's beliefs may be inscrutable, the Byronic Hero "is not a fatalist" (*The Byronic Hero: Types and Prototypes* [Minneapolis: University of Minnesota Press, 1962] 163). The frequency of "fate" and its cognates throughout the Byron canon should not distract us from the force of Byron's maxim in *Don Juan* 13, "Fate is a good excuse for our own will," which condenses arguments he had made at greater length elsewhere (e.g. *Lara*, 1:332–36). For recent theological arguments, see *Byron, The Bible, and Religion*, ed. Wolf Z. Hirst (Newark: University of Delaware Press, 1991); for psychological arguments, see Peter J. Manning, *Byron and His Fictions* (Detroit: Wayne State University Press, 1978); for arguments about commercial ideology, see Christensen, *Lord Byron's Strength*.

20. A. B. England, "Byron's *Marino Faliero* and the Force of Individual Agency," *Keats-Shelley Journal* 39 (1990): 119–20.

historical drama did bring Byron a new and compelling awareness of his own desire for autonomy.

Francis Jeffrey, reviewing *Childe Harold* canto 3, struggles to define the autonomy Byron grants his alter ego, into which the poet "enters so deeply, and with so extraordinary a fondness, that he generally continues to speak in its language, after it has been dismissed from the stage; and to inculcate, on his own authority, the same sentiments which had been previously recommended by its example."[21] It is not immediately clear why Jeffrey should object to the permeable boundary between Byron and his speakers. But the danger of Byron's self-sacrificing route to selfhood appears more clearly when his dramatic voices speak words that circumstances render politically volatile. The poet runs the risk of putting his pen into the wrong hands, as the *British Critic* suggested in tracing the conspirators in *Marino Faliero* to Cato Street: "If Thistlewood and Ings could have delivered themselves in blank verse, they would have spoken much the same words (for they did utter the same sentiments) as the doge, and his accomplice Israel Bertuccio. This is as it should be, and if Lord Byron consulted his own bosom, instead of the newspapers, it proves his deep knowledge of the worst parts of human nature."[22] Byron shares the lack of originality typical of conspirators across the ages: either he has copied from the newspapers, or the sentiments of his own bosom are as stale as those of Thistlewood and Ings. But the possibility that Byron's words reveal a "deep knowledge" permits *Marino Faliero*'s display of treasonable rhetoric to generate two incompatible judgments within the same reader: it seems at once supremely dangerous, promulgating a familiarity with "the worst parts of human nature," and altogether acceptable, "as it should be." The only position available to such a reader is an ironic detachment from what had only recently been a dire national emergency. This potential for rendering readers *indifferent* to the individuation of persons may have been what bothered Jeffrey four years earlier. The same problem can be seen in the advice given by the *Eclectic Review* to the responsible poet: "there is a mode of infusing into his personages the darkest and most hateful passions, which absolves the poet from the shame of being poetically accessory to the crime, and makes us imagine the blush of indignant virtue on his cheek, while in the act of portraying the crimi-

---

21. *Romanticism Reviewed* B:2:866.
22. Ibid. B:1:305.

nal."[23] Like Jeffrey, the *Eclectic* reviewer fears that *Marino Faliero,* in staging Byron's indifference to the allocation of responsibility for his words, might rob his readers of moral discrimination and so disable them as political agents.

Yet in writing *Marino Faliero,* Byron became, if anything, more acutely aware of his own beliefs about agency. The early scenes include an unambiguous tribute to the intact agency of even those rebels who fail in their causes, sacrificing themselves to larger historical movements:

> They but augment the deep and sweeping thoughts
> Which o'erpower all others, and conduct
> The world at last to freedom: What were we,
> If Brutus had not lived? He died in giving
> Rome liberty, but left a deathless lesson—
> A name which is a virtue, and a soul
> Which multiplies itself throughout all time.
>
> (2.2.99–105)

Six months later, however—a few days before writing Murray to protest the "usurpation" he saw in the unauthorized plan to stage *Marino Faliero* at Drury Lane—Byron used *Childe Harold*'s figure of oceanic agency to inject considerable ambiguity into the same sense of human agency in history: "But, *onward!*—it is now the time to act, and what signifies *self,* if a single spark of that which would be worthy of the past can be bequeathed unquenchedly to the future? It is not one man, nor a million but the *spirit* of liberty which must be spread. The waves which dash upon the shore are, one by one, broken but yet the *ocean* conquers, nevertheless."[24] Byron's grammar leaves it uncertain whether he really means to speak of how "one man . . . must be spread"; what remains unambiguous is the urgency and the ultimate significance of political action, which bears the spark out of history and toward utopian conflagration. Yet the promotion of an impersonal "spirit" at the expense of *every* committed "self" is double-edged. Does the Romantic *topos* of a dispersion of agency into the dynamism of nature mean for Byron that social change results from agentless actions? Or is it rather achieved in heroic acts of self-immolation? Or perhaps the glorious

---

23. Ibid. B:2:767.
24. *Byron's Letters and Journals* 8:20.

vision of agency should be seen as covering over a fear that *self* really does signify nothing? These ambiguities register in Marino Faliero's final speech, where he prays that a divine power might sustain his words, which voice the very oceanic figure Byron would make his own: "Ye elements! in which to be resolved / I hasten, let my voice be as a spirit / Upon you!" (5.3.28–30).

An important question arises from the conjunction of this passage with the two from *Childe Harold* in which Byron imagines an oceanic diffusion of agency only to override it, as the doge does, with his own rhetorical virtuosity. In his strident call for revolutionary action, Byron seems similarly to diffuse the power of change through the selfless ocean in a figure he invents to demonstrate his own power to pass on the spark of liberty. But *why* does the theme of diffused agency now accompany Byron's highly individualistic embrace of political action? My answer is that the experience of writing his first historical drama led Byron to conceive his work—the task of creating powerful but fictional voices that open broad political perspectives within the narrow precincts of the historical record—as a way of managing the writer's inevitable loss of mastery over his language in such a way as to gain access to greater powers no longer strictly his own. This pattern could be presented psychologically, as a version of the dynamic to which David Erdman traces Byron's "stage fright": "Byron asserted his ego ostentatiously, but he always managed to safeguard himself from responsibility for defeat by avoiding the initiative and by invariably 'happening' to fall into an 'impossible' situation where failure was no blame."[25] That psychological profile may seem to account for the diffusion of agency in Byron's response to the failure of *Marino Faliero,* a disappointment he claims to have experienced as "a sort of dramatic Calvinism—predestined damnation, without a sinner's own fault."[26] But the phrase "dramatic Calvinism" seems less striking as a psychological revelation than as an ironic summation of the tragic stance Byron had formulated in the play itself. For *Marino Faliero* frames the psychological oscillation between the loss and recuperation of agency within a

---

25. David V. Erdman, "Byron's Stage Fright: The History of His Ambition and Fear of Writing for the Stage," *ELH* 6 (1939): 221–22.

26. *Byron's Letters and Journals* 8:117. A "dramatic Calvinism" that discounts the salvific force of deeds is implicit in Christensen's apt description of the play as "a work wherein Romantic ambition labors in a theater of baroque inconsequence" (*Lord Byron's Strength* 264).

rhetoric that submits the individual to infinitely larger, quasi-divine agencies in a sort of dramatic Calvinism that delimits a *political* arena in which the individual's quest for autonomy must meet its damnation. The importance of *Marino Faliero* in Byron's development arises from the political circumstances, both in London and in Italy, of its writing and production. These brought Byron to an acute awareness of the political significance of a conundrum about agency that had long governed his stance toward his own writing.

Richard Lansdown has described *Marino Faliero* as "a play about itself, about the description and reenactment of historical events—by playwrights as well as by other historical personalities." Refining on Hazlitt, he sees Byron attributing his own historical consciousness to his characters, who do not merely cite historical precedents, as do the speakers in *The Fall of Robespierre,* but envision history "as a continuum in which their actions and their words will be retold and, it follows, traduced by those very tellers with whom their reputations rest."[27] I agree: in spite of Byron's avowed admiration for Joanna Baillie's dramas of the ruling passions, *Marino Faliero* strips its characters of moral motives such as jealousy and provides them instead with an almost hyperbolic awareness of the pressure of history (past, present, and future) upon motivation. I will be concerned only with one complex aspect of this historical self-consciousness, which appears in the way the play is structured to accommodate parallels between Byron and his hero, each seeking to initiate action in the gaps that open between personal and universal history. Byron's awareness of a relation between his own historical circumstances and his hero's enters the play neither as veiled autobiography nor as open polemic, but rather in the pervasive insistence of a unique dramatic structure that is responsible both for the play's historical acumen and for its critical insights into the quest for political power. That awareness is not adequately explained by the hypothesis that Byron identifies with the doge's subversive actions or republican ideals, or that the doge expresses Byron's libertarian sentiments; ideology does not go very far in accounting for the play's affective power, which depends rather on a peculiarly dynamic parallelism. *Marino Faliero* functions as a *mise en abîme* of historical reflection: Byron gazes back into the mirror of Venetian history hoping to construct an image of his own condition as political agent, only to discover

---

27. Lansdown, *Byron's Historical Dramas* 6; see also 42–44 and 135.

the doge of Venice likewise gazing into the mirror of history in order to anticipate his own recovery of political agency. *Marino Faliero* thus marks a renewed insistence on a strategy this study has placed at the heart of Romantic drama: the conception of dramatic form as a distorting mirror by means of which knowledge is transposed into action.

2.

The plot of *Marino Faliero* traces the incompletion of a process more than it imitates a complete action. That process is launched in the play's first half, which is dominated by characters who seek what is repeatedly called "redress." This term, scattered liberally throughout the first act, is generally used in the sense of "satisfaction . . . for a wrong sustained," which the OED illustrates with a line from *The Cenci:* "Think not / But that there is redress where there is wrong" (3.1.194). Marino Faliero, who feels himself treasonably slandered, declares, "I sought no vengeance but redress by law," but learns that the law will not help him: "the haughty noble / May spit upon us: —where is our redress?" When his nephew asks him: "what redress / Did you expect as his fit punishment?" he answers: "Death!" Israel Bertuccio, Chief of the Arsenal, arrives to declare his "wish to prove and urge you to redress," but not before he has laid out his own complaint: *"Doge:* Sir, you may advance —what would you? / *I.B.:* Redress." Later in the scene Israel voices, somewhat unidiomatically, "the hope I had and have, that you, / My prince, yourself a soldier, will redress / Him," referring to Barbaro, the nobleman by whom Israel has been insulted. In his first draft Byron had Israel ask not for "redress" but for "justice"; and even in the final draft, he has Faliero exclaim "You come to me for justice!" before correcting himself 18 lines later: "You ask redress of me!" Byron seems to have wanted to depict the plebeian insinuating himself with Faliero by avoiding the sweeping (and radical) connotations of "justice" in favor of the more situational "redress." The result is that even the conspirators come to speak of "the great redress we meditate for Venice," so that when the doge addresses them in his own terms, it is also on their terms: "There's not / A roused mechanic in your busy plot / So wrong'd as I, so fallen, so loudly call'd / To his redress." This last instance of "redress," paired with "fallen," makes explicit a connotation present in the term from the start: the literal sense of "raising again to an erect position." The characters who seek redress seek to prop themselves upright, to make themselves whole by supplementing what they lack as subjects and victims of an all-powerful state. To seek redress is not to seek justice or revenge, it is to seek a restoration of lost agency.[28]

The subjects of Byron's Venice sketch their own perceptions of lack early on, in a sort of dramatized *cahier de doléances*. The doge complains that his ceremonial role as head of state, bestowed in old age as a reward for lifelong service, has robbed him of freedoms and powers he had formerly known both in private life, as a husband, a father, and a feudal lord, and in state affairs, as a military commander. The conspirators ranged under Israel Bertuccio complain that their disenfranchisement has robbed them both of their human dignity and of the political role they ought to share in a liberal commonwealth. Each party comes to recognize that the state's constraints on *individual* action can only be remedied by *collective* action outside the law. Equally deprived of the means of redress, each therefore requires the other in order to reassemble an integral agency: the doge seeks in the conspirators the power of action that he has lost through his position and his old age, while the conspirators seek to construct a revolutionary cell upon the Faliero code of honor. The doge's plotting with the conspirators does not, however, cover the entire play. Their joint quest for redress is disrupted when they are betrayed by the conspirator Bertram, who justifies his defection by a private appeal to the same quasi-familial sympathies the other conspirators have invoked more ritually in justifying their actions. The plot to restore completeness is thus itself rendered incomplete by the playing out of contradictions in its logic. The doge's retrospective path of individual recuperation cannot be reconciled with the conspirators' anticipatory path of social ascent before the two vectors collide in the private apostasy that short-circuits collective action.

Act 1 offers a condensed view of the logic by which *Marino Faliero*'s failed dialectic of redress allows petty misdemeanors to generate apocalyptic wrath. The voicing of grievances in act 1 is instigated by the slanderous graffiti that Michael Steno has inscribed on the ducal throne, an epigram defaming the honor of the Dogaressa Angiolina and by implication that of the doge: "*Marin Falier dalla bella moglie: Altri la*

---

28. *Marino Faliero* 1.2.113, 110, 190, 535, 329, 338–40, 383, 401; 2.2.7; 3.1.114. "Raising again to an erect position" is the primary sense of the French *redresser,* which Littré illustrates with a verse from the gospels that might have had a particular salience for Byron: "Il avait éclairé les aveugles, guéri les paralytiques, *redressé les boiteux.*" For further reflections on "redress," see Seamus Heaney, *The Redress of Poetry* (New York: Farrar, Straus & Giroux, 1990).

gode, ed egli la mantien" ("Marin Falier, the husband of the fair wife; others kiss her, but he keeps her").²⁹ The words, which might have become the only trace of history to survive intact in the play, are ostentatiously omitted at 1.2.62, creating an effect like that of the silence that enshrines the rape in *The Cenci*. The doge needs to suppress the wording because the slur seems, almost magically, to affirm a truth simply by virtue of its having been written, a truth not about his marital life or his sexual potency, but about his position in the state. He understands the inscription as a sign pointing not to a lost integrity, but to the loss of autonomy experienced by a public man subject to being defined by others. He rightly sees the inscription not as a statement persuading his subjects of something that is not true, but as a performance that *produces* the condition of disempowerment it claims to reveal.

When the patrician "Forty" hand down a merely nominal censure of Steno, the doge feels confirmed in taking the inscription as a self-fulfilling prophecy announcing his loss of political autonomy. The sovereign inaction of the "Forty" leads him to diagnose Steno's offence as "a mere ebullition of the vice, / The general corruption generated / By the foul aristocracy" (3.2.403–5). It is that perception of a larger agency at work undermining the autonomy of all that justifies him in redirecting his wrath at Steno toward the patrician rulers. Calendaro's offer of Steno's head impaled on his sword draws from him a response that is only apparently paradoxical: "You would but lop the hand, and I the head" (3.2.416). No individual's head can be *the* head; the doge is imagining an agency that is not so readily lopped. This shift of focus from a local to a general agency, with its hypothesis of remote control, generates in the doge an apocalyptic fantasy of total redress:

> I cannot pause on individual hate,
> In the absorbing, sweeping, whole revenge
> Which, like the sheeted fire from heaven, must blast
> Without distinction, as it fell of yore,
> Where the Dead Sea hath quench'd two cities' ashes.
> (3.2.419–23)

---

29. Byron allows the doge to conceal the wording, revealing it himself only in an appendix to the play and in the moderating translation quoted here (*Poetical Works* 4:528 and 532). McGann notes another version of the inscription: " 'Becco Marino Falier dalla bella mogier' ('Cuckold Marino Falier of the fair wife')" (550).

Marino Faliero

The gratuitous mention of the Dead Sea, whose inundations are irrelevant to Sodom and Gomorrah's destruction by fire, puts the signature of *Childe Harold*'s oceanic fatalism to a sentence misleadingly begun in the first person.

The fatalistic hyperbole that must accompany the doge's wish for a "whole" agency to match his hypothesis of a general agency has been prepared by his nephew's distress at seeing his anger, "like our Adrian waves, / O'ersweep all bounds, and foam itself to air" (1.2.133). More important, we can see the fatalistic surrender of human agency to which that oceanic metaphor ultimately leads when Faliero justifies his quest for total redress:

> I act no more on my free will,
> Nor my own feelings—both compel me back;
> But there is hell within me and around,
> And like the demon who believes and trembles
> Must I abhor and do.
>
> (3.2.517–21)

Faliero's self-daemonization, his surrender to Count Cenci's refusal of personhood, appears as a reflex of the fatalistic rhetoric whose double edge is revealed in the very next scene, when Bertram speaks of "the accursed tyranny which rides / The very air in Venice, and makes men / Madden as in the last hours of the plague / Which sweeps the soul deliriously from life!" (4.1.237–40). Bertram's perception of "tyranny" as a disembodied sorcery both *diagnoses* the madness driving Faliero to act and, in repeating the denial of bodily individuation, *partakes* of the madness whose diagnosis had driven Faliero mad.

Neither a plot summary nor a review of the doge's rhetoric, however, can entirely account for the logic by which Faliero's reduction of Steno's agency passes suddenly into an apocalyptic fantasy of "absorbing, sweeping" agency, the wave of divine wrath he will ride (like a weed or a bubble) toward redress. The mechanism of history that makes small causes produce great effects (examples of which Byron catalogues in his preface, including one that Shelley would treat in *Charles the First*) appears, despite Byron's wish to downplay jealousy as a motive, to be modelled after *Othello*. As Stanley Cavell depicts Othello "trying, against his knowledge, to believe" Iago, so Byron depicts doge Faliero impelled to see at least a political truth in Steno's obviously false slur.

Cavell sees Othello's "professions of skepticism" over his wife's fidelity as "a terrible doubt covering a yet more terrible certainty," the certainty that she (and so he himself) is separate, dependent, partial, imperfect, finite; *Othello* thus dramatizes "the attempt to convert the human condition, the condition of humanity, into an intellectual difficulty, a riddle," interpreting, as Cavell puts it, "a metaphysical finitude as an intellectual lack."[30] *Marino Faliero* dramatizes a similar desire in a political rather than a sexual framework. But Byron handles the articulation of personal cause and political effect with a deftness that can only be grasped by following the dramatic development of the first act.

The theme of wounded autonomy is joined to a structure of anticipation by a short opening scene reporting the doge's feelings of powerlessness as he awaits Steno's sentencing. Two officers of the Palace describe the business of administering the state as a meaningless pastime:

> *Battista:*   How bears he
> These moments of suspense?
> *Pietro:*   With struggling patience.
> Placed at the ducal table, cover'd o'er
> With all the apparel of the state; petitions,
> Despatches, judgments, acts, reprieves, reports,
> He sits as rapt in duty; but whene'er
> He hears the jarring of a distant door,
> Or aught that intimates a coming step,
> Or murmur of a voice, his quick eye wanders,
> And he will start up from his chair, then pause,
> And seat himself again, and fix his gaze
> Upon some edict; but I have observed
> For the last hour he has not turned a leaf.
> (1.1.5–17)

The doge's struggle between present obligation and unfulfilled anticipation is rendered in the switchings between fixed gaze and wandering eye, between the pictorial stasis of his waiting immobilized "for the last hour" and the dramatic temporality of "jarring" interruptions. The trivializing catalogue of texts that make up the "apparel" of state ("petitions, / Despatches, judgments, acts, reprieves, reports"), before which the doge "sits as rapt," recalls the "Puffs, Powders, Patches, Bibles, Billet-doux" of Belinda's toilet in Pope's *Rape of the Lock*, an-

---

30. Cavell, *Disowning Knowledge* 133, 138.

other scene of rapt fascination that prepares the unfolding of a decisive drama.[31] The instruments of bureaucratic administration tempt the doge to identify himself with the trappings of power that will be figured, throughout the play, by his ceremonial robes and bonnet. Unlike Belinda, the doge rejects the reifying mirror offered to him; yet like the heroine who cannot see herself except in her array of cosmetics and commodities, Byron's doge has no means of recognizing himself beyond the meaningless texts that make up his bureaucratic world. Having been reduced by his position to "a pageant," he can only suffer from his insistence that he is still a person; and that suffering may prompt his wish to be less, or more, than human. Rejecting the apparel of state thus means suspending the quest for self-knowledge and abandoning any possible action, even such minor actions as are dictated by the protocols of his administrative role. With no means of imaging himself other than that provided by his world of illegible texts, he can only await the arrival of a new text, "the sentence" that will render his public and private roles legible.

His refusal either to *play* doge or to serve as passive spectator to that masquerade must be seen as a crucial step in initiating his quest for redress. For it is the means by which Byron arranges for us to experience the unfolding plot as an anxiety about agency. We feel Faliero's need to initiate his own plot not just in the officers' account of his restlessness, but in our partial identification with his waiting. Yet while we are made to share the doge's anticipatory anxiety, waiting for the drama to deliver on its generic promise to be meaningful, our quest for meaning is already being fulfilled. As we see the doge failing to see himself, his suspension in meaninglessness is already meaningful for us; as he awaits the messenger bearing the signs that will allow him to interpret his role, we are already receiving messages about his anticipatory anxiety. We do not just await meaning; we actively interpret that waiting as signifying the doge's passive relation to the state of which he is the nominal head. When it is announced that Steno's fate is "decided; but as yet his doom's unknown" (1.1.26), the audience recognizes not only its bond with the doge as he awaits his fate, but also its detachment from the doge's position, guaranteed by the convention that a play's meanings are only temporarily withheld. While the audience can expect suspense to be relieved as the drama is gradually delivered up to its

---

31. Alexander Pope, *The Rape of the Lock* 1:138, in *Poetry and Prose of Alexander Pope,* ed. Aubrey Williams (Boston: Houghton Mifflin, 1969) 83.

passive waiting, it sees that the doge's fate is never simply delivered but must be decisively determined by acts of which he is, in this first scene, as yet incapable.

The long second scene delivers what is promised in the first scene's description, and performance, of anticipatory anxiety: the doge's conversion from a passive waiting to an active determination of meaning. Byron plots this conversion as the movement from a reflection on the loss of power, presented in the doge's recollections of lost bodily strength and of his lost son, to his search for "other hands," "the dubious aid of strangers" he will need to determine his fate. This progression should be viewed as a dramatic unfolding of the failed specularity described in the opening scene. Starting from the doge's efforts to see himself as he is seen by others, this scene moves from his recognition of subjective lack toward his attempt to reconstitute a capacity for efficacious action. The anticipation of a meaningful sentence from the Forty is replaced by an anticipation of individual agency, which is in turn displaced into an anticipation of collective agency. The plebeian conspiracy thus makes its first appearance as a kind of prosthetic supplement demanded by the sense of lack that constitutes the doge's role.[32]

That sense of lack is nothing personal; but the action is set in motion when the doge is moved by Steno's transgression of the public/private boundary to take it personally. It finds its first expression in the doge's recollection of his earlier heroism, of a time when this head of state needed no body politic to enact its will. He sees his youth as a time when soul and body were one:

> Oh for one year! Oh! but for even a day
> Of my full youth, while yet my body served
> My soul as serves the generous steed his lord,
> I would have dash'd amongst them, asking few
> In aid to overthrow these swoln patricians;
> But now I must look round for other hands
> To serve this hoary head....
>
> (1.2.274–80)

---

32. This dramatic movement accords strikingly with Lacan's account of the mirror stage as "a drama whose internal thrust is precipitated from insufficiency to anticipation" ("The Mirror Stage," in *Ecrits: A Selection*, trans. Alan Sheridan [New York: Norton, 1977] 4). Lacan's juxtaposition of the "fragmented body" with "structures of fortified works" replicates the figuring of agency in *Marino Faliero*, and could provide an entry into a full psychoanalytic reading of the play.

The doge makes his old age represent the alienation of agency entailed by his position as a head of state that has, in a remarkable prolepsis of his fate in act 5, been detached from its body.[33] These lines provide a public equivalent for Count Cenci's private lament: "I was happier than I am, while yet / Manhood remained to act the thing I thought" (*Cenci* 1.1.96–97). The public lament cannot remain public, however, as the figurative mourning over lost youth slips toward a literal mourning for the doge's lost son, who "died in arms / At Sapienza for this faithless state" (1.2.556–57). Yet this renewed mourning returns the doge to his public role: it is voiced not as personal grief, but as a political meditation on the fracturing of the noble family in which Faliero's sense of honor, and of heroic action, is based. His expression of lack thus passes from the figure of a soul that has lost its body to the figure of a family that has lost its unity. The correlation between the two is marked by a repetition of the first lament's exclamatory "Oh!" (the rhetorical sign of lack): "Oh! that he were alive, and I in ashes! / Or that he were alive ere I be ashes! / I should not need the dubious aid of strangers" (1.2.558–60). The mourner's fantasy of changing places with the dead yields a more dangerous fantasy that the dead might, by some practical means, be brought to life. That means is offered in the connection by which the lost bond between father and son comes to signify the lost bond between soul and body.[34] The logic governing the plot dictates that once these bonds have been severed, the mourning for what is lost will pass into the melancholy of immobilization glimpsed in the first scene unless the imagination can incarnate that lost soul in a new body.

Faliero's need to recover the lost agency represented by his dead son thus provides a *personal* motive for the makeshift *social* contract that will bind him to the conspirators in what he will consider a surrogate family. His mourning passes abruptly into a meditation on the conspirators' ability to supplement his lost agency. That the doge calls their aid "dubious" signals his distrust of the purely imaginary remedies such mourning will prompt. But the gaping discontinuities he glimpses in the chain of logic that passes from son to self to society are immediately

---

33. The figure is used slightly differently in Byron's first mention of the Faliero story to Murray, where he speaks of the "head conspiring against the body" (*Byron's Letters and Journals* 5:174).

34. Byron may be recalling Dante's paradigmatic figure of schism, Bertran de Born: "Perch'io parti' così giunte persone, / partito porto il mio cerebro, lasso!, / dal suo principio che'è in questo troncone. / Così s'osserva in me lo contrapasso" (*Inferno* 28:139–42, in Dante Alighieri, *The Divine Comedy* 1:302).

repaired in the rhetoric of Israel Bertuccio. His pledge makes a guarantee out of what the doge finds most dubious, arguing that social solidarity can provide a surrogate family whose surrogate history will guarantee a surrogate honor: "Not one of all those strangers whom thou doubtest, / But will regard thee with a filial feeling, / So that thou keep'st a father's faith with them" (1.2.561–63). What is noteworthy in these crucial lines is not the familial nature of the bonds that are pledged, but the fact that they have to be pledged. In this surrogate family, the place of the "filial feeling" that reciprocates "a father's faith" must be filled by a social rather than a natural bond. Fidelity cannot merely flow from domestic affections, but must be contracted by means of a reciprocal if-then promise: "so that" does not mean that one will elicit the other, but that one is maintained *provided that* the other is maintained. The prosthetic agency that is to redress the doge's lack thus appears only in the future conditional of a reciprocal promise that carries unmistakable overtones of Lockean social-contract theory, strangely combined with reminiscences of Filmer in the matching alliterations "filial feeling" and "father's faith." It is here, in tracing out the play's treatment of anxieties about agency, that we arrive at a way of gauging its political significance. The crossing of Whig and Tory convention in Israel's lines, however, makes it impossible to reduce that political significance to the terms of partisan leanings.

Such a crossing suggests that *Marino Faliero* stages an allegorical regrounding of the modern liberal state, in the Lockean version that replaces the patriarchal ground of government with the ground of popular consent. Israel Bertuccio's conditional pledge reveals flaws that had been perceived in the social contract, notably by Hume and Godwin in their attacks on the notion of passive obligation in Locke and Rousseau. "The whole principle of an original contract rests upon the obligation under which *we are conceived to be placed* to observe our promises," writes Godwin, flourishing the double passive I have italicized. People do what they believe to be right, he argues: we keep our promises only "because it tends to the welfare of intelligent beings," not because we are obliged by our linguistic competence in uttering promises. If we are already committed to a benevolent morality, there is no need to promise that we will "do that for [our] neighbor which will be beneficial to him and not injurious to [us]"; if we are not so committed, no belief in the sanctity of promises will keep us from doing harm. Promising to act justly is superfluous because the moral code we promise to observe is the same that guarantees the promise, and it is "absurd to rest the foundation of morality thus circuitously upon promises, when it may with equal propriety be rested upon that from which promises themselves derive their obligation." Godwin's reference to the "circuitous" character of promises takes the infinite regress of obligation—the promise to keep our promise to keep our promises—as an ungrounded circulation of social energy that makes a mockery of any pretence that the liberal state is a public *thing*. Social contract theory makes it, rather, "an engagement to a non-entity, a constitution."[35]

Byron makes a specific point about partisan uses of social contract theory by alluding to such criticisms in a Venetian setting. The importance of the Venetian constitution for Whig contractarians stemmed from their sense of it as a parallel to England's "ancient constitution," since Venice was believed (by James Harrington, for example) to have "perpetuated into the modern world those principles of government which had made Rome and Sparta famous and which the ancient philosophers had enshrined in their works."[36] While not much can be said with certainty about Byron's views on the foundations of England's limited monarchy, it may be argued that *Marino Faliero,* in casting doubt on seventeenth-century Whig utopias spun from the Venetian myth, suggests that any effort to model a reformed British constitution after the Venetian commonwealth will be a search for redress that chases after a "non-entity."

But the political significance of Israel Bertuccio's promise need not depend on conjectures about Byron's views on contract theory. The doge and the conspirators may agree to found a provisional society on an artificial social contract, anticipating (or recalling) the Lockean conception of the liberal state; but at the same time they wish to secure

---

35. William Godwin, *Enquiry Concerning Political Justice and Its Influence on Modern Morals and Happiness* (1793; New York: Penguin, 1985) 216–18, 230. Godwin's argument derives from early critics of Hobbes such as Samuel Clarke, who notes that "the same law of nature which obliges men to fidelity, after having made a compact[,] will unavoidably, upon all the same accounts, be found to oblige them, before all compacts, to contentment and mutual benevolence"; quoted in Christine M. Korsgaard, *The Sources of Normativity* (New York: Cambridge University Press, 1996) 28. Carole Pateman puts the objection succinctly: "An ancient belief is that the universe rests on an elephant, which, in turn, stands on the back of a turtle; but what supports the turtle? One uncompromising answer is that there are turtles all the way down. From the standpoint of contract, in social life there are contracts all the way down." See *The Sexual Contract* (Stanford: Stanford University Press, 1988) 14.

36. Fink, *Classical Republicans* 35.

that contract with the patriarchal affects of "filial feeling" and "father's faith" that Locke had conceived the social contract as superseding.[37] The formation of the conspiracy thus appears as a regressive rehearsal of Whig ideology's primal scene, when the people first consent to be governed provided the governor's power be contractually limited by the terms of that consent. Whig idealizations of Venetian history had provided support for seventeenth-century measures designed to limit royal prerogative: Swift complains of a Whig scheme for a king "with the limitations of a Duke of Venice," and the parallel remained vivid even for Byron's disciple Disraeli, who wrote in 1836 that "had William the Third been a man of ordinary capacity, the constitution of Venice would have been established in England in 1688."[38] Such projects seem to have been based in Contarini's report that "the Duke of Venice is deprived of all means, whereby he might abuse his authority, or become a tyrant: which ancient and long continued custome from the first beginnings of the citie, even to these times, hath now taken such foundation and roote, that there is nothing whereof the citie of Venice need stand less in feare, then that their prince should at any time be able to invade their liberty."[39] In depicting a Venice whose stability can be guaranteed only by beheading that prince, *Marino Faliero* shakes the myth that Venice's stability had been maintained solely by checks and balances. At the same time it recalls not just the beheading of Louis XVI to which the parricide in *The Cenci* alludes, but the earlier beheading of Charles I that had helped to establish whatever stability the English Commonwealth could claim.[40] While Byron can hardly have wanted to suggest either that the British monarchy ought to have been left with unlimited power, or that Britain's stability might be bought with the

---

37. For persuasive arguments implicating contract theory in patriarchal domination, see Pateman, *Sexual Contract*. Pateman would help us to see that the compliant Angiolina, far from being Byron's fantasy houri, is merely the product of contractarianism taken to its psychological extreme.

38. *Examiner*, no. 36; *The Spirit of Whiggism*, in *The Letters of Runnymede*; both quoted in Fink, *Classical Republicans* 177n.

39. Quoted in Fink, *Classical Republicans* 38.

40. The contemporary force of the allusion to the Royal Martyr is considered in my reading of Shelley's *Charles the First* in Chapter 6. Here it is sufficient to note that Thomas Preston, a minor partner in the Cato Street conspiracy, was known to have "suggested that a snuff-box might be made, decorated with such revolutionary symbols as the head of Charles I and an axe. He saw it as a suitable present for the Prince Regent" (David Johnson, *Regency Revolution: The Case of Arthur Thistlewood* [Salisbury: Compton Russell, 1974] 39).

blood of George IV, he may well have wished to depict Whig pieties as historical fantasies.

When it appeared, *Marino Faliero* was constantly compared to *Venice Preserved*, less from any direct analogy between their characters, I believe, than from a sense that Byron's plot, like Thomas Otway's, was to be decoded as a commentary on partisan politics.[41] But partisan politics concerns Byron only to the extent that certain political desires, which his play traces not to partisan conflict but to anxieties about autonomy, might have carried the imprimatur of one party or another. One prominent passage can be taken as support for reading *Marino Faliero* as an ironization of Whig ideology. The doge's image of a "fair

---

41. Twentieth-century critics have labored to decode the political allegory of *Venice Preserved*. Its reputation in Byron's day is recorded in Aline Mackenzie Taylor's *Next to Shakespeare: Otway's Venice Preserv'd and The Orphan, and Their History on the London Stage* (Durham: Duke University Press, 1950): "Revolutionary and republican fervor . . . helped to sustain *Venice Preserv'd*. In 1795, when the play was revived with all new scenery and costumes, the audience cheered Robert Bensley's Pierre for his denunciation of the Venetian senate. The Lord Chancellor therewith forbade the play, and *Venice Preserv'd* was branded as a republican manifesto. In May, 1797, Napoleon marched his army into Venice and declared an end of the republic. Thereafter, Liberty, Venice, and Otway were associated in the minds of more people than Lord Byron, who wrote in 1818 that

> Ours is a trophy which will not decay
> With the Rialto; Shylock, and the Moor,
> And Pierre, cannot be swept or worn away—.

In 1821 his Marino Faliero evoked numerous comparisons with Shakespeare and Otway and [sic] Venice—just as Monk Lewis and Murray had told him it would. Indeed, after 1800 references to Otway reflect contemporary affairs quite as much as admiration for the acting of the Kemble clan or the reading of Otway's plays. Republican fervor inspired the new translations of *Venice Preserv'd* which appeared in Florence (1817), in Paris and in Utrecht (1822), as well as the two editions of Otway's complete works which appeared in England in 1812 and 1813—the last for over a hundred years" (266–67). Reviews of *Marino Faliero* that drew parallels with *Venice Preserved* include those in the *British Critic, The Drama,* the *European Magazine,* the *Examiner,* and (perhaps the source for several other reviews) the *Literary Gazette*. Byron dealt with his indebtedness in a remarkable note to 5.3.8, suggesting that his phrasings echo recent revolutionary history more than Otway: "This was the actual reply of Bailli, maire of Paris, to a Frenchman who made him the same reproach on his way to execution, in the earliest part of their revolution. I find in reading over (since the completion of this tragedy), for the first time these six years, 'Venice Preserved', a similar reply on a different occasion by Renault, and other coincidences arising from the subject. I need hardly remind the gentlest reader, that such coincidences must be accidental, from the very facility of their detection by reference to so popular a play on the stage and in the closet as Otway's chef d'oeuvre" (*Poetical Works* 4:561).

free commonwealth" contains clear echoes of Whig idealizations of Venice's mixed constitution, reinforced with the vocabulary of the beautiful codified by that arch-conservative Whig Edmund Burke:

> Not rash equality but equal rights,
> Proportioned like the columns to the temple,
> Giving and taking strength reciprocal,
> And making firm the whole with grace and beauty,
> So that no part could be removed without
> Infringement of the general symmetry.
>
> (3.2.170–75)

The aim of building a state with an architectonic coherence only *seems* to offer a practical means of fulfilling the doge's earlier wish for an intact self-image; for the continuing existence of beautifully proportioned temples implies that restoring lost agency is no more difficult than restoring the equal rights of a classical republic, something that could, however, never be accomplished except in an act of imagination. The aestheticizing of political theory provides the doge an image of a wholeness that is itself unavailable, and makes the restoration of agency seem a practical action that might be undertaken and accomplished through an act of imagination. Byron's act of imagination, however, suggests that the loss of agency entails a forfeiture of republican objectives, which in turn condemns aesthetic perfection as an illusory political ideal.

Byron's dead-end political plot thus offers a means of diagnosing the doge's wavering between his belief in Burke's inherited constitution and his contractual pledge to honor the constitution of the conspirators. This new constitution creates a performative supplement to the doge's "father's faith" toward his subjects, a supplement that forfeits the unconditioned fidelity that would follow from the acknowledgment of a patrilineal inheritance. The attempt to join a "natural" constitution to an "artificial" constitution is suspended by a contradiction; *Marino Faliero* inserts itself into contemporary political discourse by unfolding an equivocation whereby the English constitution, whose strength was supposed to lie in its requiring no codification, appeared to require at least the codification given by Burke (or Blackstone, or Hale).

The soliloquy that closes act 1 provides a neat summation of the relation between remembrance and forgetfulness of one's fathers that characterizes the contradictions of the makeshift social contract and that will shape the actions that follow:

Marino Faliero

> At midnight, by the church of Saints John and Paul,
> Where sleep my noble fathers, I repair—
> To what? to hold a council in the dark
> With common ruffians leagued to ruin states!
> And will not my great sires leap from the vault,
> Where lie two doges who preceded me,
> And pluck me down amongst them? Would they could!
> For I should rest in honour with the honour'd.
> Alas! I must not think of them, but those
> Who have made me thus unworthy of a name
> Noble and brave as aught of consular
> On Roman marbles; but I will redeem it
> Back to its antique lustre in our annals,
> By sweet revenge on all that's base in Venice,
> And freedom to the rest, or leave it black
> To all the growing calumnies of time,
> Which never spare the fame of him who fails,
> But try the Caesar, or the Cataline,
> By the true touchstone of desert—success.
>
> (1.2.579–97)

This reflection—split by the pivotal retraction "I must not think of them"—sums up the double bind that faces the doge throughout this scene. Faliero wants to present honor as a simple imperative: remember your fathers. Yet he recognizes that to do so would be to forget the duty he owes his people, to whom he stands pledged as a figurative father. His conflict entails a further double bind of remembrance and forgetting: whatever choice he makes, the doge has committed himself to an act of forced forgetfulness ("I must not think . . .") that entails an act of remembrance (". . . of them"). This speech, generated for the doge by Byron's shadowy recognition of a double bind inherent in the patriarchal metaphor of governance attacked by Locke and defended by Burke, serves as a catalogue of the acts of memory and of forgetfulness that, in the closed world of Byron's Venice, alternately create and destroy the possibility of historically significant agency.

3.

The undoing of the model of agency Byron associates with Old Whig mythography can be traced in the plot's broader contours. The artificial collective whose unity is pledged in the conspirators' contract is flawed in one significant way. Although it may be supported by a unanimity of interest, this common interest can be defined only negatively, as dissent from the forced unanimity of political opinion that has supposedly prevailed in patrician Venice. The liberal commonwealth that the conspiracy means to establish—the desired *political* end of redress—has no aim other than to abrogate the state's monopoly on political discourse. That aim is fulfilled by the very formation of the conspiracy, or rather it would be fulfilled if only the conspiracy could go public as something more than his majesty's loyal opposition. But in promoting dissent, the conspirators must allow for dissent within their own ranks, and this possibility becomes a tragic necessity; for it is the same principle that leads to a fragmenting of the unanimity both promised and presupposed by the makeshift social contract. By opening a small gap for individual freedom within the sweeping rhetoric that characterizes the unanimity of patricians and conspirators alike, Bertram's defection offers a defense of individual agency that recapitulates the logic by which *Childe Harold*'s oceanic tropes derive authorial control from the very fragmentation that appears to threaten it.

The collective agency anticipated in the conspiracy's formation claims unity on the basis not of class solidarity, which would hardly do as a means of binding the doge to the people's cause, but of a common interest staked upon shared fantasies about the inhuman. The conspirators present their enemy in images of excessive physicality, most often a monstrous assemblage of excess body parts. Byron's observance of the unities colludes in this effort by keeping the patricians physically offstage until the conspiracy has folded. The unstageable unity-in-multiplicity of the patrician rulers may thus figure as a malignant reflection of the beautifully proportioned unity-in-multiplicity of the Whig commonwealthmen, which is equally unrealizable. Pre-eminent among the excessive body parts is the hand, token of the conspirators' obsession with monstrous agency. The power of the Forty (plus the Ten) is figured, for example, as "the Briarean sceptre / Which in this hundred-handed senate rules / Making the people nothing" (1.2.268–70).[42] The people are "nothing" only because they are not a collective agent; in order to become something they must share, if nothing else, at

---

42. Another doge comes to the same conclusion in *The Two Foscari*: "The people!—There's no people, you well know it. / Else you dare not deal thus by them or me" (5.1.258–59).

least this fantasy of alienated agency. But the fantasy does little to arm them with what they need, another hundred hands; it saddles them, rather, with a hundred heads—the token not of augmented agency, but of atomized mental passivity, as in Wordsworth's use of the phrase "many-headed mass" to describe theater audiences (*Prelude* 1805 7:467).

There is classical precedent for coupling the hundred-handed giant that holds the scepter with the hundred-headed serpent that must be slain.[43] But the switch from monstrous hands to monstrous heads has a specific motive that comes to Byron from British political theory. Christopher Hill's essay on "The Many-Headed Monster" cites a wide range of early modern writers using this figure for the populace: Davenant, Dekker, Du Bartas, Massinger, Montaigne, Ramus, Sidney, and, of course, Shakespeare (in *Coriolanus*).[44] Hill's interest lies in the figure's potency during the revolutionary 1640s, when it appeared even in radical discourse. Its power resides in its traditional significance, easy to grasp in comparison with the shifting dynamics of class: "The idea that to be many-headed is the same as to be headless is easier to conceive metaphorically than literally. It relates to the theory of degree, to the conception of a graded society in which the feudal household and the family workshop or farm were the basic units. The many-headed monster was composed of masterless men, those for whom nobody responsible answered."[45] The fear expressed in this usage is that of an agency without responsibility: masterless men are hands without a head. The figure came to be used by more modern writers to cope with the diffused agency of the crowd, somewhat in the manner of the sublime tropology of *The Fall of Robespierre*. Thomas Hardy, for instance, would write of the London mob as "an organic whole, a molluscous

---

43. McGann mentions Schiller's *Fiesco* (1:13) as a source of the hydra image *Poetical Works* (4:551), but its connection with the hundred-handed giant was more readily available to Byron from classical sources such as *Aeneid* 6:287: "et centumgeminus Briareus ac belua Lernae."

44. G. Wilson Knight finds a thematic similarity between *Marino Faliero* and *Coriolanus* as plays whose heroes are driven by "a sense of honour so keen it approaches a 'vice' " (*Byron and Shakespeare* [London: Routledge and Kegan Paul, 1966] 227). Jonathan Bate develops independently the notion that "Byron saw himself as a Coriolanus who was rejected by his own people" (*Shakespeare and the English Romantic Imagination* [Oxford: Clarendon Press, 1986] 228).

45. Christopher Hill, *Change and Continuity in Seventeenth-Century England* (London: Weidenfeld and Nicolson, 1974) 182.

black creature having nothing in common with humanity, that takes the shape of the streets along which it has laid itself, and throws out horrid excrescences and limbs into neighboring alleys; a creature whose voice exudes from its scaly coat and who has an eye in every pore of its body."[46] Byron's use of the figure reverses its significance in passing it from earlier to later writers. Traditionally a hierarch's figure for the threat to hierarchy, it is used by Byron's doge, in addressing the men who would be masterless, to imagine the aristocracy from a populist viewpoint. It is the Venetian state that has become an agency without responsibility, while the people have come to bear their responsibilities with no hope of agency.[47]

The sequence of passages in which the figure appears displays its power to move men from theory to action. It appears first in the service of political theory, as a way of imagining the structure of the state which must be exchanged for a fair, free commonwealth. But political theory cannot exist apart from political rhetoric, as figures offering knowledge always threaten to initiate action. Early on, the doge agrees to hold sovereign power in a new commonwealth, provided

> that the people shared that sovereignty,
> So that nor they nor I were further slaves
> To this o'ergrown aristocratic Hydra,
> The poisonous heads of whose envenom'd body
> Have breathed a pestilence upon us all.
> (1.2.420–24)

The figure reappears in the doge's final call to action: "I tell you, you must strike, and suddenly, / Full to the Hydra's heart—its heads will follow" (3.2.238–39). As the necessity of slaying the Hydra is implicit in the very notion of a Hydra, so political theory will always entail a practical imperative. Yet who is there in Venice to "strike"? The play's

---

46. Quoted in Raymond Williams, *The Country and the City* (New York: Oxford University Press, 1973) 216.

47. I am contesting Julie Carlson's provocative argument that "*Marino Faliero* facilitates the subjection of the masses in its differential treatment of the assignment of guilt and responsibility . . . [O]nly the individual sovereign is exempt from being a sovereign individual; only he need not assume the responsibility of will. Precisely because the conspirators are a collective body, they must be viewed as individual agents. A minor character voices the necessity: 'It is the cause, and not our will, which asks / Such actions from our hands: we'll wash away / All stains in Freedom's fountain!'" (Carlson, *Theatre of Romanticism* 206–7).

political rhetoric tends not so much to project the possibility of individual action as to recall the insuperable preconditions for collective action. The fantasy of surplus body parts may be explained by the structure of the ruling bodies in Venice, which take their names from their number: "the Ten," "the Forty," and so on. A preoccupation with number, however, must be seen as a further development of the doge's discourse of lack, expressed in his claim that the people "are nothing in the state, and in / The city worse than nothing—mere machines" (1.2.301–2). Only the extremes on the spectrum of agency are occupied: as there is no place here for an agent with (say) two hands, rather than a hundred or none at all, so there is no possibility of conceiving the individual subject as a political agent capable of acting under its own direction. Political action slides repeatedly toward fiction, whether because it is not open to individuals or because, as the unimaginably absolute power of the monstrous aristocracy, it can only be localized in mythological figures.

We should not ask, as many critics have asked, whether Byron believes this, but only why the doge pretends to believe it. What purpose does the fantasy of agency serve? Like his earlier sublime diffusion of a generalized wrath, Faliero's idealization of the state's power makes agency unavailable to the individual—it is not his fault if he lacks it. Hence his need to personify the state: the state can be a character only abstractly or allegorically, and such a view allows individual characters to see their own agency as equally abstract and allegorical.[48] To say that political agency is all or nothing at all is to render individual power, which is inherently partial, inconceivable.

The necessity of a *total* revolution follows inevitably from the view that the aristocracy contains not one individual who might be singled out for mercy.[49] When the conspirators assemble in act 3, Philip Calendaro counters Bertram's appeal for pity in individual cases by allowing only

---

48. Lansdown sees this view of the state as a quality shared with Shakespeare's Roman plays (*Byron's Historical Dramas* 7).
49. See Bernard Yack, *The Longing for Total Revolution: Philosophic Sources of Social Discontent from Rousseau to Marx and Nietzsche* (Princeton: Princeton University Press, 1986). Yack's psychology of longing accounts for some of the directions revolutionary energies take in *Marino Faliero*: "while in desire our uneasiness focuses on the desired object, thus promoting attempts at its acquisition, in longing the awareness of our present incapacity to acquire the object diffuses our uneasiness. The energy produced by that uneasiness has no obvious outlet" (5).

>   such pity
> As when the viper hath been cut to pieces,
> The separate fragments quivering in the sun,
> In the last energy of venomous life,
> Deserve and have. Why, I should think as soon
> Of pitying some particular fang which made
> One in the jaw of the swoln serpent, as
> Of saving one of these: they form but links
> Of one long chain; one mass, one breath, one body;
> They eat, drink, and live, and breed together,
> Revel, and lie, oppress, and kill in concert,—
> So let them die as *one!*
>   (3.1.26–37)

Calendaro's totalizing rhetoric of terror, so graphic in its disgust for the body politic, is supported by a more remote allusion to the Hydra ("the swoln serpent"). This keynote sounds first in Faliero's voice, as he speaks an anxiety about bodily violation: "The whole must be extinguish'd; better that / They ne'er had been, than drag me on to be / The thing these arch-oppressors fain would make me" (1.2.321–23). The plebeians later pick up the figure to override the distinction between innocent and guilty: "all their acts are one— / A single emanation from one body, / Together knit for our oppression!" (3.2.285–87). Here we see the work done by the fantasy of the enemy as monstrous other: it makes that enemy not many but one. The conspirators cannot destroy the whole without destroying all its parts, just as, in the doge's image of a model commonwealth, one cannot lop off a part without mangling the whole.

Contemporary audiences, sensing the resistance of the many-headed monster to the attempt to slay it with irony, would have readily understood the slipperiness of the doge's attacks on his own class. Moreover, the dénouement makes it clear that the symmetrical opposition between a monstrous and an ideal state misrepresents the conflict between classes as a duel of equally matched agents. Such a duel can only degenerate into shadowboxing or, worse, what the doge will call "a game of mutual homicides" (4.2.289). The fantasy of a unified enemy makes the collective agent that opposes it into a double of that enemy, a phantasmatically singular agent susceptible of violent fragmentation. This false symmetry underwrites the fantasy of the patricians' total power and engenders a desire in the conspirators to seize total power for themselves. Yet this reversal only exposes the rhetoric of total revolution as an empty performance, for we can never entirely forget that the fantasy of the aristocracy as a unified enemy is belied by the bodily presence, on stage, of the doge among the conspirators.

The defection of Bertram, the apostate rebel Faliero calls "our Judas" (4.2.291), allows Byron to interpret the possibility of dissent—self-evident in the actions of the doge—as the possibility of a personal history distinct from the absorbing hegemony of political history. In remembering his childhood friendship with the patrician Lioni, whom he wishes to spare in the projected massacre, Bertram embraces the conspirators' stated faith that the highest good is to remember what is common to all humanity.[50] But his personal history leads Bertram to interpret that faith as a commitment to the inviolability of individuals rather than as an allegiance to a shared destiny. In childhood, we are led to believe, Lioni and Bertram were brought together across class lines merely by their sense of a shared humanity. Bertram clings to his belief in an inextricable bond with the aristocratic rulers whom the other conspirators would exclude from the common humanity they define in terms of a shared suffering: "the blood of tyrants is not human," they declare (4.2.163), with an extravagance matched only by Coleridge's English nobleman.

Bertram is significant in the logic of Byron's plot less for the humanistic values he voices than for preserving the last trace of recollection among the conspirators, whose rhetoric, after the initial statement of grievances, is entirely future-oriented. The conspiracy's failure to sway his affections thus appears as an instance of its more general inability to master the unpredictable interplay of anticipation and recollection, a failure we have seen in the doge's early vacillations between these two symmetrical vectors of desire. As though playing out Faliero's initial ambivalence, Bertram breaks from the movement toward a future social unity because he is moved to recollect (or invent) a past social unity. His actions close off a future by maintaining the power of the past,

---

50. Daniel Watkins emphasizes this somewhat platitudinous humanism in judging that the conspirators and their aristocratic leader "must learn to set particular class differences aside and explore their common social needs as human beings ... only by developing a social rather than simply a class perspective can they hope to mount a revolutionary campaign that will do more than merely reverse existing class structures" (*A Materialist Critique of English Romantic Drama* [Gainesville: University Press of Florida, 1993] 160).

even though his motivations bear a surprising resemblance to those of the other conspirators. Indeed, Bertram's humanist values can be traced to the same makeshift contract that first establishes the conspiracy. The plebeians and their doge come together on exactly the same grounds that bring Bertram and Lioni together: the possibility of common desires that cross class lines.

Bertram, then, does not reject the moral grounds on which the conspiracy is formed; he dissents from its conception of history. The conspirators' belief that the future can be entirely cut off from the past follows, as Rivers's utopian vision of "these disputed tracts" followed, from an assumption that individual histories are entirely absorbed in larger and more inexorable processes. They assume that the orphaned Bertram, absorbed either within the regime of repression or within the movement that opposes it, can have no private past that might obstruct the forward march of revolution. Bertram's being constrained by affective bonds thus, paradoxically, contributes to Byron's effort to rescue a sliver of personal freedom from a vision of absolute historical fatality. Just as Bertram can move against the flow of history *because* he is constrained by the past, so Byron gladly saddles himself with the constraints of historical fact in order to discover, in a newly politicized context, the freedom *Childe Harold* had formulated in its image of the banner that "Streams like the thunder-storm *against* the wind" (4.98).

The undoing of the stillborn conspiracy may be understood as refuting in advance Nietzsche's dictum that "forgetting is necessary for action of any kind."[51] *Marino Faliero* might seem, in many places, rather to confirm that maxim, above all in dramatizing the doge's vacillation between anticipation and recollection. Byron expresses his reservation, however, by making forgetfulness unavailable except in the form of moral blindness. Forgetting appears in *Marino Faliero* as an action that (turning Nietzsche's logic against itself) can never quite get underway except by means of a passive forgetfulness that degrades action into the customs and habits by which the past maintains its grip. Thus the speech that commits the doge to embracing the future is itself entirely directed toward the past:

---

51. Friedrich Nietzsche, "On the Uses and Disadvantages of History for Life," in *Untimely Meditations,* trans. R. J. Hollingdale (New York: Cambridge University Press, 1983) 83.

> Farewell all social memory! all thoughts
> In common! and sweet bonds which link old friendships,
> When the survivors of long years and actions,
> Which now belong to history, soothe the days
> Which yet remain by treasuring each other,
> And never meet, but each beholds the mirror
> Of half a century on his brother's brow,
> And sees a hundred beings, now in earth,
> Flit round them whispering of the days gone by,
> And seeming not all dead, as long as two
> Of the brave, joyous, reckless, glorious band,
> Which once were one and many, still retain
> A breath to sigh for them, a tongue to speak
> Of deeds that else were silent, save on marble—
> Oimé! Oimé!—and must I do this deed?
>
> (3.2.327–41)

Bertram's betrayal is thus, from a certain point of view, not a betrayal at all; indeed, in an echo of the doge, he claims that it is not even an act: "I did not seek this task; 'twas forced upon me" (5.1.130).[52] His defection merely translates into plot the recoil from agency already conceived by the doge, who is no more able to act on this conception than he is on any other. In this anti-Nietzschean reading, which might be tested on any number of passages about the desire for oblivion in Byron, the deformation of collective agency is built into the process of its formation as its mirror image, and the catastrophe of *Marino Faliero* is merely the plotting of this reflection.

4.

That universal recoil from action provides a context for interpreting the remarkable diagnosis Bertram delivers to Lioni identifying, in a metaphor of sorcery, what drives political action in Venice: "the accursed tyranny which rides / The very air in Venice, and makes men / Madden as in the last hours of the plague / Which sweeps the soul deliriously from life!" These lines might stand for the powerfully realistic form of magical thinking by which words are understood to cast a

---

52. Manning notes the echo of the Doge's line "the task / Is forced upon me, I have sought it not" (3.1.9–10); see *Byron and His Fictions* 120.

spell over political realities, as they are shown to do throughout the play but for the first time explicitly in Bertram's scene with Lioni. Lioni's celebrated nocturne, a calm before the storm unleashed by Bertram's defection, intimates this new understanding of the powerful spell cast by words.

Hazlitt criticized Lioni's speech as being too overtly concerned with its own diction, labelling it "a running allusion to the pending controversy between his Lordship, Mr. Bowles, and Mr. Campbell, on the merits of the natural and artificial style in poetry."[53] Lioni begins by recalling his feelings of uneasiness amidst the artificial splendors of a patrician ball, in a neo-Augustan style well suited to evoke "a dazzling mass of artificial light" (4.1.33). He then turns to describe the calm of the moonlit scene he now views, a scene still dominated (and here is the polemical allusion Hazlitt protests) by manmade objects:

> The high moon sails upon her beauteous way,
> Serenely smoothing o'er the lofty walls
> Of those tall piles and sea-girt palaces,
> Whose porphyry pillars, and whose costly fronts,
> Fraught with the orient spoil of many marbles,
> Like altars ranged along the broad canal,
> Seem each a trophy of some mighty deed
> Rear'd up from out the waters, scarce less strangely
> Than those more massy and mysterious giants
> Of architecture, those Titanian fabrics,
> Which point in Egypt's plains to times that have
> No other record. All is gentle: nought
> Stirs rudely; but, congenial with the night,
> Whatever walks is gliding like a spirit.
> (4.1.74–87)

Byron polemicizes not just in providing artificial objects made to the order of the descriptive poet, but also in borrowing for his poetry of artifice the historical weight of the monuments it describes, the indispensability of "a trophy of some mighty deed" that has left "no other record." This monumental aura of recollected agency is cast, ironically, by the moonlight "serenely smoothing o'er" both the visible scene and its verse description, blurring distinctions to the point where one

---

53. Hazlitt, *Works* 19:45.

scarcely perceives the oceanic fatalism in the claim that "mighty deed[s]" rear themselves up from the waters. Byron's verse leaves a momentary impression that "all is gentle" and that "nought / Stirs rudely," charming away Lioni's justified uneasiness with a poetic spell whose power will not be underestimated by an audience that has spent the evening watching a conspiracy unfold.

   The confrontation between Lioni and Bertram in the rest of the scene quickly evacuates the conspiracy plot, helping to clear a space for Byron to account, in his dénouement, for the political power of such spells. The conspirators' mistake, it now appears, lay in thinking that actions directed toward the future can break the spell of the past. That mistake appears in an exchange between Philip Calendaro and Israel Bertuccio:

> *Calendaro:* Better bow down before the Hun, and call
> A Tartar lord, than these swoln silkworms masters!
> The first at least was man, and used his sword
> As sceptre: these unmanly creeping things
> Command our swords, and rule us with a word
> As with a spell.
> *I.B.:*   It shall be broken soon.
>   (2.2.114–19)

The aggressive posture in which Israel draws his sword on the patrician spell of words nearly allows one to forget that that spell of words outlasted the threat of the Hun, proving its superior power. The ambiguous antecedent of Israel's "It" should make readers uneasy, with its hint that the conspiracy intending to break the *spell* can itself be undone if any of the conspirators breaks his *word*—a reminder that the conspiracy, too, is founded upon a spell of words. The difference between the patrician spell of words and that upon which the conspiracy is founded might be seen as identical to the difference between the absolutist's faith in the king's divinely sanctioned decrees and the Whig view of the government's foundation upon the performative efficacy of the people's consent. Without confirming the Tory argument—for at this point he has yet to show us a single patrician—Byron strips away the Whig illusion by showing that contractual performatives assume a freedom from the sway of magic spells that they are also supposed to bring about.

It would not be quite right to say that Byron is of the patricians' party without knowing it, as Hazlitt would have us think of any poet who trades in power. For Byron is fully aware of the power of spells, a power he has himself exercised in the fatalistic deconstructions of agency that recuperate power on the level of stylistic control. His awareness can be gauged from lines the doge speaks shortly after the exchange just quoted, when confronting Israel before a statue we are to take as a monument to the dead Falieri: "I tell thee, man, there is a spirit in / Such things that acts and sees, unseen, though felt; / And if there be a spell to stir the dead, / 'Tis in such deeds as we are now upon" (3.1.95–98). The doge understands how the patrician spell works. A spell that would stir the dead, here, can only be something that would stir the spell of the dead, enabling the dead to act and to see, unseen though felt in every effort to break their gaze. "Deeds" cannot break the spell of the past that constrains action in the present; they can only help keep that spell alive.

The doge's suspicion that deeds merely reinforce the spell of words leads, in his final speeches, to his counsel that "true *words* are *things,* / And dying men's are things which long outlive, / And oftentimes avenge them; bury mine, / If ye would fain survive me" (5.1.289–92). The juxtaposition of Faliero's full confession with his ironic plea to be silenced adds a strange twist to Byron's drama of agency. Silencing the doge (by keeping the people away from the scene of his execution) will help disarm any further threats to aristocratic power. Marino Faliero, the erstwhile patrician, wishes to acquiesce in this effort to silence him, even as the politically shrewd doge of Venice announces the futility of trying to break the spell of words. But the necessity of having him break his silence *here* does not eliminate Byron's desire to allow him his silence. "True *words* are *things* . . . bury mine": these lines convey the urgency of Byron's wish to confront us with what he is least able to dramatize, the silencing of his hero. A passing into permanent silence can hardly be accommodated to dramatic language, any more than an eternity of future history can be presented on a stage governed by the unity of time. Like the conspirators' fidelity to their social contract, the silence of the doge can only be promised in a prolepsis that can never assume either textual or stage presence.

Byron is left allowing the spell of his own dramatic words to help maintain the grip of Venice on the modern imagination, which he had described in canto 4 of *Childe Harold:*

> But unto us she hath a spell beyond
> Her name in story, and her long array
> Of mighty shadows, whose dim forms despond
> Above the dogeless city's vanish'd sway;
> Ours is a trophy which will not decay
> With the Rialto; Shylock and the Moor,
> And Pierre, cannot be swept or worn away.
>
> (4:4)

The fact that Byron characterizes this spell as being cast by fictional *persons* may help to explain why he wished to present the movement of history in terms of a fictive rendering of the conflicted *person* identified twice in his play's oxymoronic title: *Marino Faliero, Doge of Venice*. Byron's performances of fatalism always meant to overcome the diffusion or absorption of agency with a stylistic reassertion of his own biographical subject. In the political context into which *Marino Faliero* entered when it was staged in April 1821, that recuperation of personhood may be understood in terms of François Furet's view of the French Revolution as "the collective subordination of manifold, contingent individual life courses to the idea of an inevitable historical event, which is imagined as a massive effect that answers to a single, overpowering cause." Christensen extrapolates from this view that "the end of the Revolution, considered not as a conceptual break occurring within the terrain of French historiography but as a moment of change executed by Englishmen whose history had been bound up with the course of the Revolution, might begin with the renewal of biography."[54] *Marino Faliero* thus appears not just to mark the end of the Revolution but to satirize the unwitting conservatism of those who have failed to notice.

The *New Edinburgh Review* remarked of *Marino Faliero* that "the story of a commonwealth is not the fit subject of a tragedy."[55] Byron can be understood as demonstrating his profound agreement. As Shelley would realize in his effort to write a tragedy on the events that established England's short-lived commonwealth, the story of a com-

---

54. Christensen, "Ecce Homo: Biographical Acknowledgment, the End of the French Revolution, and the Romantic Reinvention of English Verse," in *Contesting the Subject: Essays in the Postmodern Theory and Practice of Biography and Biographical Criticism*, ed. William H. Epstein (West Lafayette: Purdue University Press, 1991) 54; paraphrasing Furet, *Interpreting the French Revolution*.

55. *New Edinburgh Review*, July 1821 (*Romantics Reviewed* B:2:807).

monwealth can become tragic only by being presented as the story of a person who stands for, *and* against, that commonwealth, in a position the *Monthly Magazine* shrewdly identified as "a solecism of state, a kind of political paradox." Faliero, that reviewer writes, "commits, as it were, high treason against himself; and leagues with a band of malcontents, who by discomfiture became rebels, to cut down the overgrown aristocracy of his city, and set up in its place, the likeness of a free government in his own person." [56] Committing high treason against himself, the Suicide King claims an absolute sovereignty whose political correlate is at best "the likeness of a free government." It is this *likeness* that Byron attacked by tracing the simulacrum of liberty to anxieties of impaired agency on the part of whomever would aspire to institute it in his own person, whether it be the Prince Regent or Arthur Thistlewood. In doing so, he displays both the political force and the limitations of the gesture by which he had, so often, diffused his own agency into a spell of words that can be buried but not broken.

56. *Monthly Magazine*, July 1821 (*Romantics Reviewed* B:4:1677).

6

History's Lethean Song: *Charles the First* and *The Triumph of Life*

> To see all human race, from the beginning of time, pass, as it were, in review before us; appearing in their true colours, without any of those disguises, which, during their life-time, so much perplexed the judgment of the beholders: What spectacle can be imagined, so magnificent, so various, so interesting? What amusement, either of the senses or imagination, can be compared with it?
> —HUME, "Of the Study of History"

At a turning point in *The Triumph of Life* when Rousseau, Shelley's guide to the hell of history, is recalling his own entrance into that hell, it becomes suddenly unclear—as it had for Mortimer in *The Borderers* —whether his story is about what he has done or what has been done to him. Historical narrative, the attractive packaging in which we wrap our beliefs about agency, appears in this passage as a Romantic defense against the randomness of life:

> I among the multitude
> Was swept; me sweetest flowers delayed not long,
>   Me not the shadow nor the solitude,
>
> Me not the falling stream's Lethean song,
>   Me, not the phantom of that early form
> Which moved upon its motion,—but among

> The thickest billows of the living storm
> I plunged....
> (460–67)

The solitary autobiographer mirrors himself in the flowers, music, and visionary phantoms he claims to have outgrown, delaying or dallying once again, though "not long." Shelley's anaphoric arrangement of this verbal meandering calls attention to the commanding position of Rousseau's self-objectifying "me not," exposing the rhetorical sleight of hand by which the "Lethean song" of personal history converts passivity into activity, "I was swept" into "I plunged." Rousseau can hardly be condemned for revising his story to replace the passive with the active voice, but he does provide an opportunity to reflect on the moral problem that rhetorician's trick conceals. In a poem that presents the sweep of history not merely as all that *exists* in the past, present, and future, but as "the sphere / Of all that is, has been, or will be *done*" (104–5, emphasis added), Rousseau's shift seems to hollow out the active voice, suspending whatever certainties the narrative grammar might have been conveying about history's being governed by decisive actions. Shelley is not asking his reader to choose between the active and the passive aspect of Rousseau's account; he is foreclosing both alternatives, to make his reader share in the unaccountability of what he has called "Life."[1]

Shortly after finishing *The Cenci,* Shelley had argued in his essay "On Life" that "*I,* and *you* and *they* are grammatical devices invented simply for arrangement and totally devoid of the intense and exclusive sense usually attached to them" (478). Now he extends the observation to the narrative grammar of agency, implying that *active* and *passive* are only fictive impositions divvying up an undifferentiated unity of Life. In the first case Shelley follows Hume's assertion in "Of Personal Identity" that "All the nice and subtle questions concerning personal identity

---

1. Shelley does not simply endorse the Derridean yearning for "a system that no longer tolerates the opposition of activity and passivity" in having Rousseau grope toward the middle voice that Derrida accuses philosophy of having "distributed into an active and a passive voice, thereby constituting itself by means of this repression" ("Différance," in *Margins of Philosophy,* trans. Alan Bass [Chicago: University of Chicago Press, 1982] 9, 16). He uses Rousseau's equivocation, rather, to show that an inability to *tolerate* the opposition of activity and passivity leads not to an overcoming but to an intensification of repression, occasioned by a moral disorientation that is debilitating rather than liberating.

can never possibly be decided, and are to be regarded rather as grammatical than as philosophical difficulties."[2] In the second he seems to respond to Thomas Reid's attempt, in his *Essays on the Active Powers of Man,* to identify a grammatical rather than a philosophical difficulty in Hume's claim that "we have no idea of power." Reid contends that we *must* have an idea of power because "there is no language so imperfect, but that it has active and passive verbs . . . the one signifying some kind of action; the other the being acted upon." Anticipating objections —"that active verbs are not always used to denote an action, nor is the nominative before an active verb, conceived in all cases to be an agent, in the strict sense of the word; that there are many passive verbs which have an active signification, and active verbs which have a passive"— Reid admits that languages retain traces of the mythical thinking by which, "to a child, or to a savage, all nature seems to be animated," because we "judge of other things by ourselves, and therefore are disposed to ascribe to them that life and activity which we know to be in ourselves." Such thoughts led an active life among the poets of the first generation, where they assumed considerably greater power than Reid's critique of them. Shelley might, on that basis, have been ready to see how Reid's recourse to grammar in affirming the clarity of our ideas about agency ends up qualifying commonsensical beliefs about agency as myths that language constructs out of experience. "An active and a passive are the capital [voices]," Reid asserts; "some languages have more, but no language so many as to answer to all the variations of human thought." One can imagine Shelley reading this as a confirmation of Hume: we have no idea, only various inchoate experiences, of power.[3]

When *The Cenci* allows Beatrice to suspend judgment on her own deed—"Which is or is not what men call a crime, / Which either I have done, or have not done; / Say what ye will" (5.3.84–85)—Shelley reminds us not of the middle voice(s) Reid has in mind, but of the logical axiom of the excluded middle. Beatrice's wish, bound up with her earlier derivation of agency from the suspension of identity pro-

---

2. Hume, *Treatise* 310.
3. Thomas Reid, *Essays on the Active Powers of Man* (Edinburgh, 1788), essay 1, chap. 2; quoted from the Garland facsimile reprint (New York, 1977) 13–22. Shelley reported to Godwin his early reading in "Locke, Hume, Reid & whatever metaphysics came in my way" (Shelley, *Letters* 1:303); he was also familiar with Drummond's attacks on Reid in the final chapter of *Academical Questions.*

voked by her suffering of embodiment, is *to avoid* excluding that middle—her persecutors will exclude it for her. Rousseau's gesture in *The Triumph of Life,* by contrast, signals not a problem in the grounding of justice posed by a case of discontinuous identity, but a problem in the rhetorical generation of beliefs about agency. Shelley's turn from questions about identity to beliefs about action should be understood in terms of his attempt, toward the end of his career, to strengthen his poetry's political claims by immersing himself in historical study. He may have been encouraged by Byron's attempts to place modern revolutionary movements in a historical perspective; *Marino Faliero*'s performances of fatalism should prepare us to see that Rousseau's equivocation exemplifies a rhetorical gesture that has a central place in both Byron's and Shelley's late explorations of history. Byron gives similar treatment to the "cloud of witnesses" that appears in *The Vision of Judgment:* "Like an aërial ship it tacked, and steered, / Or was steered" (st. 57). In a poem offering a last judgment on George III, it should make all the difference to know whether the people direct their own movements or are led by the nose; but who, asks Byron's grammatical equivocation, can make that distinction with any authority? The problem is more pervasive than such local instances can suggest. In *The Triumph of Life,* the juggernaut of history *either* moves under its own power *or* is driven along by its "Janus-visaged Shadow" (94): who can be sure which? Nor can the problem be confined within Shelley's text: while writing *The Triumph of Life,* Shelley *either* fell victim to a boating accident and tragically died *or* suicidally gave his sails to the tempest and sailed into Eternity. Rousseau's story suggests that we construct such narratives because we are unable to conceive life (or death) as a random process in which our involvement is never finally settled as active or passive.

With such skeptical cautions in mind, what can we venture to say Shelley *did* in attempting to grapple with the place of the individual agent in larger historical patterns? How will we determine whether Rousseau, or Shelley, performs or merely suffers the equivocation in which history catches him? Such are the complex questions—partly historical, partly aesthetic, partly moral—posed by the politically-charged poetics that emerged from Shelley's relation to the skeptical tradition, as explored in Chapter 4. Whether Shelley answered such questions, or how he managed to evade them, can be judged from his late attempts to dramatize the pressures that history exerts on persuasions about agency. Shelley's late understanding of history is best approached, however, not (as many critics have tried to approach it) by examining *The Triumph of Life* in isolation, but by tracing, in the broader context of the end of Shelley's career, how he followed Hume's turn from skeptical epistemology to political history.[4] If Humean skepticism provides the background for Shelley's first attempt at stage drama, Humean historiography provides the background for his last: *Charles the First,* the historical drama Shelley began writing in January 1822, whose fragmentary drafts provide an indispensable context for reading *The Triumph of Life*.[5]

What survives of *Charles the First* cannot afford any sure view of Shelley's project. Aside from a sketch of the first two acts and various disconnected fragments, Shelley left four more or less complete scenes. The first recreates a pageant both celebrating and subtly challenging the power of King Charles and his court; the second moves into the court for an exposition of the religious, political, and economic causes of the Civil War, punctuated by prophetic jests from the court fool; the third offers the Gothic spectacle of the Star Chamber; the fourth shows the principal Puritan leaders on the verge of departing for America. These four scenes, while they do not convey a dramatic structure, do act out different aspects of political language, focusing on a single

---

4. In his essay "Apocalyptic Scepticism: The Imagery of Shelley's 'The Triumph of Life'" (*Keats-Shelley Journal* 27 [1978]: 70–86), Lloyd Abbey promises to show how Shelley's final poem can be read as "the poetic portrayal of total Humean scepticism" (70), but he pays almost no attention to Hume.

5. *Charles the First* was conceived before *The Cenci* but begun in earnest only in 1822. Shelley initially regarded the subject as a project for Mary, probably as a result of having heard of Godwin's plans to write a book on *The Lives of the Commonwealth Men*. The plan is recalled in letters of July 1820, January 1821, and October 1821, but real work on *Charles the First* probably did not begin until January, 1822; Shelley's program for the first two acts survives in a notebook in the Huntington Library dating from this time. Nora Crook gives an excellent account of the fragments' composition in the introduction to *The Bodleian Shelley Manuscripts*, vol. 12 (New York: Garland, 1991). The relevant manuscripts are: MS. Shelley adds. e. 17, pp. 33–52, 55, 93b, 185rev.–93b, and c. 4, f. 136. Ancillary materials will be found in two of the three Shelley notebooks held by the Huntington Library, San Marino, California: the manuscripts are catalogued as HM 2111, and the relevant locations are notebook I, *12r, p. 185 and notebook III, 10v–11v, pp. 19–20. Since I have consulted both Crook's facsimile and the original manuscripts for the passages I quote from *Charles the First,* my citations refer both to pages in the manuscript and to scene and line numbers from the most commonly available redaction, in *The Complete Poetical Works of Percy Bysshe Shelley,* ed. Thomas Hutchinson (New York: Oxford University Press, 1965).

concern: the relation between the power of political language and the power of dramatic spectacle. *Charles the First* reveals Shelley's attempt to displace the allure of spectacle with a language capable of undoing the complicity between power and its representation in the spectacular manipulation of words and bodies, and so to remove historical drama from the vicious ironies of power that it displays. In *The Triumph of Life*, which exhibits history *sub specie aeternitatis*, Shelley is free to declare that "God made irreconcilable / Good and the means of good" (230–31) and can thus simply assume—whatever the political consequences—an ironic relation between utopian aspirations and their historical outcomes. *Charles the First* can make no such assumption, for Shelley's aim was to exhibit, on the politically charged Regency stage, the relation of freedom to bondage, using whatever means history offered.

It might then be said that the vision of history eclipsed in *The Triumph of Life* shines forth in *Charles the First*. The exact shape of the unfinished poem's political darkness can be made visible only by referring its scenes of posthistorical destruction, in which "Life" cannibalizes agency, back to the scenes of the historical drama in which Shelley brings that agency to Life. It would be hard to exaggerate his disappointment, a month before his death, at finding himself unable to go on with the play: "I write little now," he confessed in a letter to John Gisborne; "I do not go on with 'Charles the First.' I feel too little certainty of the future, and too little satisfaction with regard to the past, to undertake any subject seriously and deeply."[6] His decision not to go on with the play, tied as it was to his work on the new poem, was itself a deep and serious undertaking. Rousseau's ghostwritten autobiography in *The Triumph of Life* surely implies a rejection of the humanistic premises of historical drama, which is bound to represent history with the actions of significant individuals. But what motivated Shelley's rejection of drama? The generic shift toward Shelley's final poem entails a movement away from the bodies on stage that had threatened to drag down his utopian imaginings in *The Cenci*, and toward those disembodied powers of language that can be glimpsed in a drama but that cannot be confined to the stage. Yet Shelley knew better than simply to deny or renounce embodiment, a condition always acknowl-

---

6. 18 June 1822; Shelley, *Letters* 2:436.

edged in his own political struggles, however utopian. The significance of Shelley's movement away from drama can come to view only in a full account of the relation between *Charles the First* and *The Triumph of Life,* an account that might begin with a catalogue of themes and images they share as a result of their having been composed, to some extent, together during Shelley's last spring.[7] But these common elements explain little unless one has a sense of what Shelley learned from the historical research he undertook in preparing to write *Charles the First*. I will begin, therefore, by reconstructing Shelley's understanding of history with an eye to the relation between its manifestations in *The Triumph of Life* and in the opening scene of *Charles the First,* which (unlike other drafted scenes) Shelley left in something like a final version. Stuart Curran has compared this scene to the experiments of Pirandello, calling it "Shelley's most ambitious attempt yet to present a drama that looked continually into itself as into a mirror even as it represented itself to readers or auditors as a spectacle to contemplate and through which to contemplate themselves."[8] What he does not remark upon is Shelley's motive for building his house of mirrors in the amusement park of British historiography. It has sometimes been thought (first by Shelley's friend Thomas Medwin) that *Charles the First* is riven by the Shelleyan ambivalence Peacock's *Nightmare Abbey* expressed hyperbolically in the character Scythrop, who loves both Stella and Marionetta, both the passionate revolutionary star and the puppet of civil society. The complex relations between Shelley's sources, however, reveal in his project a far more intractable irony.

---

7. Few critics have even begun to note the shared elements. Neville Rogers ventures that the procession in *Charles the First* "may not be a wholly unrelated predecessor in Shelley's mind of the 'Sad pageantry' of *The Triumph of Life*" (*Shelley at Work: A Critical Inquiry* [Oxford: Clarendon Press, 1967] 281). Richard Holmes traces similarities in imagery to the carnivals in Pisa, where the Shelleys resided intermittently between 1820 and 1822 (*Shelley: The Pursuit* 577, 697, 718). R. B. Woodings offers the most provocative lead: "confronted alone by history Shelley either must gesture towards the protection of the ever-returning cycles of the ages or admit to being trapped in the horror itself. The ambiguities of the latter position he treated in *The Triumph of Life,* and not the least of the claims of *Charles the First* is that its composition led Shelley to the imagery and concepts that were to be explored in that last remarkable poem" (" 'A Devil of a Nut to Crack': Shelley's *Charles the First,*" *Studia Neophilologica* 40 [1968]: 237).

8. Stuart Curran, "Shelleyan Drama," in *The Romantic Theatre: An International Symposium,* ed. Richard Allen Cave (Totowa, N.J.: Barnes and Noble, 1986) 68.

I.

Scholars have identified the histories Shelley read in preparing to write *Charles the First* but have done little to probe his understanding of them. Alhough he consulted the Restoration memoirs of Bulstrode Whitlocke and Edward Hyde, Earl of Clarendon, his two main sources were the mid-eighteenth-century histories written by Hume and by Catharine Macaulay.[9] Hume's skeptical method seems to have appealed to Shelley, for he used Humean terms in describing his project to Medwin: "I mean to write a play, in the spirit of human nature, without prejudice or passion, entitled 'Charles the First.' "[10] Hume had conceived his *History of England* as a critical intervention in the historiographic mythmaking of the Walpole administrations, showing how historical narratives organize "prejudice or passion" to produce historical agents: not the phantom agents of personal histories like Rousseau's, but agents defined by everyday political maneuverings. By extending the skeptical method of the *Treatise of Human Nature* to a critique of partisan myths about England's past, Hume meant to establish a foundation for defending the legitimacy not of any particular theory of government (Whig or Tory) but of accepted customs and practices. Reading the skeptical Hume in an atmosphere permeated by Burkean conservatism, Shelley might well have felt discomfort with Hume's qui-

---

9. Kenneth Neill Cameron has identified four sources for Shelley's play: Whitlocke's *Memorials of the English Affairs* (1682), Clarendon's *History of the Rebellion* (1702–7), Hume's *History of England* (1754–62) and Macaulay's *History of England* (1769–72); see "Shelley's Use of Source Material in *Charles I*," *Modern Language Quarterly* 6 (1945): 197–210 and *Shelley: The Golden Years* (Cambridge: Harvard University Press, 1974) 411–21. Woodings contests and augments Cameron's arguments in "Shelley's Sources for *Charles the First*," *Modern Language Review* 64 (1969): 267–75. Shelley seems to have used the "Regents Edition" of Hume's history; his notes are preserved in Bodleian Library, MS Shelley adds. e. 7, now available in *The Bodleian Shelley Manuscripts*, vol. 16, ed. Donald H. Reiman and Michael J. Neth (New York: Garland, 1994). The accounts of Shelley's sources have neglected at least one source I think likely: William Allen's "well-known pamphlet" *Killing No Murder* (1657), which Shelley asked Thomas Medwin to send him in 1819; see Medwin's *Life* 340. This text's revolutionary afterlife is detailed in Olivier Lutaud, *Des révolutions d'Angleterre à la révolution Française* (The Hague: Martinus Nijhoff, 1973): it was was reissued in 1792 by the Society for Constitutional Information, and the 1658 French translation was reprinted in 1793 with the original title page. Byron has Marino Faliero allude to the title when he speaks of stabbing Israel Bertuccio "to save / A thousand lives, and, killing, do no murder" (3.2.505).

10. July, 1820; Shelley, *Letters* 2:219–20.

etism. Macaulay's radical critique of Hume would have confirmed Shelley's suspicions, although her dogmatic simplifications might also have renewed his respect for Hume's method.

It was once thought that Hume wrote his political essays, and ultimately his *History*, in a fit of alarm at the force of his own skepticism in the *Treatise*.[11] Hume's defense of habit and custom as sources of political stability seemed a conservative defense against rationalist destroyers of old faiths, among whom Hume might have come to count himself. More recently, Hume's *History* has been taken as a salutary extension of his epistemological skepticism in book 1 of the *Treatise*, following the path of books 2 and 3 in erecting out of habit and custom a bulwark not against doubt but against abstract political dogmas. Hume's critique of "the Whig interpretation of history" is now understood, as it was by few when the *History* began to appear in 1754, as applying the skeptical method equally to historical myths promulgated by both Whigs and Tories.[12] Nicholas Phillipson characterizes Hume's approach as "a philosophical whiggery bent on playing off the crude anti-intellectualism of ministerial propagandists against the intellectual strengths of opposition historiography."[13] Hume deemed himself "a Whig, but a very sceptical one," and saw his politics as having split his subject matter along two opposed vectors: "My views of things are more conformable to Whig principles; my representations of persons to Tory prejudices." He attributed misconceptions of his politics to a stylistic difficulty Shelley would discover for himself, the unwarranted affective power of the moments in any history that dramatize the actions of persons. "Nothing can so much prove that men commonly regard more persons than things," he wrote, "as to find that I am commonly numbered among the Tories."[14]

---

11. Carl Becker, *The Heavenly City of the Eighteenth-Century Philosophers* [New Haven: Yale University Press, 1959] 83.

12. For critical perspectives on the view of Hume as a Tory, see E. C. Mossner, "Was Hume a Tory Historian? Facts and Considerations," *Journal of the History of Ideas* 2 (1941): 225–36 and H. R. Trevor-Roper, "Hume as a Historian," in *David Hume: A Symposium*, ed. D. F. Pears (New York: St. Martin's Press, 1966) 89–100.

13. Nicholas Phillipson, *Hume* (London: Weidenfeld & Nicolson, 1989) 85.

14. To John Clephane (?1756); *The Letters of David Hume*, ed. J. Y. T. Grieg (Oxford: Clarendon Press, 1932) 1:237. Leo Braudy explains that "the Tory view of history concentrated upon personalities, while the Whig emphasized the teleological growth of abstract principles, like liberty," but he sees Hume's emphasis on personalities as distinct from both lines in having a moral rather than a political aim (see *Narrative Form in History and Fiction: Hume, Fielding, and Gibbon* [Princeton: Princeton University Press,

Among the *things* Hume sought to establish was that the ancient or Saxon constitution was a myth promulgated to support the Whig interpretation of 1688, an argument that would have seemed backward to reformers in Shelley's time. In 1754, however, Hume's *History* would have accorded well with recent Whig efforts to shift the grounding of government from a mythical medieval precedent (then being invoked by the Tories) to a notion of rights established by nature and reason. But the *History*'s consonance with the updated Whig line could not override the affective power of the doings and sufferings of *persons* in Hume's dramatic recreations, particularly his account of the martyred Charles I, which was decisive in shaping the *History*'s reception. As Hume later recalled, in an ironic voice close to that of the *History* itself: "I was assailed by one cry of reproach, disapprobation, and even detestation; English, Scotch, and Irish, Whig and Tory, churchman and sectary, freethinker and religionist, patriot and courtier, united in their rage against the man, who had presumed to shed a generous tear for the fate of Charles I."[15] Hume himself came to realize the naiveté of his early pose as "impartial," although Voltaire, a suspicious reader if there ever was one, always agreed with that judgment. Assumptions about Hume's Tory leanings, then, are largely the result of partisan anxieties stirred by the *dramatic* component of a project begun as an exercise in political irony.[16]

Such a project might have held a strong appeal for the Shelley of *A Philosophical View of Reform*. Yet the *History*'s reputation among Shelley's acquaintance had been forcefully diminished by Catharine Macaulay's critical response. The introduction to her *History of England* positions her as one of the partisan enthusiasts Hume had written his *History* to disarm. When she was a child reading about England's

---

1970] 50). Hume's remark about being a very skeptical Whig is quoted in Rodney W. Kilcup's introduction to Hume, *The History of England*, abridged edition (Chicago: University of Chicago Press, 1975) xviii. By far the best overview of Hume's politics is to be found in Duncan Forbes, *Hume's Philosophical Politics* (New York: Cambridge University Press, 1975); for background on the narrower question of the politics entailed by an epistemological skepticism, see John Christian Laursen, *The Politics of Skepticism in the Ancients, Montaigne, Hume, and Kant* (New York: Brill, 1992).

15. Hume, "My Own Life," in *Essays Moral, Political, and Literary*, ed. Eugene F. Miller (Indianapolis: Liberty Classics, 1987) xxxvii.

16. For Voltaire's views on Hume, see Victor G. Wexler, *David Hume and the History of England* (Philadelphia: American Philosophical Society, 1979) 20–21. On the general relation between Hume's historical style and his wish to maintain a political detachment, see John Valdimir Price, *The Ironic Hume* (Austin: University of Texas Press, 1965).

past, she recalls, "Liberty became the object of a secondary worship in my delighted imagination." She writes now to convey that enthusiasm:

> With regret do I accuse my country of inattention to the most exalted of their benefactors: Whilst they enjoy privileges unpossessed by other nations, they have lost a just sense of the merit of the men by whose virtues these privileges were attained; men who, with the hazard and even the loss of their lives attacked the formidable pretensions of the Stewart family, and set up the banners of Liberty against a tyranny which had been established for a series of more than one hundred and fifty years; and this by the exertion of faculties, which, if compared with the barren produce of modern time, appear more than human.

Macaulay's first motive is to set the record straight where it has been distorted by the so-called impartiality of historians who "confound together in one undistinguished group the exalted patriots who have illustriously figured in this country, with those time-serving placemen who have sacrificed the most essential interests of the public to the baseness of their private affections." But she also hopes her *History* will alert readers to the lurking enemies of liberty: "This faction has not only prevented the establishing any regular system to preserve or improve our liberties; but lie at this time in wait for the first opportunity which the imperfections of this government may give them to destroy those rights, which have been purchased by the toil and blood of the most exalted individuals who ever adorned humanity."[17] Such claims would speak to the Shelley who was predisposed, with some justice, to see a conspiracy of secret agents behind every new step in his government's march of repression.

Given Macaulay's republican enthusiasms, it was inevitable that her chief difference from Hume, on the matter of the ancient constitution and the Norman Yoke, would appear most clearly in their disagreement on the causes of the Civil War. This was certainly the point of most heated contestation in the political climate of the mid-eighteenth century, and it was the problem Hume had chosen as the starting point from which he would ultimately construct his narrative both forwards and backwards. "I commenced with the accession of the House of Stuart," he wrote in his autobiography, "an epoch when, I thought, the

---

17. Catharine Macaulay, *The History of England from the Accession of James I to the Elevation of the House of Hanover*, 3d ed. (London, 1769) 1:vii, vi, xii.

misrepresentations of faction began chiefly to take place."[18] Responding to his complimentary copy of Macaulay's *History*, Hume again chose the matter of Stuart prerogative as the ground on which to defend himself:

> I cannot but think, that the mixed monarchy of England, such as it was left by Queen Elizabeth, was a lawful form of government, and carried obligations to obedience and allegiance; at least it must be acknowledged, that the princes and ministers who supported that form, tho' somewhat arbitrarily, could not incur much blame on that account; and that there is more reason to make an apology for their antagonists than for them.

Macaulay's retort was forthright in diagnosing the political consequences of Hume's skeptical detachment:

> Every kind of government may be legal, but sure all are not equally expedient; and an individual, who rigorously maintains and enlarges his power, in opposition to the inclination and welfare of a people, is, in my opinion, highly criminal. Your position, that all governments established by custom and authority carry with them obligations to submission and allegiance, does, I am afraid, involve all reformers in unavoidable guilt, since opposition to established error must needs be opposition to authority.[19]

The anti-Burkean animus of the reform movement would, on this point, have made Shelley's agreement with Macaulay nearly automatic.

Macaulay's *History* was popular among the dissenters who had made up the intellectual circle of Shelley's father-in-law, William Godwin. Joseph Priestley was explicit in presenting "the very masterly history of Mrs. Macaulay" as "a good antidote to what is unfavourable to liberty in Mr. Hume."[20] Mary Wollstonecraft characterized her as "the

---

18. Hume, "My Own Life" xxxvi. The major defenders of the "ancient constitution" in the Romantic period were Burke and Coleridge. The best source on Burke's antecedents is J. G. A. Pocock, "Burke and the Ancient Constitution," in *Politics, Language and Time* (New York: Atheneum, 1971). David Aram Kaiser calls *On the Constitution of Church and State* "Coleridge's cumulative attempt to present a *theoretical* account of the traditional ancient Constitution, of which Burke was a prominent and often *antitheoretical* defender" (" 'The Perfection of Reason': Coleridge and the Ancient Constitution," *Studies in Romanticism* 32 [1993]: 32).

19. Quoted in "Account of the Life and Writings of Mrs. Catherine [*sic*] Macaulay Graham," *The European Magazine and London Review* 4 (1783): 331.

20. Joseph Priestley, *Lectures on History and General Policy* (1803) 1:340; quoted in Bridget Hill, *The Republican Virago: The Life and Times of Catharine Macaulay, Historian* (Oxford: Clarendon Press, 1992) 40.

woman of the greatest abilities, undoubtedly, that this country has ever produced."[21] Godwin himself spoke for the milieu loyal to Macaulay when he wrote, in 1809, of recent attempts to varnish the character of Charles I:

> The years of his reign are a momentous period to the friends & the enemies of the liberties of mankind, & the latter are deeply interested in having him painted as the most innocent & unoffending of his species. Hume, I should hope, had a soul superior to the base desire of paying court to the men in power of his time; but he was influenced, partly by a motive very familiar to his temper, the love of paradox, & the inclination to support what at least looked like falshood, & partly by the feeling that the tragic fate of his hero afforded the materials of an elegant & pathetic tale.[22]

The indignation that met the publication of Hume's *History* in the generation preceding the French Revolution resonated in the echo chamber of the generation following it, establishing an atmosphere in which Shelley's preference for Macaulay's *History* might seem assured.

Yet skeptical tendencies within the same milieu might have prompted Shelley to take Hume more seriously than Godwin seems to take him. Godwin himself might more justly have considered his own debt to Hume's *History*, whose most lasting effect was to instill in free-thinking readers a skepticism toward all historical accounts. Godwin's rebuttal of Hume does not dissent from Hume's method, but extends to Hume the same skepticism that Hume had been the first to apply to English history. That method can be seen, for example, in Hume's remarks on available accounts of Cromwell:

> The writers, attached to the memory of this wonderful person, make his character, with regard to abilities, bear the air of the most extravagant panegyric: His enemies form such a representation of his moral qualities as resembles the most virulent invective. Both of them, it must be confessed, are supported by such striking circumstances in his conduct and fortune as bestow on their representation a great air of probability.[23]

21. Mary Wollstonecraft, *A Vindication of the Rights of Woman*, 2d ed., ed. Carol H. Poston (New York: Norton, 1988) 105.
22. William Godwin, "Interview of Charles I & Sir William Davenant," in *Shelley and His Circle*, ed. Kenneth Neill Cameron (Cambridge: Harvard University Press, 1961) 1:448–49.
23. Hume, *The History of Great Britain* (Edinburgh, 1754), chap. 61, 7:295–96. Braudy gives considerable attention to Hume's treatment of Cromwell (see *Narrative Form* 51–61).

Hume's use of the term "wonderful" is ironic, not because Hume hated Cromwell but because a contradictory character would appear, in Hume's history, not as some miraculous prodigy but as an epitome of the problem of locating bundles of perceptions within the order of history—as a typical case, that is, of the difficulties that justify the skeptical method. Godwin makes this point explicit in an essay of 1797, turning the screw of Hume's irony to argue that history is merely a form of romance generically prohibited from acknowledging its fictionality. He cites competing accounts of the Civil War as the most obvious support for his definition of history as a kind of fiction subject to disagreement:

> Whitlocke and Clarendon, who lived upon the spot, differ as much in their view of the transactions, as Hume and the whig historians have since done. Yet all are probably honest. If you be a superficial thinker, you will take up with one or another of their representations, as best suits your prejudices. But, if you are a profound one, you will see so many incongruities and absurdities in all, as deeply to impress you with the skepticism of history.[24]

Here Godwin confirms Hume's method by impugning his politics. But what is the political significance of this attempt to amalgamate history and romance? Is "the skepticism of history" a function of Godwin's early radicalism, or is it what ultimately suspended that radicalism? Was it in spite of the dubiousness of all Civil War histories, or was it out of a fascination deriving from "the skepticism of history," that Godwin would prompt Shelley to add another fiction to the pile before adding his own in *The History of the Commonwealth* (1824–28)?

Shelley's use of both Hume and Macaulay might be seen as following the advice of Joseph Towers, an early reviewer who expressed a hope that readers, "after they have perused Mr. Hume's *History* . . . will qualify it with a *quant. suf.* of Mrs. Macaulay's; and the real state of truth and things may probably be found in the mean between them."[25] No serious reader of Hume's *Treatise* would presume that "the real state of truth" could be easily located by balancing two accounts. After

---

24. William Godwin, "Of History and Romance," first published as an appendix in *Things As They Are, or The Adventures of Caleb Williams*, ed. Maurice Hindle (New York: Penguin, 1988) 371.

25. Joseph Towers, *Westminster Magazine* 6 (1778): 230; quoted in B. Hill, *Republican Virago* 43.

the 1790s there was, however, a more pressing reason to read Hume with Macaulay, for both had become well known for the use that had been made of them during the French Revolution. Hume's *History*, translated immediately into French by the Abbé Prévost, came to be widely regarded in France as the masterwork of "the English Tacitus," and was generally prized by the ancien régime for its "impartial" report on the fall of King Charles and his French queen. By the 1790s, Hume had gained a vast audience in France, including the king himself, who was said to have read the *History* while awaiting execution. Macaulay's *History* did not appear in French until 1791, but it was an immediate success in Brissotin circles, to which it was recommended by its translator Mirabeau. Mirabeau reportedly made a direct correlation between Macaulay's account of the Civil War and the ongoing events in France: "In our present circumstances, this translation is no ordinary work. There are so many points of contact, so many relations between these events and personages and us, that to note them all would be to write a parallel history of the two revolutions."[26] Shelley's use of both Hume and Macaulay does not indicate an "impartial" attempt to cover the range of available partisan perspectives; Macaulay might have taught him to discern a reactionary politics in any such claim to impartiality, had he not already taught others, in *The Cenci*, the meaning of the pope's claim to a "blameless neutrality" (2.2.40). It indicates, rather, Shelley's awareness of the inescapable topicality not only of his material but also of his method.

That topicality was still ineluctible in the early 1820s, for attempts to correlate the English and French Revolutions had become central to the Reform movement's search for a history in which its own efforts might meet greater success than the French had found.[27] Shelley himself

26. Catharine Macaulay, *Histoire d'Angleterre*, avis de l'éditeur, I.ix; quoted in Laurence L. Bongie, *David Hume: Prophet of the Counter-revolution* (Oxford: Clarendon Press, 1965) 114–15; my translation. My account of the French reception of Hume and Macaulay derives from Bongie.

27. *Charles the First* offers an early example of the nineteenth-century use of seventeenth-century rebellions to illuminate the French Revolution. The topic has been canvassed in many places, most recently by Kenneth R. Johnston and Joseph Nicholes in "Transitory Actions, Men Betrayed: The French Revolution and the English Revolution in Romantic Drama," *The Wordsworth Circle* 23 (1992): 76–96 and in a special edition of *The Wordsworth Circle* (25:3, Summer 1994) edited by Johnston, Nicholes, and Thomas Prasch. It is worth distinguishing two lines of influence emanating from the eighteenth-century historians. One line is compulsively analogical: it runs from radical intellectuals in France to the London Corresponding Societies, touching lightly on Words-

made such a comparison in *A Philosophical View of Reform,* where he declares that France "has undergone a revolution (unlike in the violence and calamities which attended it, because unlike in the abuses which it was excited to put down) which may be paralleled with that in our own country which ended in the death of Charles the 1st. The authors of both revolutions proposed a greater and more glorious object than the degraded passions of their countrymen permitted them to attain."[28] Shelley's attempt to blend Macaulay's Whiggish enthusiasm for the "glorious object" and Hume's indignation at the limits placed by human "passions" only begins to suggest the difficulties he faced when he tried to give shape to their accounts in *Charles the First.* I believe that Shelley found a way around those difficulties only by sacrificing his political ambition to dramatize history in the actions of persons and moving on to the apocalypse of agency in *The Triumph of Life.* I will proceed to the latter after a brief detour through its dramatic predecessor, by which I hope to show its implication in Shelley's new awareness of the complexities of history.

2.

Charles the First acknowledges from the start the difficulties posed by the partisan mediation of historical knowledge by opening with the dramatic self-consciousness of a Shakespearean play within the play. On 3 February 1633, at the height of Charles's power, the Inns of Court presented to the king a masque called *The Triumph of Peace,* "the most magnificent that hath been brought to court in our time," according to

---

worth's *Letter to the Bishop of Llandaff,* then passes through superficial readings of Scott on to a wide range of Victorian novelists, culminating in Benjamin Disraeli's tribute to Charles I as "the holocaust of direct taxation" (*Sybil,* ed. Sheila M. Smith [New York: Oxford University Press, 1981] 230) and passing into decline with *David Copperfield*'s Mr. Dick and his pathetic obsession with the Royal Martyr's head. The other line insists just as fiercely on marking distinctions between the two periods: it culminates in Scott's best historical novels, but its source is Edmund Burke, who observed that Richard Price and his dissenting circle, "in all their reasonings on the Revolution of 1688, have a revolution which happened in England about forty years before, and the late French revolution, so much before their eyes, and in their hearts, that they are constantly confounding all the three together. It is necessary that we should separate what they confound" (*Reflections* 99–100).

28. Shelley, *Prose* 236.

Charles the First and *The Triumph of Life*

its author James Shirley.[29] The procession through the streets to Whitehall featured chariots patterned after those of the Roman triumphs, decorated with feathers and silver and illuminated by an almost supernaturally bright light: "the Torches and flaming huge Flamboys born by the sides of each Chariot, made it seem lightsom as at Noon-day, but more glittering, and gave a full and clear light to all the streets and windows as they passed by."[30] There was darkness, too: as one of several antimasques, there appeared a pack of fake cripples and "Beggars in timorous looks and gestures, as pursued by two Mastives that came barking after them." These were aesthetically functional, as "the Habits and properties of these Cripples and Beggars, were most ingeniously fitted . . . by the Commissioners direction."[31] For a fleeting moment, English society was transformed into an aesthetic unity expressing the totality of royal power. The protests of the people lining the streets could be easily incorporated: costumed marshallmen were on hand to "restrain the rudeness of people, that in such triumphs, are wont to be insolent, and tumultuary," so that the forcible suppression of conflict appeared as one more element of the aesthetic display.[32] Even the temporary and occasional nature of the pageant could be seen as contributing to its effect. "Thus was this earthly Pomp and Glory, if not Vanity, soon past and gone, as if it had never been," wrote Whitlocke, who was Master of the Revels on that day he would recount in his *Memorials of the English Affairs,* the history mentioned by Godwin and consulted by Shelley. *Sic transit gloria mundi:* if the illusion of a unified society passed away, it seemed to do so almost by decree of the organizers.[33]

The opening scene of *Charles the First* recreates this earlier attempt to stage political history. But in spite of the stage direction setting the scene at "The Masque of the Inns of Court," Shelley's overture displaces spectacle with a critical commentary by the masque's spectators. One of them states Shelley's aim: "When lawyers masque 'tis time for honest

---

29. James Shirley, *The Dramatic Works and Poems of James Shirley,* ed. William Gifford and Alexander Dyle (New York: Russell and Russell, 1966) 6:284.
30. Bulstrode Whitlocke, *Memorials of the English Affairs* (London, 1682) 20.
31. Shirley, *Dramatic Works* 6:259; Whitlocke, *Memorials* 19.
32. Shirley, *Dramatic Works* 6:260.
33. Whitlocke, *Memorials* 21. Whitlocke writes after the fall of both Charles and Cromwell, whom he served in succession.

men / To strip the vizor from their purposes" (1.76–77). The procession that passes offstage does allow Shelley to name the major figures who will appear in his drama, yet he concentrates less on the spectacle than on its audience of "honest men." By forcing *his* audience to imagine the spectacle described by these spectators, Shelley attempts to cope with the ambiguities of his historical research by making an overt theme of the partisan filters through which dramatic spectacle delivers historical knowledge. That acknowledgment sets the aims of *Charles the First* against those of *The Triumph of Peace,* presenting the power of spectacle in the wavering light cast by the remarks of its politically divided spectators.

Shelley's hope that historical drama might empower political agents is signalled in one of those remarks: "Canst thou discern / The signs of seasons, yet perceive no hint / Of change in that stage-scene in which thou art / Not a spectator but an actor?" (1.33–35). What became of that hope in *The Triumph of Life* might be gauged from the reworking of these lines in Rousseau's advice to the narrator: "Follow thou, and from spectator turn / Actor *or victim* in this wretchedness" (305–6, emphasis added). The main puzzle posed by the proximity of *Charles the First* to *The Triumph of Life* is how Shelley moved from an apparent assurance of clear distinctions between passivity and activity to the apparent indifference toward them in Rousseau's narrative. But other questions arise as well. How does Shelley's effort to display the motives behind the spectacle of history in *The Triumph of Peace,* by displacing and deferring his own drama, inform the spectacle of history described in *The Triumph of Life*? Does the narrative fragment carry forward the project of the dramatic fragments, or does it reveal flaws in that project? These questions justify a detailed comparison of the two texts, which will prepare us to approach a verdict on the political aspirations of romantic drama.

The triumphal chariots that course through Shelley's two late historical fragments establish their most obvious similarity. In *Charles the First,* a Royalist Youth describes the procession in the language of imperial artifice:

> How glorious! see those thronging chariots
> Rolling, like painted clouds before the wind,
> Behind their solemn steeds: how some are shaped
> Like curved sea-shells dyed by the azure depths

> Of Indian seas; some like the new-born moon;
> And some like cars in which the Romans climbed
> (Canopied by Victory's eagle-wings outspread)
> The Capitolian—See how gloriously
> The mettled horses in the torchlight stir
> Their gallant riders, while they check their pride,
> Like shapes of some diviner element
> Than English air, and beings nobler than
> The envious and admiring multitude.
> (1.137–49; 162 rev.-161 rev.)

The newborn moon, the clouds, the almost divine horses, the wings, the strange illumination, and the ignoble multitude are also present in the first appearance of the car in *The Triumph of Life,* but in grotesque:

> Like the young Moon
>   When on the sunlit limits of the night
>   Her white shell trembles amid crimson air
>   And whilst the sleeping tempest gathers might
>
> Doth, as a herald of its coming, bear
>   The ghost of her dead Mother, whose dim form
>   Bends in dark ether from her infant's chair,
>
> So came a chariot on the silent storm
>   Of its own rushing splendour, and a Shape
>   So sate within as one whom years deform
>
> Beneath a dusky hood and double cape
>   Crouching within the shadow of a tomb,
>   And o'er what seemed the head a cloud like crape
>
> Was bent, a dun and faint etherial gloom
>   Tempering the light; upon the chariot's beam
>   A Janus-visaged Shadow did assume
>
> The guidance of that wonder-winged team.
>   The Shapes which drew it in thick lightnings
>   Were lost. . . .
> (79–97)

The new description of the pageant arrives, so to speak, cradled in the old description's arms, presaging, as in *The Ballad of Sir Patrick Spence,* "a deadly storm." No longer delivered by a dramatic voice speaking from an identifiable worldly perspective, the description is now more heavily laden with emblematic meanings derived not from historical incident but from other allegorical texts. As the language of cavalier luxuriance gives way to the language of the Old Testament prophets, the light that bathed the historical stage on which the earth's glories passed away becomes a very different light that eclipses those earthly appearances.

Interpreters agree that the main difficulty of *The Triumph of Life* lies in establishing the significance of the light that recurs throughout the poem, and it is here that we find the most important relation between the two fragments. Its first major occurrence frames *The Triumph of Life* as a supernatural vision, as remote as possible from the world of history, which seems to vanish as "a cold glare, intenser than the noon / But icy cold, obscure[s] with [   ] light / The sun as he the stars" (77–79). This description may not, however, be so remote from *Charles the First*. It can be traced to Whitlocke's report of the pageant preceding *The Triumph of Peace,* in which "the Torches and flaming huge Flamboys born by the sides of each Chariot, made it seem lightsom as at Noon-day, but more glittering." In Shelley's source, the pageant's artificial illumination does not merely turn the night to day, but outshines the light of day itself. This becomes a recurrent pattern in *The Triumph of Life,* in which the metaphysical light of vision effaces the natural light of phenomena, much as the Wordsworthian Imagination makes its appearance "when the light of sense / Goes out, but with a flash that has revealed / The invisible world" (*Prelude* 1805 6:534–36). *The Triumph of Life* thus presents as a vision what *Charles the First* can only gesture toward: a power deliberately placed, like the Wordsworthian Imagination, beyond the natural world to which stage drama, especially historical drama, must remain confined.

These early occurrences of unnatural light in *The Triumph of Life* also illuminate Shelley's movement from the dramatic conventions of *Charles the First* toward the conventions of visionary poetry by calling attention to the way in which the cycles of natural light structure the temporal framework that is observed (or pointedly violated) in all narrative. The opening lines of *Charles the First* give an account of the footlights going up, in the First Citizen's remark on the masque, "which turns, / Like morning from the shadow of the night, / The night to day" (1.2–4; 181 rev.). *The Triumph of Life* opens with a parallel passage substituting the imperfect tenses of historical narrative and so placing a fuller emphasis on sequence: "Swift as a spirit hastening to his task / Of glory and of good, the Sun sprang forth / Rejoicing in his splendour, and the mask / Of darkness fell from the awakened Earth" (1–4). The relation between these two dawns, one masquing and one unmasking, can be seen in the strange grammar of the lines in *Charles the First*. The simile of the First Citizen is structured, or broken apart, by an anacoluthon: the masque that transitively turns night to day cannot, except in a violently antinatural figure of speech, be placed in grammatical parallel with the morning as it intransitively turns (itself) away from the night. The solecism that opens Shelley's play poses a crucial thematic alternative: to assimilate the impositional "turning" of the pageant's tropes to the natural turning of the earth is either to remove all artifice from the pageant or to remove all naturalness from the dawn. The first lines of *The Triumph of Life* develop the latter possibility by immediately denaturalizing what might have been a nature description. In a later passage that returns to this opening—one of many moments of *déjà vu* in this poem—Rousseau will present sunrise as the moment when "Day upon the threshold of the east / Treads out the lamps of night" (389–90). As in the opening description of the sun springing forth, here dawn is not the gradual process of night giving birth to day but the sudden violence of day obliterating night.

The superseding of natural light has a specific motive shared by both fragments. Shelley's daemonized *aubade* explicitly revises a topos of revolution poetry: the appearance of the day's new light as an emblem of a new age abruptly dissociated from the time of an ancien régime. This topos informs Wordsworth's "Bliss was it in that dawn to be alive" (*Prelude* 1805 10:692), which Shelley might have known from its publication in *The Friend* (1809), and it organizes the plot of Keats's revolutionary epic *Hyperion*. The political stakes of the revolutionary dawn, and of its critical negation in Shelley, are clearly stated by Georg Lukács: "The defenders of progress after the French Revolution had necessarily to reach a conception which would prove the historical necessity of the latter, furnish evidence that it constituted a peak in a long and gradual historical development and not a sudden eclipse in human consciousness."[34] Shelley's republican precursor here is Milton in the *Hymn*

---

34. Georg Lukács, *The Historical Novel*, trans. Hannah and Stanley Mitchell (Lincoln: University of Nebraska Press, 1983) 27.

on the Morning of Christ's Nativity, whose theme is the cultural revolution enacted with the advent of Christianity, seen as "the supersession of one ground of values by a new ground."[35] The old gods are defeated by the new Son of God, figured in Milton's hymn as the sun that brings light:

> So when the Sun in bed,
> Curtain'd with cloudy red,
>   Pillows his chin upon an Orient wave,
> The flocking shadows pale
> Troop to th'infernal jail;
>   Each fetter'd Ghost slips to his several grave,
> And yellow-skirted Fays
> Fly after the Night-steeds, leaving their Moon-lov'd maze.
>
> (229–36)

Sunrise figures the end of false surmise, in a climactic moment of achieved cultural enlightenment. This climax requires the gradual build-up visible in Milton's description of the emergence of dawn out of the bed of ocean, in a continuous movement that gives graphic evidence of the necessity (in Lukács's terms) of a progressive rather than a sudden enlightenment.[36]

In *The Triumph of Life,* where no new light is ever granted authority to organize history into an old regime and a new one, the appearance of the sun must be emptied of this natural necessity. Shelley hyperbolizes the conventions of nature description to show that historical process is unlike natural process. For the springing forth of Shelley's sun

---

35. A. Grossman, "Milton's Sonnet, 'On the late massacre in Piemont,' " *Triquarterly* 23–24 (1972): 194. The comment is applied to the *Nativity Hymn* by Christopher Hill in *Milton and the English Revolution* (New York: Penguin, 1979) 21, from which I quote the phrase.

36. In *The Statesman's Manual,* Coleridge uses the figure of the sun as Milton does, but with a modification that brings it close to Shelley's figure: "The natural Sun is . . . a symbol of the spiritual. Ere he is fully arisen, and while his glories are still under veil, he calls up the breeze to chase away the usurping vapours of the night season, and thus converts the air itself into the minister of its own purification: not surely in proof or elucidation of the light from heaven, but to prevent its interception" (*Collected Works,* vol. 6, ed. R. J. White [Princeton: Princeton University Press] 10). Leslie Brisman's comment on this passage goes to the heart of its political use in Shelley's hands: "It is one idea of progress that is being compared to another, and so the deep truth that Christianity is an idea of progress (philosophy plus history) is buried in the very condition of the analogy" ("Coleridge and the Supernatural," *Studies in Romanticism* 21 [1982]: 148).

figures historical rather than natural processes: the Sun, "rejoicing in his splendour," is a tyrannical Sun King, modelled not, as critics have suggested, after Louis XIV, but after Charles I rejoicing in his courtly spectacles.[37] The historical coding of nature in these opening lines colors Shelley's metaphysical account of the sun's relation to the natural world. As the lines unfold they reveal how, "at the birth / Of light," following a hierarchical "succession due,"

>   Continent,
> Isle, Ocean, and all things that in them wear
> The form and character of mortal mould
>   Rise as the Sun their father rose, to bear
>
> Their portion of the toil which he of old
>   Took as his own and then imposed on them.
>   (6–7, 15–20)

Toil, the condition of mortal history, is imposed simultaneously with the stamping of "form and character," the transformation of eternal essences into mutable phenomena: the sun imposes upon "all things" the appearance they must wear. The natural order, as soon as it appears as an order, is thus already subject to the imposition of a temporal as well as a hierarchical (coded as monarchical) "succession due" which, like the pageant's "turning" of night to day, describes history rather than nature.

But as the sun becomes a figure for earthly power, it ceases to be solely a figure for the cyclical renewal of history. It now generates an alternate metaphorical system that disrupts the symbolic import of the sun's diurnal course. This alternate system develops out of another passage in *Charles the First* which in turn expands upon a specific historical source that may help in identifying the political implications of the metaphorical system that conflicts with the temporal pattern of day and night. In scene 2 of *Charles the First,* Charles describes himself as being, like the sun, an intermediary between God and the world. In his present state he is not a setting but a darkened sun, a sun that has passed behind a cloud:

---

37. Johnston and Nicholes take the image of the rising sun that opens *Charles the First* to be "an oblique reference in the iconographic tradition of the 'Sun King' of Versailles" ("Transitory Actions" 84). But Louis XIV was not born until 1638, and, as I argue below, Shelley had better authority for having Charles compare himself to the sun.

> For a king bears the office of a God
> To all the under world; and to his God
> Alone he must deliver up his trust,
> Unshorn of its permitted attributes.
> [It seems] now as the baser elements
> Had mutinied against the golden sun
> That kindles them to harmony and quells
> Their self-destroying rapine. The wild million
> Strike at the eye that guides them. . . .
> (2.139–47; 140 rev.–139 rev.)

Charles thinks of his realm as an organic (ecological) whole, like an aesthetic construct (such as the pageant) that attempts to appropriate the unity of the natural world. In a properly unified realm, the light of the "golden sun" should "kindle" the "harmony" of music, as in the opening of *The Triumph of Life*: "The smokeless altars of the mountain snows / Flamed above the crimson clouds, and at the birth / Of light, the Ocean's orison arose / To which the birds tempered their matin lay" (5–8).[38] What arises on the historical stage of *Charles the First*, however, is not harmony but a discord that, in a reversal of this synaesthetic image, blots the light that kindled it. That darkness is presaged by a figure in an uncompleted passage in the first scene:

> This Charles the First
> Rose like the equinoctial sun [   ]
> By vapours, through whose threatening ominous veil
> Darting his altered influence he has gained
> This height of noon—from which he must decline
> Amid the darkness of conflicting storms,
> To dank extinction and to latest night.
> (1.146–52)

The speaker of these lines is not yet able to distinguish, as the king will, between the natural law that brings an end to the monarch's day and the "conflicting storms" of revolution that can swallow the sun.

The traces of Shelley's research for *Charles the First* allow us to identify a subtext for the King's sun–eye metaphor. Shelley took it from

---

38. Cf. Shelley, *Prometheus Unbound* 2.1.24–27: "through yon peaks of cloud-like snow / The roseate sunlight quivers: hear I not / The Æolian music of her sea-green plumes / Winnowing the crimson dawn?"

a passage he bracketed in his copy of *Eikon Basilike,* in which Charles speaks of Strafford and likely of himself as well: "While moving in so high a spheare {and with so vigourous a lustre, he must need, [as the sun] raise many envious exhalations, which condensed by a popular Odium, were capable to cast a cloud upon the brightest merit and integrity.}"[39] This conceit and its development in *Charles the First* surely owe something to the opening lines of *Richard III,* where the cloud covering the royal sun is dispersed, "In the deep bosom of the ocean buried." As in Shakespeare, the burden of the conceit is that obscuring clouds must inevitably be dispersed by the sun that called them into being.[40]

The Triumph of Life consistently presents the obscuring of the sun's light not as the cyclical replacement of day by night, but as a movement that develops *Eikon Basilike*'s metaphor of the cloud passing over the sun: as "tempering" and "eclipse," or in passages describing the waning of one light in the supervening "splendour" of another. There is, however, a difference between the sun's being temporarily obscured by a passing cloud, or "tempered" as a keyboard might be, and its passing into eclipse. The shift from clouding in *Charles the First* to eclipse in *The Triumph of Life* is condensed in Milton's famous simile describing

---

39. See Walter Edwin Peck, *Shelley* (New York: Houghton Mifflin, 1927), appendix F 2:363; I follow Peck in reproducing Shelley's brackets and braces. Another annotation reads: "How beautiful the language / of Liberty even in a King's [illegible]" (364; the bibliographical note in the Pforzheimer Collection conjectures the illegible word as "person"). There is some evidence that Shelley read *Eikon Basilike* through Milton's *Eikonoklastes,* whose preface argues (in Christopher Hill's summary) that "so far from being a tragic drama . . . Charles's execution was 'a ridiculous exit'; Marshall's engraving of the royal martyr was 'like a masking scene.' It was all a sham, 'devices begged from the old pageantry of some Twelfth-Night's entertainment at Whitehall'" (*Milton* 177). The evidence runs as follows. Mary includes "Milton's Speech on Unlicensed Printing" in her reading list for 1815 (see Newman I. White, *Shelley* [New York: Knopf, 1940] 2:541), and it is likely that she and Percy read *Areopagitica* in an edition of Milton's *Prose Works* requested from Thomas Hookham on 29 July 1812 and received 17 August. That edition was probably one of two published since the turn of the century, either the 1806 complete edition in seven volumes or, more likely, the two-volume 1809 selection. The latter, which Shelley owned at the time of his residence at Marlow, prints a much compressed text of *Eikonoklastes* but includes the whole of the preface.

40. Though the voice of Richard III is not audible in the king's transformation of the *Eikon Basilike* conceit, the identification is supported by the line that initially opened scene 2. The cancelled line reads: "Where, in the envious winter [of this] its glory. . . ." Woodings comments that "the *Richard III* echo again refers to the world of civil wars, but more generally it summarises the conflicting views that, in Shelley's eyes, surround any monarch" (" 'A Devil of a Nut to Crack' " 225.)

Satan rising up in hell, to which Shelley had alluded in *A Philosophical View of Reform* and to which the figures of both late fragments are indebted. It continues a simile I quoted in Chapter 1 from the first book of *Paradise Lost*:

> As when the Sun new ris'n
> Looks through the Horizontal misty Air
> Shorn of his Beams, *or* from behind the Moon
> In dim Eclipse disastrous twilight sheds
> On half the Nations, and with fear of change
> Perplexes Monarchs.
> (1:594–99, emphasis added)[41]

The first part of this simile is allusively present in *Charles the First* where the king echoes "Shorn of his Beams" in his phrase "Unshorn of its permitted attributes"; the second part may appear in *The Triumph of Life* as the "eclipse" of line 290. Since we are considering Shelley's movement from one figure to the other, however, the most important element is the simile's passage from clouding to eclipse, effected by Milton's troubling "or." Satan is like a clouded sun, *or* like the sun in eclipse: the threat to royal power may be temporary, *or* it might be a portent of disaster. Shelley's perplexing metaphor of eclipse, likewise, is not so much an alternative as a corrective to the more reassuring metaphor of clouding. Milton's sense of political and cosmic disaster is partly present whenever the figure of obscured light occurs in *The Triumph of Life*, and his dubious "or" (which resounds powerfully throughout Shelley's poem) leaves indeterminate what might have seemed, on the stage of *Charles the First*, a decidedly passing twilight.[42]

But the pattern of eclipse in *The Triumph of Life* cannot be limited to the political significance supplied by Milton's simile. The conceit of obscured light that structures the king's political credo in *Charles the First* becomes, in *The Triumph of Life*, a more inclusive metaphor for history in general, including the history from which we began, that of the individual mind. In being broadened the figure becomes more com-

---

41. Shelley alludes to Milton's lines in *A Philosophical View of Reform*: "these events, in the present condition of the understanding and sentiment of mankind, are the rapidly passing shadows which forerun successful insurrection, the ominous comets of our great republican poet perplexing great monarchs with fear of change" (*Prose* 238).

42. For more on the Miltonic "or," see Leslie Brisman, *Milton's Poetry of Choice and Its Romantic Heirs* (Ithaca: Cornell University Press, 1973).

plex, especially when it is juxtaposed with the conventional metaphoric system of the rising and setting sun. The complexity may be seen in Rousseau's condemnation of those who are chained to Life's chariot: "their lore / Taught them not this—to know themselves; their might / Could not repress the mutiny within, / And for the morn of truth they feigned, deep night / Caught them ere evening" (211–15). "Morn of truth," like many of the solar metaphors in the poem, probably refers to those (like Rousseau's friend and enemy Hume) who thought of themselves as bringing on an age of Enlightenment. The figure is their figure, not necessarily Rousseau's; "deep night" is Rousseau's ironic completion of the metaphoric "lore" adopted by the advocates of Enlightenment. The term "evening," however, in spite of its congruity with this rejected metaphorics of darkened Enlightenment, belongs to a metaphorical system Rousseau does endorse: it suggests death, the even-ing of Life, and thus presupposes some authentic morn (birth) that precedes and grounds the metaphor of the feigned "morn of truth." Rousseau's morning–evening scheme, reinforced by his subsequent reference to "our mortal day" (229), recapitulates the opening use of dawn to figure temporality in general. In the new context, however, it subsumes within a scheme of rise and fall the figures of Enlightenment that perpetuate the illusion of progressive renewal condemned by the man who began his career with a *Discourse* repudiating Enlightenment meliorism.[43] The irony of "deep night," however—the incongruity that gives the passage its power—is that it precedes "evening": Rousseau's temporal metaphor of day and night is interrupted by the nontemporal metaphor of obscured light. "Deep night" suggests not death but benightedness, and belongs not with the cyclical replacement of day by night but with the perplexing "eclipse" effected by the instituted church as it throws "shadows between Man & god" (289–90), and with the "strange night" later brought on "ere evening" as the throng of shadows, like a cloud of vampire bats, obscures the sun (484–86). The metaphor of the obscuring cloud in *Charles the First*, then, contributes to the separation effected in *The Triumph of Life* between a traditional metaphor depicting history as the temporal succession of night and day, and a very different metaphorical system presenting history as a

---

43. Edward Duffy's *Rousseau in England: The Context for Shelley's Critique of the Enlightenment* (Berkeley: University of California Press, 1979) offers a detailed reading of *The Triumph of Life* as a critique of the Enlightenment; see esp. chap. 5.

nontemporal repetition of obscurings that blot a light shining from a realm beyond time.

Shelley gradually transforms the passing figure from *Charles the First* into a major narrative device. As one reads through *The Triumph of Life*, the temporal symbolism of its opening sunrise is repeatedly disrupted by the metaphor of obscuring. The differing systems within which one might place the poem's figures of light thus gradually lose their quality of alternatives and become, if not (in Paul de Man's phrase) "mutually obliterating," at least mutually suspending, like two points of view in a skeptical debate. How does Shelley orient his reader amid these conflicting understandings of history? The answer can again be traced to *Charles the First,* specifically to the means by which it points toward a resolution of the spectators' debate about the political meaning of *The Triumph of Peace.* For the two fragments share another remarkable feature, one that counters their similarly skeptical tactics for averting resolution: the apparition, in the midst of each poem's pageantry, of the disfigured Dantean specter of a historical personage. For the figure of Rousseau in *The Triumph of Life* derives, in important ways, from the figure of Alexander Leighton in *Charles the First.* In order to understand the significance of Rousseau, it is essential to understand the importance of Leighton's entrance into the pageant that dominates the opening scene of *Charles the First.*

3.

The lavish performance of *The Triumph of Peace* in 1633 arose out of a wish by City lawyers to defend the court's spectacles from the antitheatrical attacks of Puritan iconoclasts like their colleague William Prynne, whose massive *Histriomastix* helped stimulate revolutionary agitation in the early 1630s.[44] To all who recognized the political stakes

---

44. The significance of the masque's being presented by the Inns of Court is clarified by Laurence Stone's observation that "the most numerous, wealthy and influential professional group [at this moment] was the lawyers, whose numbers [had] increased dramatically" during the Stuart reign (*The Causes of the English Revolution, 1529–1642* [London: Routledge and Kegan Paul, 1972] 75). Stephen Orgel claims that many saw Prynne's book "as a call to revolution"; see *The Illusion of Power: Political Theater in the English Renaissance* (Berkeley: University of California Press, 1975) 44. Orgel has written more extensively on *The Triumph of Peace* in Orgel and Roy Strong, *Inigo Jones: The Theatre of the Stuart Court* (Berkeley: University of California Press, 1973) 2:539f.;

of antitheatrical agitation, the court's amateur theatricals were more than entertainment; some would even have shared Stephen Orgel's view that "the stage at Whitehall was [Charles's] truest kingdom, the masque the most accurate expression of his mind."[45] Both Hume and Macaulay describe the sequence of events by which the power of the sovereign, violated by Prynne's attack, came to be reasserted in a visible form: first, by the "magnificent" expression of power in the performance of *The Triumph of Peace;* second, by a visible inscription of power upon Prynne's body, most famously in the clipping of his ears, commemorated in a sonnet by Milton.[46] Macaulay reverses the actual order of events:

> The illegal, barbarous punishment which had been inflicted on Prynne, instead of rousing the half-subdued spirit of the English, gave rise to a pompous performance of the same sort as the unfortunate barrister had with so much hardiness condemned. Noy the attorney-general, Sir Edward Finch the speaker of the house of Commons, and other dependents of the court, had so much influence on their brethren, as to instigate them to offer a mask to the King and queen, to wipe off the stain of being thought disaffected to their favourite amusement.[47]

In reversing the order of events, Macaulay makes a direct connection, of a sort that Foucault would make more systematically, between the expression of power on the body of Prynne and the public display of power in the "pompous performance" of *The Triumph of Peace*.[48]

Orgel and Strong reproduce many documents including Whitlocke's report. For further details, see Murray Lefkowitz, *Trois masques à la cour de Charles Ier d'Angleterre* (Paris: Centre National de la Recherche Scientifique, 1970) 27–109.

45. Orgel, *Illusion of Power* 79. In Orgel's view, "much of Caroline legal and political history has the quality of a court masque" (89).

46. Milton, "On the New Forcers of Conscience under the Long Parliament" (1646?), in John Milton, *Complete Poems and Major Prose,* ed. Merritt Y. Hughes (1957; Indianapolis: Bobbs-Merrill, 1980) 144–45. The line "Clip your Phylacteries, though baulk your Ears," which declines (in an obvious *occupatio*) to name Prynne, replaces a line cancelled in the Trinity MS: "Clip ye as close as marginal P——'s ears" (Hughes 145n). Hughes gives the occasion for Prynne's punishment as the 1637 publication of a pamphlet attacking Bishop Wren.

47. Macaulay, *History* 2:154–55.

48. On corporal punishment as an expression (or inscription) of power, see Michel Foucault, *Discipline and Punish: The Birth of the Prison,* trans. Alan Sheridan (New York: Pantheon, 1977). A similar motive of celebrating the restored integrity of the sovereign's power prompted a masque celebrating the 1638 conviction of Hampden: William Davenant's *Britannia Triumphans,* staged by Inigo Jones. Its naval theme alluded unmistakably to the levying of ship money, which Hampden had unsuccessfully resisted.

Recreating this moment in the first scene of *Charles the First,* Shelley reinforces the connection by structuring his pageant symmetrically around a stand-in for Prynne placed at the center of the scene. That stand-in is Leighton.

Shelley knew that the performance of *The Triumph of Peace* was meant to vindicate courtly spectacle. To judge from his opinions about the "disgusting splendours" of the Prince Regent's spectacular entertainments, Shelley probably enjoyed Macaulay's sarcastic diagnosis of Charles's court masques: "The King, the Queen, and the whole court, entered with glee into a species of entertainment, which, whilst it varied the action of the idle business of a monarchical life, helped to dissipate that reflection in the public which is so formidable to ill-designing princes."[49] He would also have understood that Prynne's attack on such entertainments had been seen—mainly at the prompting of Archbishop Laud—as a direct attack on the integrity of the court. But Shelley could hardly have made his *dramatic* interpretation of these historical materials turn on the fate of the antitheatricalist Prynne.[50] Moreover, he probably knew, in spite of Macaulay's mistake, that Prynne had not yet been punished at the time of the masque's performance. He therefore replaced Prynne with the fleeting apparition of Alexander Leighton, notorious sower (or stirrer) of sedition, who steps on stage with

---

49. Macaulay, *History* 2:148. Richard Holmes writes that "Shelley attacked the Prince Regent's lavishly extravagant fete at Carlton House on 19 June [1811], which included a 200-foot banqueting table along the length of which ran an artificial stream encased in banks of silver and pumped from intricately ornamented silver fountains at one end. 'What think you of the bubbling brooks, & mossy banks at Carlton House?' he exclaimed to Miss Hitchener, grimly enumerating the ludicrous magnificence and 'disgusting splendours'" (*Shelley* 73).

50. The persistence of antitheatrical attitudes in the Regency era is treated as common knowledge in Jane Austen's *Mansfield Park,* though critics have discovered it in more roundabout ways. Prynne's arguments were alive and well in the *Christian Observer* of April 1813, which declared in its generally approving review of Coleridge's *Remorse* that "we adhere firmly to the puritanical tenet of the unlawfulness of stage amusements" (*Romantics Reviewed* A:1:283). In an example somewhat closer to Shelley, Mary Russell Mitford's *Charles the First* has the villainous Cromwell denounce the queen in terms certain to arouse the laughter of theatergoers: "A rank idolater; a mumming masquer; / A troller of lewd songs; a wanton dancer; / A vain upholder of that strength of Satan / The playhouse" (2.2.49–53; *The Works of Mary Russell Mitford, Prose and Verse* [Philadelphia, 1854] 658). The politically moderate Mitford rejects Puritan antitheatricalism as the same passion that led to regicide; hence the irony with which she treats Cromwell's attack on the court theatricals. Elsewhere, Cromwell voices Mitford's liberal convictions, defending "freedom of act, / Of speech, of will, of faith" (5.2.15–6; 670); this may explain the refusal of a license in 1825.

the mark "S.S." visibly branded on each cheek.[51] Macaulay herself introduces the episode of Prynne and the masque by picking up her narrative "whilst the terrors of Leighton's punishment hung yet on the mind of the public."[52] Shelley's characters treat Leighton and Prynne as interchangeable: the Old Man who leads the debate about the pageant attacks maypoles in an echo of Prynne's *Histriomastix* and recommends "Smiting each Bishop under the fifth rib" in a verbatim quotation from Leighton's *Plea against Prelacy*.[53] If Prynne's antitheatrical writings and his punishment provide a key to understanding the political aim of staging history in *The Triumph of Peace*, then the appearance of the disfigured Leighton offers a key to interpreting Shelley's triumphal procession.

A key is required because Shelley presents the pageant only through the conflicting interpretations of its spectators. Masque and pageant forms appear in Shelley's poetry both as instances of the oppressive power of aesthetic illusion and as models for a historical process that might undo that power: "The Mask of Anarchy," the final act of *Prometheus Unbound*, and *The Triumph of Life* are only the best known instances. The procession in *Charles the First* was meant to express the totality of absolute earthly power even as it passes away; Shelley therefore structures the debate about its political function with a dialectic of monumentalism and obliteration that can be traced directly to his earlier rehearsals of the Revolutionary festivals, which had offered monumental summations of history that depended for their effect on the forfeiting of any claim to lasting value. Gerald McNiece registers a curious mix of opinion about such festivals among Shelley's acquaintance:

> Shelley had available to him a good many specific descriptions of the fetes [*sic*]. Helen Maria Williams mentioned their value. . . . Mrs. Wollstonecraft, like Godwin, criticized such devices as fetes and associations for resorting to mysterious appeals to the imagination, a faculty which be-

---

51. Shelley leaves the details of Leighton's branding to the imagination; I supply details from Macaulay (*History* 2:93).

52. Macaulay, *History* 2:147. Prynne was apparently scheduled to make an appearance in scene 2 of Shelley's play, but he does not appear; perhaps the lines substituting Leighton for Prynne in scene 1 postdate the lines at the head of scene 2 that indicate Prynne's appearance on stage.

53. As Woodings notes, Shelley adds. e. 7 indicates that Shelley found the phrase in Hume ("Shelley's Sources" 268).

trays men into irrational follies by supporting 'the enthusiasm of the moment....' The fetes, garlands, and altars, which in France lent dramatic energy 'to the conviction of truth and justice,' and seemed to observers like Hazlitt a judgment on French superficiality and sensuality, reappeared in Shelley's revolutionary poetry in the service of a richer, more comprehensive faculty of knowledge than Godwin's discursive reason.[54]

Shelley's awareness of two contrary views current among progressive thinkers can help us understand his developing poetic use of masque, pageant, and festival forms. Canto 5 of *The Revolt of Islam* (1817–18) provides the most extended early example. Here the poem's nonviolent revolution is celebrated and consolidated in a popular festival, begun in stanza 14 with "A glorious pageant, more magnificent / Than kingly slaves arrayed in gold and blood / When they return from carnage, and are sent / In triumph bright beneath the populous battlement" (1842–45).[55] This festival is characterized only as a negation or revision of the traditional imperial triumph, in which the conventions once employed by victorious tyrants are reversed. The "nation / Made free by love" initiates its own celebration without being forcibly and passively "sent / In triumph." Its celebration is conducted without those material traces of power, "gold and blood," with which the imperial triumph commemorates the tyrant's power: as the festival simply occurs, rather than being staged, props are no longer necessary. And since the trappings that had served as reminders of tyrannical power are absent, the monumentalizing function of such public displays is wholly undone. In "Ozymandias," written a few months after *The Revolt of Islam*, Shelley would attribute the aesthetic of monumentalism to the delusions of a tyranny that believes its "might" can be made as permanent as "pas-

---

54. Gerald McNiece, *Shelley and the Revolutionary Idea* (Cambridge: Harvard University Press, 1969) 117–19. For another perspective on the Revolutionary festivals, as they relate to the English theater, see Carlson, *Theatre of Romanticism* 9–11.

55. Shelley, *Poetical Works* 82 (abbreviated hereafter in text as *PW*). See also McNiece, *Shelley* 204: "Like the fetes of the French Revolution, Shelley's ritual Mass in canto V celebrating the descent of Equality invokes multitudes of worshipers; models its procedures on older techniques using altars, hymns, impressive statues, and veiled images; and has a presiding priestess, Laone, who, like the actress representing Liberty at the Feast of Reason, chants a hymn to Equality.... Like the fetes and pageants of the French Revolution, the rituals which Shelley describes were designed to consolidate and inspire the liberated masses, make them live the revolution ideally and emotionally so as to become one with the divine general will and escape the pull of ages of reaction, corruption, and indolence."

sions . . . / stamped on . . . lifeless things."[56] Shelley's festival, by contrast, means to facilitate forgetting rather than remembrance: its historical function is not expressive or commemorative, like Ozymandias's inscription, but performative, fostering not memory but what Foucault calls "countermemory."[57]

Such features of Shelley's early work provide a context for interpreting the debate in *Charles the First* between two opposed views of the relation between spectacle and power. On the one hand, Shelley presents *The Triumph of Peace* as an attempt to give visible form to the power of Stuart absolutism by *commemorating* the material grip of the past over the present's ability to imagine a future. In his staging of "material power," Shelley would be thinking less of *The Revolt of Islam*'s symbolic "gold and blood" than of his historical sources' emphasis on conspicuous expenditure in a time of economic crisis—the "blood and gold" on which, a spectator remarks, Archbishop Laud has become drunk (1.60). This economic motivation would hardly have placed Shelley outside the mainstream of English drama; the extravagance of the Stuart courts has been offered by at least one modern

---

56. Shelley, "Ozymandias" 6–7. Carl Woodring finds a similar critique of monumentalism in *Prometheus Unbound*, act 2: the "emblems of forgotten mysteries and tyrannies . . . were captured and re-erected in Rome, under subsequent tyrannies, as emblems of the power of later kings and priests. All these once-potent mysteries, which were as strange, 'savage, ghastly, dark and execrable' as the forms of Jupiter they enveloped, have left only their astonishing monuments, *which will no longer deceive and tempt*" (*Politics in English Romantic Poetry* 302). Woodring then argues that Shelley "does not design the poem merely as 'an astonishment,' like the hieroglyphics on an obelisk whose meaning is lost; he tries to dissolve the manners, morals, and issues of his own day in the moving beauty of myth" (309).

57. Similar ideas can be found in documents relating to the festivals of the French Revolution; one of the women erecting a triumphal arch in a 1793 festival play, for example, explains the monument's function as engendering a kind of countermemory: "Ce monument proscrit l'odieuse mémoire / D'un tyran féroce et pervers" (Gabriel Bouquier and P.L. Moline, *La Réunion du dix-août, ou l'inauguration de la république française* . . . [Paris: An 2], act 2). Shelley's festival distills from such moments something like the Nietzsche slogan, "Forgetting is necessary to action of any kind" ("The Use and Abuse of History for Life," in *Untimely Meditations,* 83). That slogan has reached postmodernism via Foucault, who argues that "History becomes 'effective' to the degree that it introduces discontinuity into our very being . . . knowledge is not made for understanding; it is made for cutting" ("Nietzsche, Genealogy, History," in *Language, Counter-Memory, Practice: Selected Essays and Interviews,* ed. Donald F. Bouchard [Ithaca: Cornell University Press, 1977] 154). But postmodern proponents of "countermemory" have their precursors in the eighteenth century, such as the philosophical historian Chastellux, who declared that in order to be happy there is "far greater need of forgetting than of remembering" (quoted from Becker, *Heavenly City* 94).

critic as a background for King Lear's opening wager that "the signs of royal power can outlast their material base."[58] Reformers could easily imagine the Regent—or the "old, mad, blind, despised, and dying king" of "England in 1819"—sharing that attitude with the Royal Martyr. On the other hand, the interpretation given to the pageant by Shelley's characters suggests that such a display can *obliterate* the past. The conflict among those characters may therefore be understood as a reappraisal of *The Revolt of Islam*'s rewriting of a Revolutionary debate about the power of spectacle. *Charles the First*, as it represents historical reality and not an ideal revolution, must work out its position in this double interpretive context by posing a question that is not answered in *The Revolt of Islam:* How can the inscriptions of power, the currency with which Charles makes his wager, be liberated from their oppressive task of commemorating the state's monopoly on the means of social control, from conspicuous consumption to violence? Can a tyrant's *Triumph* be turned into a Revolutionary festival?

The two sides of this debate are argued by representatives of two generations: the "Old Man" or "Second Citizen" and "A Youth" who addresses him as "father." The difference in age contributes to the debate's ambiguity, for Shelley's usual apportioning of liberality to youth and rigidity to age runs contrary to what he evidently knew of the generational lines of conflict during Charles's reign.[59] The Second Citizen opens with a Prynne-like sneer at the "vanity" of public display, to which the Youth responds by taking the triumph as a festival, in tones that echo the early ("ineffectual angel") Shelley:

58. Richard Halpern, *The Poetics of Primitive Accumulation: English Renaissance Culture and the Genealogy of Capital* (Ithaca: Cornell University Press, 1991) 232. Halpern adds that "the consumption-sign really came into its own in the urban environment of London, where it not only achieved an unprecedented intensity but decisively detached itself from economic production and hence from its own reproduction. Many Elizabethan and Stuart courtiers consumed their economic resources as stars consume their own fuel, throwing off a brilliant light of consumption-signs as they slowly collapsed from within" (237). His vocabulary of the consumption-sign is borrowed from Jean Baudrillard, *For a Political Economy of the Sign*, trans. Charles Levin (St. Louis: Telos Press, 1981).

59. Laurence Stone notes that "the dissident Parliamentary leaders, both at Westminster and in the only two counties where it has been tested, were significantly older, by a medium of about ten years, than the loyal Cavaliers," so that in the 1640s—as also, perhaps, in Regency England—"the old were more radical than the young" (*Causes of the English Revolution* 133).

Charles the First and *The Triumph of Life*

> —'tis like the bright procession
> Of skiey visions in a solemn dream
> From which men wake as from a Paradise,
> And draw new strength to tread the thorns of life.
> If God be good, wherefore should this be evil?
> And if this be not evil, dost thou not draw
> Unseasonable poison from the flowers
> Which bloom so rarely in this barren world?
>   (1.17–24; 179 rev.)

He ends by advising the Old Man to forget all that these appearances might recall, since only forgetting can bring the future out of the shadow cast by the past: "Oh, kill these bitter thoughts which make the present / Dark as the future!" (1.25–26; 178 rev.). Shelley has his "Youth" embrace the historical amnesia for which F. R. Leavis attacked the mature poet: "Shelley represents most nearly in the period (if we leave out Blake) the complete rejection of the past."[60] But *The Revolt of Islam* had offered an argument, not merely amnesiac slogans: Laon's exhortation to "let the past / Be as a grave which gives not up its dead / To evil thoughts" (st. 12, 1819–21; *PW* 82) admits that we *must* have reminders of the past, but hopes they might—like the graves that serve as permanent reminders of impermanence—help us to overcome the materialism that binds us to that past. Revolution seeks to discard such "bitter thoughts" like the outworn garments that bind the triumph's "kingly slaves *arrayed* in gold and blood" (emphasis added); as though acting upon Beatrice Cenci's advice that her family should "put off as garments overworn" all that has kept them in thrall (3.1.208), the popular festival functions as a ceremonial divestiture, a casting off of the materialism of tyranny and the tyranny of materialism.[61] The sensory immediacy of the festival effaces all memory traces: "To hear, to see, to live, was on that morn / Lethean joy! so that all those assembled / Cast off their memories of the past outworn" (st. 42; 2089–91; *PW* 88). With this predecessor of *The Triumph of Life*'s "Lethean song," the festival frees its participants from the weight of history by engendering an experience of pure presence unburdened with duration. This is the

---

60. F. R. Leavis, *Revaluation: Tradition and Development in English Poetry* (New York: George W. Stewart, 1947) 8.
61. *A Philosophical View of Reform* envisions a "just and necessary revolution" to ensure that tyranny is "*divested* of its most revolting attributes" (*Prose* 236, emphasis added).

interpretation Shelley has his Youth deliver to the incredulous Old Man.

Shelley seems to want to retract, or at least to suspend, the argument of his own youth about the value of history; for *Charles the First* makes the perspective of *The Revolt of Islam* complicit with royalist propaganda. Shelley's revolutionary Puritans argue that an agency capable of effecting change requires a firm grasp of the historical past. The interpretive challenge here arises from Shelley's skeptical use of dramatic form, which follows the method Earl Wasserman identifies in *Julian and Maddalo:* "Having no first principles, the skeptic can understand essential human nature and the foundation on which to build only by watching first the abrasive interaction of opposing doctrines."[62] What Wasserman says of the skeptic holds doubly true for the dramatist, except that Shelley's concern, after reading Hume and Macaulay, is no longer "essential human nature" but the relation between power and its mode of appearance. The difficulty posed by the political spin imparted by Hume and Macaulay is that *Charles the First* must also open doubts about the skeptical suspension of judgment itself, particularly its power to disarm historical agents of the rhetorical means by which they adopt beliefs they can act upon. Is it not politically regressive, in the context sketched in this scene, to use dramatic form to suspend judgment on the importance of remembering the past? Or did the King's appropriation of that skeptical strategy as a means of social control actually accelerate the drift among his subjects from the position of spectators to the position of actors?

Shelley's skeptical poetics may seem to leave the debate unresolved by undermining the integrity of each speaker; but Shelley provides another set of terms in which the conflict can be understood. The appearance of the disfigured Leighton—and his brief speech, which in Shelley's manuscript answers the question "What image of our fairest country / Canst thou be?" (169 rev.)—returns the pageant to its historical context in order to point a way out of the bondage in which its partisan interpreters are languishing. Leighton's entrance focuses the conflict between the pageant's two functions: his "S.S." offers a material reminder of the power that has reduced him to an allegorical Sower of Sedition, even as his words encourage us to forget that power by reading past the single interpretation it seeks to impose on him. Like the Dantean specters he

---

62. Wasserman, *Shelley* 74.

resembles, Leighton supplies the terms in which his appearance must be read:

> I was Leighton: what
> I *am* thou seest. And yet turn thine eyes,
> And with thy memory look on thy friend's mind,
> Which is unchanged, and where is written deep
> The sentence of my judge.
>
> (1.88–92; 169 rev.)

Leighton's appeal to "memory" as a means of breaking the spell of appearance must be understood dialectically, as incorporating the appeal to countermemory in *The Revolt of Islam*. Like all appearances, Leighton's has changed: what "I *am*" is no longer what "I was," but only in terms of mere appearance, what "thou seest." His appeal to memory is an appeal to what "is unchanged" beneath appearance, an appeal that resonates strikingly with Orsino's description of "vile disguise" in *The Cenci*: "these must be the masks of that within, / Which must remain unaltered" (5.1.92–93). An emblem of Shelley's own antitheatrical idealism, Leighton dislocates the terms of the debate over the signs of power, tersely redescribing the issue from a prophetic standpoint that makes visible images point beyond the historical stage to which they seem bound, toward another realm in which their bondage to worldly power is undone.

The political force of such a standpoint might be judged from Leighton's echo of Robespierre, who speaks of "the reign of eternal justice whose laws are engraved not on marble or stone but in the hearts of all men, even in the heart of the slave who has forgotten them or of the tyrant who disowns them."[63] But Leighton's role can be understood apart from any such allusion, merely from the way in which, although his remarks may refer obliquely to the pageant, he seems strangely unassimilable to the scene in which he appears. His role is to defeat his persecutors' aim in marking his face by counselling resistance to the semiotic order of the reigning powers, of which the pageant is only the

---

63. Quoted by Roe, *Wordsworth and Coleridge* 209, from *The Documentary History of Western Civilisation: The French Revolution*, ed. Paul Beik (London, 1971) 278. There is a similar phrasing in the passage from Hume's *History* reprinted with *Wat Tyler* in 1817; Hume calls the doctrines of the "seditious preacher" John Ball "conformable to the ideas of primitive equality which are engraven in the hearts of men" (*Wat Tyler* [Oxford: Woodstock, 1989] xviii).

first of many instances that might have followed in Shelley's play. While Leighton's entrance must call attention to the ways in which power can be made visible, his words ask us to turn away from power's material inscription. His branding is a fixed mark, to be sure; but from the unstageable perspective he invokes, it is merely an illusory appearance, as fleeting as *The Triumph of Peace* and the tyranny it commemorates. The innocence of his mind, by contrast, is as permanent as Prometheus's "written soul," "that form / Which lies unchanged within" (2.1.110 and 64–65). Leighton's speech tells us that his marks are not the permanent inscription of power, but a passing show; not material evidence of historical necessity, but a staged illusion; a reminder, indeed, but a reminder of the need to forget.[64]

Whether or not the echo of *Prometheus Unbound* can stand as evidence that Shelley endorses Leighton's argument, the remainder of the scene shows that the Puritans cannot even hear it. Capable of seeing power only in its most spectacular manifestations, the Third Citizen makes a gesture of pity that replicates the literalism of tyranny: "Are these the marks with which / Laud thinks to improve the image of his Maker / Stamped on the face of man? Curses upon him, / The impious tyrant!" (1.92–95; 168 rev.).[65] To ignore the injunction not to look with the eyes is merely to accept and repeat the literalism that dictated Leighton's torture and, by implication, the clipping of Prynne's ears.

64. The Dantean resonances of Leighton's speech point to a specific parallel: the figure of Manfred, whose shade appears with a cleft brow in Canto 3 of *Purgatorio*. Manfred's wounds are the scars of history, John Freccero argues, but his smile indicates a grace denied in the world where he had been excommunicated and marks his triumph over the apparently mortal wounds of history: "In God's book, Manfred's brow is clear." Leighton interprets his own wounds similarly, in his exhortation to turn our eyes away from the letter of the law inscribed on his face. Here Leighton echoes a passage Shelley marked heavily in his copy of *Inferno,* at the moment in canto 9 where Virgil warns Dante of the Medusa: "Turn your back, and keep your eyes shut; for should the Gorgon show herself and you see her, there would be no returning above" (9:55–57; see Peck, *Shelley* 2:357). Freccero's reading of this passage shows petrification to figure idolatrous literalism, the very threat against which Leighton unsuccessfully warns the Puritan citizenry. See John Freccero, *Dante: The Poetics of Conversion* (Cambridge: Harvard University Press, 1986) 195, 198, 199, 206, and 119–35. Freccero also notes the relation between Manfred's wounds and Christ's wounds, as they bear witness to the resurrection, and compares them to the marks inscribed on penitent souls at the entrance to Purgatory. The marks signify the appearance of sins in historical time, to be effaced when history is left behind.

65. The manuscript suggests that two different citizens may speak these lines. Whether their speaker is one or many, their attempt to read Leighton's face as a palimpsest, with God effacing the traces of violence written upon His image, voices a recurrent concern in Shelley. *A Philosophical View of Reform* uses the same figure to speak of "slavery" as having "created this thing which has extinguished what has been called the likeness of

Leighton's speech serves as a reminder that this is the same literalism that dictated Prynne's own attack on the theater.[66] In Shelley's subtle handling of this historical allusion, the literalism of stage representation is used to argue for the undoing of that literalism. Yet is not this literalism exactly what Shelley could have expected of a contemporary audience, which *The Cenci* had characterized as "the misdeeming crowd / Which judges by what seems" (5.1.87–88)? Perhaps what blocked Shelley's progress in writing his historical drama was a fear that dramatic form, as it must present history in terms of binding appearances, would flatten his ironic intentions into a propaganda piece that would inspire in his contemporaries the same literalism he shows as the ruling passion of tyrants and rebels alike.[67]

How, then, are we to understand *The Triumph of Life*'s transfiguration of Leighton into Rousseau? The apparition of Rousseau, following the pattern established by Leighton's fleeting appearance, is directly related to the figures of obliterated light. Here is how the narrator describes Rousseau taking shape:

> what I thought was an old root which grew
> To strange distortion out of the hill side
> Was indeed one of that deluded crew,
>
> And . . . the grass which methought hung so wide
> And white, was but his thin discoloured hair,
> And . . . the holes it vainly sought to hide
>
> Were or had been eyes.
>
> (182–88)

God in man" (*Prose* 236); *The Cenci* figures Count Cenci's deeds as inscribing the faces of his children: "you fear to read upon their looks / The shame and misery you have written there" (1.1.41–42). *Charles the First* adds an ironic twist by placing together the "marks" inscribed by Laud and the "image" "stamped" by his Maker.

66. Thomas H. Luxon has discussed this matter in his excellent study of Bunyan: "Literalism, even at times a kind of hyperliteralism, was the rallying cry of advanced Puritans"; see *Literal Figures: Puritan Allegory and the Reformation Crisis in Representation* (Chicago: University of Chicago Press, 1995) ix.

67. Donald Reiman reads *Charles the First* in a similar fashion, claiming that Shelley saw his play "not in terms of the simple categories of the oppressors and the oppressed that had governed *The Cenci*, but rather as a drama of the irony of historical necessity in which Charles is to be crushed by the Jacobin-like violence of the Second Citizen, whose bloodthirstiness matches that of Archbishop Laud" (*Percy Bysshe Shelley* [New York: Twayne, 1969] 150). My suggestion that the violence shared by Laud and the citizens is the violence of literalism would make *Charles the First* a further elaboration, rather than a repudiation, of *The Cenci*.

The apparition may be brought back to the poem's images of obliterated light if we attend to Rousseau's missing eyes, which recall Shelley's development of the figure from *Eikon Basilike* in which the metaphor of the clouded sun is joined to the metaphor of the body politic by way of the sun's identification with light and thus with the eye. In the king's lines from *Charles the First,* "The wild million / Strikes at the eye that guides them" (2.146–47): the king, traditionally the head of the body politic, can be the eye of the people because, being also the sun, he sheds the light by which they see their way. Like Oedipus, however, the body politic strikes out its own eye, according to a counter-metaphor that makes permanent the temporary darkness in *Eikon Basilike*'s metaphor of a cloud passing over the sun. Rousseau's missing eyes in *The Triumph of Life* may have a similar significance. Here "the wild million" of *Charles the First* becomes "the loud million" (437) and "the million with fierce song and maniac dance / Raging around" (110–11), the throng of Life that not only obscures but permanently extinguishes the illumination Rousseau might have shed. The eclipse metaphors that run through the poem, seen from the blinded Rousseau's point of view, take on a sense of permanent darkness that further removes them from the metaphor of night's temporary obscurity. These eclipses give Rousseau's disfigurement the permanence Leighton is so eager to disclaim in his own; for while Leighton may argue that his markings must vanish with the passing of worldly appearances, Rousseau's blinding figures that very passing of appearances, and so cannot be undone by viewing history in some otherworldly light. Rousseau has no eyes to turn. This specific revision has a broader parallel in the imagery of *The Triumph of Life:* light never disappears; it cannot disappear. Even in his blindness, Rousseau must struggle in vain to hide the gaping holes that, like Prometheus's "lidless eyes" (1.479), doom him to an endless exposure to a light which, to use a phrase that appears in *Charles the First* and recurs obsessively in Shelley, "cannot die."

The relation between Rousseau's disfigurement and the pattern of obliterated light reveals the most striking similarity between Leighton and Rousseau. In each case, the appearance of the disfigured figure occasions a reflection on remembrance and forgetting, presented in the Lockean image of stamping and effacing impressions on a blank surface. As the "stamped" traces of historical violence—his branding— may be effaced according to Leighton's speech in *Charles the First,* so in *The Triumph of Life* the "form and character" stamped by the sun

Charles the First and *The Triumph of Life*

on "all things" may be similarly effaced. The repeatedly defaced palimpsest of the face, stamped by God and defaced by Laud, resembles the shore in the simile with which Rousseau describes the process of forgetting that sustains the momentum of Life:

> ". . . suddenly my brain became as sand
>
> "Where the first wave had more than half erased
> The track of deer on desert Labrador,
> Whilst the fierce wolf from which they fled amazed
>
> "Leaves his stamp visibly upon the shore
> Until the second bursts—so on my sight
> Burst a new Vision never seen before.—"
>
> (405–11)[68]

That this simile deals with forgetting as well as with the parallel obliteration of light is clear from a line cancelled in the manuscript, offering a different simile: "like Stars at sunrise are forgot." Rousseau's simile can thus be read as a revision of Leighton's speech: if the face of man in *Charles the First* is like the sand of the "brain" in *The Triumph of Life*, the stamped image of Leighton's Maker is like the track of the deer, washed by time's waters and replaced by the traces of violence, the stamp of the "fierce wolf" (from *Charles the First*'s "grim wolf") which is itself effaced by the same process.[69] *The Triumph of Life* makes this

---

68. *Charles the First*'s thematics of monumentalism are revisited here by way of borrowings from "Ozymandias": "stamped" (7), "the lone and level sands" (14).

69. Donald Reiman's facsimile edition of the manuscript (*The Triumph of Life: Shelley's Rough Draft Holograph Manuscript, MS Shelley adds. c. 4, folios 19–58* [New York: Garland, 1986]) shows, at folio 44r (pp. 234–35), that Shelley conceived the visible stamp of the wolf as a legible trace or inscription, and provides a startling parallel between this stamp and the stamping in *Charles the First*. Shelley seems initially to have written: "Whilst the wolf's track, from which they fled amazed / Was legible, until the second broke." He replaced "legible" with "visible," then cancelled the line and wrote what we take to be the final version. The "stamp" retained in this final version may be a displacement of a "stamp" cancelled in one of the poem's most important passages. The final version of lines 228–31 reads: "much I grieved to think how power & will / In opposition rule our mortal day— / And why God made irreconcilable / Good & the means of good . . ."; the line beginning "And why God made" initially began "And why God stamps." If Shelley wrote the cancelled words remembering *Charles the First*, the context of Leighton's speech would carry over in the lines on the deer and the wolf. Shelley may also have wanted to establish a connection between God's stamping His image onto the face of man, and His having made irreconcilable good and the means of good.

effacement the result of the "new Vision, and its cold bright car, / With savage music, stunning music"—the result, that is, of the pageant borrowed from *Charles the First* and running through the entire poem. An absolute visionary light, with the discordant harmony it kindles, effaces the visible traces of power, the form and character that a subordinate natural light has stamped on all things. In *Charles the First*, it is the transcendental pageant of universal history implicitly invoked by Leighton—with its capacity to efface the court's pageantry and the bodily markings of visible power—that may restore to those who remember it the face of man. In *The Triumph of Life* it is the excess of a nonphenomenal, visionary light—more readily available in this Dantean afterworld than on the Regency stage—that restores the sand of the brain, and presumably the ideal nature of all things, to their blank purity. The passage in *The Triumph of Life* may, then, be read as eclipsing the "political and ethical" element in the line from "On Life" I would apply to the skeptical project of *The Cenci*, claiming that philosophy "leaves, what is too often the duty of the reformer in political and ethical questions to leave, a vacancy" (477).

4.

In rewriting *Charles the First*, *The Triumph of Life* might be said to privatize its arguments, to depoliticize or even to cancel them. The conclusion my reading justifies is simpler and less judgmental. In *Charles the First*, Shelley wants to make a claim for the power of an ironic detachment from the awareness of being situated in history. That claim is complicated by his attempt to establish it in the public forum that requires him to assign his words to bodies on a stage. *The Triumph of Life* takes away the bodies.

The visionary poem can be seen as providing a suitable vehicle for an irony so pervasive that it prevented Shelley from completing his drama. But *Charles the First* commemorates a desire for agency that *The Triumph of Life* has abandoned. It makes us wonder whether that loss is regrettable. This is, in a sense, *the* question posed by Romantic drama: whether the bodies drama puts on exhibit allow for a public articulation of private irony that might make irony do the political work of turning spectators into actors. Richard Rorty has asked, in the context of modern liberalism, a question lurking behind Shelley's late fragments: Is there not a fundamental incompatibility between private irony and liberal hope? "There is at least a prima facie tension," Rorty suggests, "between the idea that social organization aims at human equality"—one of Shelley's radical objectives—and the ironist's view that "human beings are simply incarnated vocabularies." Drama would seem to run counter to that ironic argument: the suffering of Beatrice Cenci, even if we understand it as allegorizing an epistemological problem, must nonetheless make us feel, when we see or even imagine her body on stage, that she is something more than Hume's "bundle or collection of different perceptions, which succeed each other with an inconceivable rapidity, and are in a perpetual flux and movement." That "something more" is what Shelley wanted to make us feel by writing her story as a play; and if we say that *The Cenci* is nothing more than *A Treatise of Human Nature* argued with bodies, then in stumbling on those bodies we have gone some distance toward accounting for the difference in political tendency and force between those two texts. As Rorty acknowledges, there is something inescapable in the arguments of those who view irony as politically regressive: "if men and women were, indeed, nothing more than sentential attitudes—nothing more than the presence or absence of dispositions toward the use of sentences phrased in some historically conditioned vocabulary—then not only human nature, but human *solidarity,* would begin to seem an eccentric and dubious idea."[70]

The Triumph of Life solves some of the problems into which Shelley was led by his research for *Charles the First.* As he struggled to write the play, those problems grew beyond the dissatisfaction that had compelled Hume, in Leo Braudy's account, to shift his *History* from a dramatic method assuming "that moral action is the center of history" to a narrative method better equipped to capture the "unimpeded flow of time."[71] The generic shift from *Charles the First* to *The Triumph of Life* suggests that Shelley needed to figure change not in the fleeting discontinuities of scene changes, but in the more permanent form of a narrative that effaces its own tracks but *preserves the evidence of that effacement.* There can be no claim in *The Triumph of Life,* as there must be on stage, that one can *see* the agency that brings change:

---

70. Richard Rorty, "Private Irony and Liberal Hope," in *Contingency, Irony, and Solidarity* 88–89.
71. Braudy, *Narrative Form* 44, 37.

conflicts between systems of figurative language, for example those that support the judgments "active" and "passive," do not make good dramatic material. By the same token, however, the changes effected within *The Triumph of Life*, although their agency may be invisible, will always be available to be read and can thus be called, in an important sense, permanent. *Charles the First* reaches toward a permanence lying beyond the historical stage, but it cannot sustain a language touching upon what the *Defence of Poetry* calls "the universal element with which [the mind] has perpetual sympathy" (485). For the representational space of the stage is generically incompatible with the prophetic spaces sought out in Shelley's visionary poems, such as the cave in *Prometheus Unbound* "where we will sit and talk of time and change, / As the world ebbs and flows, ourselves unchanged" (3.3.23–24).

Charles the First, however, like Romantic drama considered as a whole, prompts a question neither *Prometheus Unbound* nor *The Triumph of Life* can answer: How will we ever bring outselves to *do* anything, except hide, in those caves of immutability? That is the question Shelley allows his Puritans to ask. For he wants the question asked —by persons with bodies—even if he cannot bring himself to endorse an answer. It is asked, I think, in the following exchange from the Star Chamber scene, in which the revolutionary prophecy of the Puritan Bastwick confronts the immediacy of bodily pain:

> Bastwick. Were I an enemy of my God and King,
>   And of good men, as ye are;—I should merit
>   Your fearful state and gilt prosperity,
>   Which, when ye wake from the last sleep, shall turn
>   To cowls and robes of everlasting fire.
>   But, as I am, I bid ye grudge me not
>   The only earthly favour ye can yield,
>   Or I think worth acceptance at your hands,—
>   [   ] even as my Master did,
>   Until Heaven's kingdom shall descend on earth,
>   Or earth be like a shadow in the light
>   Of Heaven absorbed—some few tumultuous years
>   Will pass, and leave no wreck of what opposes
>   His will whose will is power.
> Laud. Officer, take the prisoner from the bar,
>   And be his tongue slit for his insolence.
> Bastwick. While this hand holds a pen—
> Laud.   Be his hands—

Juxon.   Stop!
   Forbear, my lord! The tongue, which now can speak
   No terror, would interpret, being dumb,
   Heaven's thunder to our harm [   ]
   And hands, which now write only their own shame,
   With bleeding stumps might sign our blood away.

The political commitments of such a scene are overt, not only in Bastwick's forceful prophecy, but even more in the linkage of writing and bodily pain that is borrowed from *Titus Andronicus,* which Shelley read in the month before he began writing *Charles the First.*[72] But its political commitments are at odds with each other: Bastwick's immutable prophecy cannot save him from the bodily pain it would bring to an end. "His will whose will is power" must sound terribly hollow, not just in comparison with *The Triumph of Life*'s decree that "God made irreconcilable / Good and the means of good," but more obviously in the face of a bodily suffering that is unimaginable for Shelley's Rousseau. The point is not that Shelley agreed with Bastwick and then changed his mind, but rather that the drama's ability to draw on the political force of arguments he could not personally endorse seems inextricable from the drama's generic commitment to embodiment. In turning away from both, Shelley turned away from politics, at least politics of a certain kind.

Bastwick's argument might be characterized with Rorty's description of the liberal commitments of the metaphysician, who "thinks that there is a connection between redescription and power, and that the right rede-

---

72. From the Stocking edition of *The Journals of Claire Clairmont* (514–15), which relies on the reading list in *Letters* 2:467–88 and on the Frederick L. Jones edition of *Mary Shelley's Journal,* we can trace at least part of Shelley's reading in Shakespeare during the period in which *Charles the First* was being contemplated:

January 1820	*The Tempest*
December 1821	*Julius Caesar*
	Cymbeline
	Henry IV
	Titus Andronicus
January 1822	*King Lear*
	All's Well That Ends Well
March 1822	*Hamlet*
	Romeo and Juliet

The plays most clearly present in *Charles the First* are *The Tempest, Titus Andronicus, King Lear,* and *Hamlet.*

scription can make us free."[73] Shelley, at this point in his career, might be characterized with Rorty's contrasting description of the ironist, who learns "that our chances of freedom depend on historical contingencies which are only occasionally influenced by our self-redescriptions." Rorty's adjudication of these competing stances can help clarify Shelley's motives in writing, and in suspending, *Charles the First:*

> There is no reason the ironist cannot be a liberal, but she cannot be a "progressive" and "dynamic" liberal in the sense in which liberal metaphysicians sometimes claim to be. For she cannot offer the same sort of social hope as metaphysicians offer. She cannot claim that adopting her redescription of yourself or your situation makes you better able to conquer the forces which are marshaled against you. On her account, that ability is a matter of weapons and luck, not a matter of having truth on your side, or having detected the "movement of history."[74]

Shelley's conflicted position toward drama arises as his intellectual irony is increasingly, and unbearably, qualified by his appeal to human solidarity. *The Triumph of Life* suggests that he chose irony over solidarity. Why he made that choice can be gathered by looking at one final passage from *Charles the First,* in which Shelley shows how an audience might approach the "signs" that are displayed on a stage in such a way as to turn them from bearers of meaning into agents of change.

Shelley allows the Old Man to back his argument about the nefarious political powers exhibited in *The Triumph of Peace* with an interpretation of the antimasque. His speech compares the bond between wealth and misery to the bonds tying cause to effect and signifier to signified:

> Here is health
> Followed by grim disease, glory by shame,
> Waste by lame famine, wealth by squalid want,
> And England's sin by England's punishment.
> And, as the effect pursues the cause foregone,
> Lo, giving substance to my words, behold

---

73. Rorty filters the metaphysician's position through the voice of the ironist; what the metaphysician would say, in His own voice, is that *"the truth* may make us free" (John 8:32; emphasis added). Rorty may be attempting to root his metaphysician in one line of Romanticism, for Coleridge took this verse as a motto for his shortlived periodical *The Watchman.*

74. Rorty, "Private Irony" 90–91.

> At once the sign and the thing signified—
> A troop of cripples, beggars, and lean outcasts,
> Horsed upon stumbling jades, carted with dung,
> Dragged for a day from cellars and low cabins
> And rotten hiding-holes, to point the moral
> Of this presentment, and bring up the rear
> Of painted pomp with misery!
> (1.162–74; 159 rev.-157 rev.)[75]

" 'Tis but the antimasque," says Shelley's Youth, as many critics have said of *The Triumph of Life* as a whole. The antimasque's generic reversal may well prefigure the ironic reversal of genre (celebration become tragedy) with which Shelley seems to have wanted to conclude his play. But the Old Man's speech is less important for what it suggests about Shelley's dramatic irony than for its idea of history as an ironic necessity, an idea that will provide the narrative structure of *The Triumph of Life*. The Old Man reads "this presentment" as a chain of signifiers providing its own interpretation by a logic of negation: what is seen signifies (the absence of) what is hidden, with the consequence that what is hidden must appear as a new signifier. His understanding of visible appearances as a system of signification belongs to a tradition of biblical exegesis that can be traced to the Puritan divines, but it also belongs to a philosophical tradition much closer to Shelley, for it is an axiom of Berkeley's epistemology that "Visible ideas ... signify ... after the same manner that words of any language suggest the ideas they are made to stand for."[76] The Old Man does not, however, grasp Berkeley's critical recognition that "the connection of ideas does not imply the relation of *cause* and *effect*, but only a mark or *sign* with the thing *signified*"; rather, he adopts Thomas Reid's "common sense" assurance that "What we commonly call natural *causes* might, with more propriety, be called natural *signs,* and what we call *effects,* the

---

75. The extensive manuscript revisions show that Shelley struggled to formulate this set of analogies: cancelled lines include "turning words to things" and "the image & the object signified." For a general consideration of "succession" in this scene and in other works, see Steven Jones, "'Choose Reform or Civil War': Shelley, the English Revolution, and the Problem of Succession," *The Wordsworth Circle* 25 (1994): 145–49.

76. George Berkeley, *Principles of Human Knowledge*, ed. T. E. Jessop (New York: T. Nelson and Sons, 1945), par. 43; quoted from Terence Allan Hoagwood, *Prophecy and the Philosophy of Mind: Traditions of Blake and Shelley* (University: University of Alabama Press, 1985) 28.

thing signified."[77] The slippage into "common sense" philosophy that Shelley introduces in his phrasing of the Old Man's response suggests that he wants to turn the commentary on the pageant into an interpretation not just of the ironies that structure the outcomes of political decision-making, but also of the limitations of the common-sense, unironical mind that turns such structural ironies into binding necessities. What overtly signifies wealth can turn out covertly to signify want without committing us to a belief in the necessity by which wealth *must* cause want. Indeed, the ability to read the signs of wealth as signs of want should allow one to intervene in the process by which wealth might cause want; but the Old Man stands idly by.

Drama can play to common sense by putting bodies on stage, and it can facilitate skepticism by staging a conflict of voices. Suspending the spectators' debate with the entrance of Leighton's damaged body might have been part of Shelley's effort to combine these elements in a way that helps the spectators of *Charles the First* understand themselves as actors. Leighton's damaged body comes onstage, however, not as a body like the spectator's, but as a legible sign, just as the "troop of cripples, beggars, and lean outcasts" are absorbed into the play of signs organized by the Old Man. Shelley clearly wants to present damaged bodies as "substance," not as "sign" but as "thing signified"; but he knows that the stage only *seems* to allow him to do this, and the Old Man's speech exposes the futility of pretending that interpreting bodies on stage is the same as caring about people.

The postdramatic, posthistorical execution of *Charles the First* carried out by *The Triumph of Life* makes the latter a "phantom of that early form / Which moved upon its motion" (464–65). Shelley's phantom poem can have no proper end, any more than Rousseau can find an end to the thick billows of equivocation in which Shelley envelopes him. The endlessness of *The Triumph of Life*—the bad infinity of phantom agency—far from instilling the mastery of a skeptical *contemptus mundi,* engenders an unquenchable nostalgia for the doings and sufferings that could once be found in history. It suggests that Shelley learned, from writing *Charles the First,* that to put suffering on stage is not to stop it but only to endow it with the phantom agency Shelley called

77. Berkeley, *Human Knowledge* par. 65, quoted from Hoagwood, *Prophecy* 29; Reid, *An Inquiry into the Human Mind on the Principles of Common Sense,* quoted from Andrew Cooper, *Doubt and Identity* 20; quoted also in Hoagwood, *Skepticism and Ideology* 67.

Charles the First and The Triumph of Life

Life. It is only within the history one is living that one can choose to stop exhibiting cripples, beggars, and lean outcasts, to stop using that exhibition as an occasion for moral and political commentary, however enlightened. The limits of such writing are evident in a single, fragmented line I have already quoted from the Star Chamber scene:

> *Bastwick.*   While this hand holds a pen—
> *Laud.*   Be his hands—
> *Juxon.*   Stop!

The political power claimed for writing runs up against the limit of bodily suffering, even as that suffering is being folded back into Shelley's powerful writing, which was, in *Charles the First*—but is not, in *The Triumph of Life*—made to seem dependent on his having a body. *The Triumph of Life,* which marks Shelley's withdrawal from the body, can be called a political poem only in the sense that it allows us to see the intractable political dilemma commemorated in his unfinished historical drama. It shows why Shelley had to stop.

Index

Abbey, Lloyd, 209n.
Absolutism, 105, 201, 235–37
Accident, 30, 89, 97
Acknowledgment, 14–15, 44, 49, 57, 71, 75, 99–100, 122–24, 126, 130, 144, 150, 162, 190, 210–11, 220–22; and avoidance, 15, 39, 125, 127, 137, 141, 144, 153–59; and disavowal, 112, 152–54, 157–59
Addison, Joseph, 170n.
Alienation, 75–79, 161, 185, 193
Allegory, 90–91, 119, 128–31, 142–43, 157–58, 168, 171, 173, 186, 189n., 195, 240, 247
Allen, William, 212n.
Allison, Henry E., 157n.
Althusser, Louis, 7, 45
Ambivalence, 29, 32–34, 62, 76, 82, 89, 112, 122–23, 173, 197–98, 211, 250–52
Anderson, Perry, 7
Anti-Jacobin, 45n.
Appiah, Anthony, 7–9
Arac, Jonathan, 46–47
Arendt, Hannah, 44–45
Aristotle, 92
Austen, Jane, 234n.
Austin, J. L., 92n.
Authoritarianism, 165, 170–71
Autonomy, xiii, 2, 4, 7, 10, 28, 33, 44, 46, 49, 62, 72, 81–83, 101, 111, 118, 130, 138, 173–74, 177, 180–82, 189, 195, 208

Baer, Marc, 6n.
Baillie, Joanna, 38n., 100, 124, 128, 177
Bakhtin, Mikhail, 11
Ball, Patricia M., 111n.
Ballad of Sir Patrick Spence, 223
Barrell, John, 40n.
Barrish, Jonas, 121n.
Bate, Jonathan, 16n., 193n.
Baudrillard, Jean, 47, 238n.
Beacon, 167n.
Becker, Carl, 213n., 237n.
Beer, John, 100, 113
Belief, 99–103, 106–7, 114–15, 117–21, 125–30, 137–38, 207–8; disbelief, suspension of, 100, 111, 144. *See also* Skepticism
Bellingham, John, 130–31
Belsey, Catherine, 81n., 91n.
Bennett, Arnold, 74n.
Berkeley, George, 251–52
Berlin, Isaiah, 62n.
Black Dwarf, 56
Blackstone, William, 190
Blake, William, 67, 76n., 251n.
Bloom, Harold, 67
Blum, Carol, 44n.
Bodies, embodiment, xii–xiii, 3–4, 9, 16–17, 19, 50, 56, 84, 98, 100, 108, 112–13, 122–23, 130, 135–37, 140–45, 149–52, 155–59, 181, 184–85, 192, 195–97, 208–10, 233, 246–53; body politic, 50, 156, 184, 196, 244; disembodiment, 16, 50, 130, 158–59, 210

255

Bonaparte, Napoleon, 12
Bongie, Laurence L., 219n.
Booth, Stephen, 1
Bouquier, Gabriel, 237n.
Bowles, William Lisle, 34n., 200
Bradley, A. C., 90n.
Brandl, Alois, 117n.
Braudy, Leo, 213n., 217n., 247
Brisman, Leslie, 114, 226n., 230n.
British Critic, 174, 189n.
British Review, 125, 128, 153n., 170n.
Bromwich, David, 71, 82n.
Brooks, Peter, 60, 153n.
Brutus, 24–28, 130 (sculpture); 41 (character); 175 (historical personage)
Büchner, Georg, 42
Bunyan, John, 243n.
Burckhardt, Jacob, 12
Burke, Edmund, 29, 51n., 66, 118, 190–91, 212, 216; *Letters on a Regicide Peace,* 29; *Reflections on the Revolution in France,* 80, 220n.
Burroughs, Catherine B., 101n.
Burwick, Frederic, 111n., 114, 122–24
Butler, E. M., 167n.
Butterfield, Herbert, 167, 213
Byron, George Gordon, Lord, 19, 160–63, 165–204, 208; *Childe Harold's Pilgrimage,* 142, 160–63, 172–75, 181, 192, 198, 202–3; *Don Juan,* 173; *The Giaour,* 143; *Lara,* 173n.; *Marino Faliero,* 165–204, 208, 212n.; *The Two Foscari,* 192n.; *The Vision of Judgment,* 208

Cameron, Kenneth Neill, 212n.
Campbell, Thomas, 200
Carlson, Julie, 101n., 103n., 117, 166n., 194n., 236n.
Carlson, Marvin, 46n.
Carlyle, Thomas, 2
Cause, causality, 82, 87, 93–95, 145–51, 155, 169, 203
Cavell, Stanley, 9, 13–15, 91, 181
Chandler, Alice, 74
Chastellux, François Jean, Marquis de, 237n.
Chew, Samuel, 168
Christensen, Jerome, 170–72, 203
Christian Observer, 13n., 234n.
Circumstance, 27–28, 52, 55, 70, 84, 114, 118, 142

Clairmont, Claire, 249n.
Clarendon, Earl of, 212, 218
Closet drama, 23, 78
Cobbett, William, 74
Cole, Stephen E., 8–9
Coleridge, John Taylor, 130
Coleridge, Samuel Taylor, xi–xii, 2, 4, 13, 18, 23–57, 62n., 82–85, 90, 99–131, 216n.; *Biographia Literaria,* 34–36, 111; *Conciones ad Populum,* 35n., 44; "Critique of Bertram," xii; "Destiny of Nations," 112–14, 118; "Effusion XX," 117; *Essays on his Times,* 52; "The Eolian Harp," 83, 111–12; *The Fall of Robespierre,* 28–49, 54, 62, 96, 177, 193; *The Friend,* 24–28, 48n., 197, 225; "Frost at Midnight," 111, 126; "Kubla Khan," 111–12; *Lectures on Shakespeare,* 60n., 90; *Notebooks,* 24; *On the Constitution of Church and State,* 216n.; *Osorio* and *Remorse,* 13, 99–131, 234n.; "Religious Musings," 114; "Sonnets on Eminent Characters," 36; *Statesman's Manual,* 226n.; *Watchman,* 250n.
Collaboration, 28–32, 49, 68, 85, 112–14
Collings, David, 4n., 64n.
Collins, William, 38n.
Compulsion, 2, 58–61, 68, 75–77, 80–81, 171; to repeat, 81, 85–88. *See also* Fate, fatalism
Confession, 58–61, 64–66, 124–25, 202
Conspiracy, 168, 174, 178–79, 185, 190–202; Cato Street Conspiracy, 167n., 168–69n., 174, 188n., 204, 215
Contagion, 44, 52, 80
Contarini, Gasparo, 188
Contract, 16, 185–91, 198, 201
Cooper, Andrew M., 156n., 252n.
Corbett, Martyn, 167n.
Covent Garden, 16, 140n.
Cox, Jeffrey, 45
Critical Review, 34
Cromwell, Oliver, 217
Crook, Nora, 209n.
Crowds, 42–49, 52–56
Curran, Stuart, 211
Curry, Kenneth, 30n., 40n.

Index

Dante (Alighieri), 149, 185n., 232, 240, 242n., 246
Davenant, William, 193, 233n.
Davidson, Donald, xii
De Bruyn, Lucy, 44n.
Dekker, Thomas, 193
Deleuze, Gilles, and Felix Guattari, 82
De Man, Paul, 98, 232
Dennett, Daniel C., 8n., 27n.
De Quincey, Thomas, 75n., 159n.
Derrida, Jacques, 206n.
Desire, 5, 8, 47, 61, 81–82, 85, 115, 119, 136, 144–45, 246
Desmond, Robert W., 31n.
Determinism, 119, 173
Dialogue, 124–25, 136–38, 149–51, 154
Dickens, Charles, 220n.
Disraeli, Benjamin, 188, 220n.
Dobrée, Bonamy, 76n.
Donohue, Joseph W., 5n., 104n.
Drama, The, 189n.
Drummond, William, 2, 207n.
Drury Lane, 111, 131, 175
Du Bartas, Guillaume, 193
Duffy, Edward, 231n.

Eclectic Review, 174
Edinburgh Monthly Review, 143n.
Eikon Basilike, 229, 244
Eliot, George (Mary Ann Evans), 135
Empson, William, 78n., 84n.
England, A. B., 173
Engle, Lars, 90n.
Enlightenment, 61, 66, 103n., 116–20, 148, 156, 163, 226, 231, 253
Enthusiasm, 109–16, 126, 214–15, 236
Erdman, David, 34n., 176
European Magazine, 189n.
European Magazine and London Review, 216n.
Ewen, Frederic, 119
Examiner, 189n.

Fancy, 109–18, 123–26, 129
Fate, fatalism, 45, 160–63, 165–73, 181, 198, 201–3, 208
Ferriss, Suzanne, 158n.
Feudalism, 55, 69–70, 73–76, 179, 193
Filmer, Robert, 186
Fink, Z. S., 170n., 187–88n.
Fischer, David James, 45n.

Fletcher, Richard, 6n.
Forbes, Duncan, 214n.
Foucault, Michel, 12, 158, 233, 237
Fragments, fragmentation, 25, 154, 162, 192–96, 209, 222, 224, 246–47, 253
Freccero, John, 242n.
Freedom, x–xi, 14, 17, 29, 44, 52–56, 58, 62, 68–80, 84–88, 109–12, 121, 138, 152, 159–60, 166, 170–77, 181, 188, 192, 194n., 198, 204, 215–17, 250; from action, 14; in Kant, 14; of religion, 105–9; and servitude, 58, 210, 241
Freud, Sigmund, 61n., 81, 86–88, 90, 93, 173
Friedman, Michael H., 73
Fry, Paul H., 148n.
Furet, François, 42, 203

Galignani, A. and W., 169n.
Gallagher, Catherine, 16–17
Gamer, Michael, 34n.
Garrick, David, 119, 157n.
Gaull, Marilyn, 5n., 140n.
Gelpi, Barbara Charlesworth, 154n.
Giannotti, Donato, 28n.
Giddens, Anthony, 5
Gill, Stephen, 63n.
Godwin, William, 77, 148, 186, 207n., 209n., 216–18, 221, 235–36
Goethe, Johann Wolfgang von, 105, 166–67
Goldman, Michael, 92n.
Goldmann, Lucien, 26
Gold's London Magazine, 158
Greenblatt, Stephen, 15n., 23
Greever, Garland, 34n.
Gross, Kenneth, 107
Grossman, A., 226n.
Guérard, Albert, x, 3
Guilt, 38–40, 54, 68, 71, 108, 121–24, 130–31, 196

Hadley, Elaine, 6n.
Hale, Matthew, 190
Halévy, Elie, 31n., 73–74
Halpern, Richard, 69n., 238n.
Hardy, Thomas, 193–94
Harrington, James, 187
Hart, H. L. A., 8n., 92n.
Hartman, Geoffrey, 63n., 82n., 85n.

Hazlitt, William, xii, 2, 23, 33, 50, 125, 166–67, 169, 170n., 177, 200, 236
Heaney, Seamus, 179n.
Hegel, G. W. F., 12
Hill, Bridget, 216n.
Hill, Christopher, 193, 226n., 229n.
Historical drama, 31, 37, 51, 210, 222, 224
Historicism, 10–12, 78
Historiography, 209–19
Hoagwood, Terence, 139n., 251–52n.
Hobbes, Thomas, 35
Hobhouse, Henry, 168n.
Hobhouse, John, 168
Holcroft, Thomas, 40n.
Holmes, Richard, 30n., 33n., 211n., 234n.
Huet, Marie-Hélène, 159
Hugo, Victor, 47
Human, humanism, 8–9, 15, 182–83, 197, 210; dehumanization, 145; inhuman, 158, 192
Hume, David, xii, 3, 136n., 146–47, 150, 154n., 155–57, 186, 205–9, 212–99, 231–33, 240–41, 247
Hunt, Leigh, 49n., 165

Iconoclasm, 121–22, 127
Identity, xiii, 12, 19, 47, 136–39, 144, 150, 154–63
Imagination, 33, 61, 83–85, 90n., 112–14, 137, 141, 144, 151, 155–57, 163, 185, 190, 215, 224, 235–37. *See also* Fancy
Impersonation, 141–43, 157, 165
Individuals, 3, 23, 29–31, 40–44, 47, 49–50, 53, 62, 66, 113, 170, 174–76, 179, 181, 184, 192, 195–98, 203, 210
Insanity, 8, 78, 89–92, 96, 123–28, 130–31, 138, 144, 153–60
Instrumentality, 55, 93, 103, 105, 166
Integrity, 26, 50, 179–80, 190, 229, 234, 240
Intention, 5, 52–53, 90–92, 129, 148, 151
Intentional systems, 8–9
Irony, 148n., 214, 218, 231, 243, 246, 250–51
Izenberg, Gerald, 29, 33n., 63

Jacobinism, 34, 44, 45n., 49–50, 62, 78, 243n.
Jacobus, Mary 16n., 83

Jeffrey, Francis 174–75
Johnson, Barbara, 162
Johnson, David, 188n.
Johnson, E. D. H., 169
Johnson, Samuel, 157n.
Johnston, Kenneth, 219n., 227n.
Jones, Steven, 251n.
Justice, 53–54, 58, 66, 72, 78, 108, 142, 158–60, 169, 186, 208

Kaiser, David Aram, 216n.
Kant, Immanuel, 2, 14, 157
Kean, Edmund, 137n.
Keats, John, x–xi, 14; "The Fall of Hyperion," x–xi; "Hyperion," 225; "On Sitting Down to Read King Lear Once Again," 14
Kelley, Theresa M., 76
Kelsall, Malcolm, 169n., 170
Kemble, John Philip, 16, 189n.
Kibbey, Ann, 122n.
Kilcup, Rodney W., 214n.
King, Martin Luther, 140n.
Knapp, Steven, 37, 127n.
Knight, G. Wilson, 193n.
Korsgaard, Christine M., 187n.

Lacan, Jacques, 45, 152n., 154n., 184n.
La Fayette, Marquis de, 168–69
Lamb, Charles, 121n.
Langbaum, Robert, 124n.
Lansdown, Richard, 135n., 169n., 177, 195n.
Laplanche, Jean, 33n.
Laud, Archbishop, 234, 243n., 245
Laursen, John Christian, 214n.
Law, 58, 67, 72–77, 78n., 80–81, 131, 139, 152–53, 158–60, 178–79, 214–16, 221, 228, 232, 241; canon law, 90
—concepts of law:
constitution, 46, 73, 187–90, 214–16
habeas corpus, 40, 75
heriot, 73n., 74n.
Magna Carta, 73–76
mens rea, 92
negligence, 89
rights, 53, 190, 215
trial by jury, 62
trial by ordeal, 75
Leavis, F. R., 153, 239
Lefkowitz, Murray, 233n.

Index

Leighton, Alexander, 232–35, 240–46, 252
Levinson, Marjorie, 26n.
Lewis, Wyndham, 9–10
Liberalism, 14, 141–42, 151, 164, 185, 242–43
Literalism, literalization, 14, 141–42, 151, 164, 185, 242–43
Literary Gazette, 169n.
Liu, Alan, 11–12
Locke, John, 3, 157n., 186–88, 181, 207n., 244
Lockridge, Laurence, 5, 44n.
London Chronicle, 30n., 41n.
Lonsdale, James Lowther, Lord, 74, 75n.
Lowes, John Livingston, 117n.
Lukács, Georg, 45, 225–26
Lutaud, Olivier, 212n.
Luxon, Thomas H., 243n.
Lyric, xi, 40, 48, 111, 137–38
Lytton, Edward Bulwer-Lytton, Baron, 167n.

Macaulay, Catharine, 212–19, 233–34, 241
Machines, mechanicity, x, 23, 39–48, 58, 82, 84–85, 130, 151, 158, 169–71, 181, 195
MacPherson, C. B., 75n.
Magic, 99–100, 113, 117–25, 159, 180, 199–203
Magnuson, Paul, 128n.
Mann, Thomas, 97
Manning, Peter J., 173n., 199n.
Marat, Jean-Paul, 168
Marshall, David, 80n.
Marx, Karl, xii, 17–18
Massinger, Philip, 193
Maturin, Charles, 78n.
McFarland, Thomas, 26n., 83n., 111n.
McGann, Jerome J., 17, 170, 180n., 193n.
McNiece, Gerald, 235
McWhir, Anne, 152n.
Medici, Alessandro de', 24n.
Medwin, Thomas, 25–26, 211, 212n.
Melodrama, 60, 63, 69, 140, 153
Melville, Herman, 140n.
Memory, 150, 154–57, 184, 191, 197–201, 242, 246; and countermemory, 237, 240; and forgetting, 191, 198–201, 235–45

Michelangelo (Buonarroti), 24–28
Michelet, Jules, 12
Milton, John, 36–38, 44, 225–26, 229–30, 233
Mirabeau, Comte de, 168–69, 219
Mirrors, 32, 64–65, 68, 70, 78–79, 158n., 160, 177–78, 184n., 199, 206, 211
Mitford, Mary Russell, 234n.
Moline, P. L., 237n.
Moniteur Universel, 46n.
Montaigne, Michel de, 193
Monthly Magazine, 204
Monthly Review, 105n.
Montrose, Louis, 10–12
Monuments, monumentalism, 26, 200–202, 235–36
Moorman, Mary, 72
Mossner, E. C., 213n.
Motive, 5, 8–9, 59, 67, 81–82, 90, 94–95, 177
Muller, John P., 152n.

Narrative, ix, 8, 13, 42, 80, 83, 91–92, 97, 114, 129, 143, 155, 169, 205–8, 224, 232, 247
Nashe, Thomas, 15
Necessity, xii, 25, 68, 146–47, 169, 225–26, 242, 251–52
New Edinburgh Review, 203
New Monthly Magazine, 136–37, 151, 158
News, newspapers, 30, 34, 40–43, 46–48, 174
Nicholes, Joseph, 219n., 227n.
Nietzsche, Friedrich, 9, 18, 92, 198–99, 237n.
Novels, 13, 16–17, 23, 117–20

O'Neill, Eliza, 3, 141, 143, 157
Orgel, Stephen, 232n., 233
Orwell, George, ix–xi
Otway, Thomas, 189, 203

Paranoia, 88, 118
Parker, Reeve, 71n., 95n., 99n., 102, 107n., 130
Parrish, Stephen Maxfield, 128n.
Pascal, Blaise, 26
Passion, passions, 83, 100–101, 113, 119, 124, 128, 220

Passivity and activity, ix–xi, 6–7, 13, 16, 61, 82–91, 155–57, 161, 172–73, 183, 193, 206–8, 222, 248; passive and active voices, ix–xi, 135n., 206–7; middle voice, 83, 207
Pateman, Carole, 187–88n.
Paulson, Ronald, 121–22
Peacock, Thomas Love, 141, 160, 211
Peck, Walter Edwin, 229n., 242n.
Performance, 136, 138, 153–59, 163–64, 184, 197
Perry, James, 30n.
Personhood, 8–9, 53, 142–43, 150, 161, 174, 181, 183, 203–4, 213, 220
Personification, 47, 49, 89, 113–14, 127, 158, 195; and depersonalization, 169; and impersonality, 175. *See also* Impersonation
Phillipson, Nicholas, 213
Pirandello, Luigi, 211
Pitt, William, 40, 75
Plato, 35
Pocock, J. G. A., 216n.
Political parties (Whig and Tory), 170, 186–92, 201, 212–22
Pope, Alexander, 66, 182–83
Prasch, Thomas, 219n.
Prévost, Abbé, 219
Price, John Valdimir, 214n.
Priestley, Joseph, 216
Priestman, Donald G., 71n.
Private, privacy, 23–24, 40, 42, 53–55, 64, 66, 96, 136, 171, 179, 184–85, 198, 215, 246
Prynne, William, 232–35, 238, 242–43
Psychoanalysis, 33n., 60–61, 86–88
Psychology, 60–62, 65–67, 77, 85, 90, 96, 128, 142
Psychomachia, 60n., 99, 137. *See also* Allegory
Psychosis, 152n., 159
Pückler-Muskau, Prince Herman von, 142n.
Pulos, C. E., 139n., 146
Purinton, Marjean D., 72n.

Quarterly Review, 50–51, 130
Quinney, Laura, 81n.

Radcliffe, Ann, 34n.
Rajan, Tilottama, 40

Ramus, Peter, 193
Rationality, 8, 55, 68n., 114, 117–18
Redress, 55, 178–83, 192
Reform, 51, 55, 75n., 121, 216, 219
Regicide, 26–28, 53, 130
Reid, Thomas, xii, 2–3, 207, 251
Reik, Theodor, 58, 90, 93, 173
Reiman, Donald, 243n., 245n.
Repetition, 64, 81, 85–86, 97, 151, 185. *See also* Compulsion
Repression, 33n., 89, 142
Responsibility, xiii, 10, 39–41, 47–49, 61, 70, 92, 96, 174, 193–94
Revolution, 23, 45n., 105, 107, 159, 168, 169n., 176, 179, 189n., 195, 198, 211, 212n., 226, 229, 232, 236–40; French Revolution, 29–49, 72, 80, 84, 96, 158, 203, 217–20, 225, 235–38
Revolutionary theater, 45–47
Reynolds, John Hamilton, 29
Richardson, Alan, 5, 154
Robespierre, Maximilien, 31–33, 44, 72, 168, 241
Robinson, Charles, 165–66
Roe, Nicholas, 32, 36, 40, 241n.
Rogers, Neville, 211n.
Rolland, Romain, 45
Rorty, Richard, 15, 246–50
Ross, Marlon, 81–82
Rossington, Michael, 158n.
Rousseau, Jean-Jacques, 60, 186; as character, 205–12, 225, 231–32, 243–45, 249, 252
Rubin, Merle R., 136n.
Rudé, George, 45n.
Russell, Gillian, 6n.

Sade, Marquis de, 60
Sammons, Jeffrey, 119n.
Sanuto, Marino, 169
Satirist, 128
Sayre, Robert, 34n.
Schiffer, Ed, 92n.
Schiller, Friedrich, 95n., 105, 116–19, 126, 193n.
Scott, Walter, 13, 33n., 125, 220n.
Searle, C. E., 75n.
Sedgwick, Eve, 101n.
Sennert, Daniel, 35
Seward, Anna, 46n.

Index

Shakespeare, 23, 121n., 165, 170, 195n.; 220; *All's Well That Ends Well,* 249n.; *Coriolanus,* 193; *Cymbeline,* 249n.; *Hamlet,* 12, 33n., 65, 84, 88–92, 97, 137n., 249n.; *Henry IV,* 249n.; *Julius Caesar,* 41, 88, 249n.; *King Lear,* 13, 69–70, 135, 161, 238, 249n.; *Macbeth,* 16, 88, 90n., 94, 136, 160; *The Merchant of Venice,* 203; *Othello,* 9, 60n., 68, 181, 203; *Richard the Third,* 119, 157n., 229; *Romeo and Juliet,* 77, 91, 249n.; *The Tempest,* 249n.; *Titus Andronicus,* 249
Shelley, Mary Wollstonecraft Godwin, 25, 93, 137n., 140, 147, 148n., 158, 209n., 229n., 249n.
Shelley, Percy Bysshe, 3, 14, 19, 25–26, 135–64, 172, 203–4, 205–53; *The Cenci,* 3, 6, 135–64, 165, 178–80, 185, 188, 206, 209n., 210, 219, 239, 241–43, 246–47; *Charles the First,* 14, 25–26, 181, 188n., 209–53; *A Defense of Poetry,* 136, 248; *Julian and Maddalo,* 160–61, 165, 240; "The Masque of Anarchy," 235; "Mont Blanc," 147n.; "Ode to Liberty," 163–64; "Ode to the West Wind," 144, 161; "On Life," 147, 159, 206, 246; "Ozymandias," 26, 236–37; *A Philosophical View of Reform,* 75n., 139, 166, 214, 220, 230, 239n., 242n.; *Prometheus Unbound,* 137, 149, 152–54, 228n., 235, 242, 244, 248; *Queen Mab,* 142–43, 152; *A Refutation of Deism,* 146; "Review of Mary Shelley's *Frankenstein,*" 147n.; *The Revolt of Islam,* 236–41; "Sonnet: England in 1819," 163, 238; *The Triumph of Life,* 164, 205–11, 220–32, 235, 239, 243–53
Sheridan, Richard Brinsley, 104, 112, 115
Shirley, James. *See Triumph of Peace*
Sidmouth, Henry Addington, Viscount, 168n.
Sidney, Philip, 193
Silence, 140, 145, 170, 180, 202
Simpson, David, 73, 83n.
Skepticism, 3, 18–19, 61, 109, 117–22, 135–36, 139, 145–47, 150, 153–55, 159–61, 164, 208, 212–13, 216–18, 232, 240, 246, 252

Smith, Paul, xi, 5
Smith, William, 51
Social energy, 10, 23, 28, 30, 49, 53, 56, 187
Solidarity, xiii, 15, 53, 186, 192, 247, 250
Solipsism, 81, 111, 125, 145, 150–51, 154
Somnambulism, 97, 130, 160
Southey, Robert, xii, 74; *The Fall of Robespierre,* 28–49, 54, 57, 96, 177, 193; *Joan of Arc,* xii, 112–14, 118, 126–27; *Letters from England,* 77; *Wat Tyler,* 49–57, 62, 69, 71, 96, 113, 241n.
Spivak, Bernard, 60n.
Stagecraft, 100–102, 116–26, 242; stage directions, 43, 73
Stekel, Wilhelm, 60–61, 86n.
Sternbach, Robert, 127n.
Stocking, Marion Kingston, 249n.
Stone, Laurence, 232n., 238n.
Storch, R. F., 63n.
Strong, Roy, 232–33n.
Subjectivity, xi, 7–8, 96, 170–71; structural determination of, 7–8, 11, 83n.
Sublime, sublimity, 28, 33, 37–49, 114, 117, 127, 193–95; countersublimity, 48–49
Suicide, 81, 142, 204, 208
Suleri, Sara, 104n.
Superstition, 86–88, 99, 114–15, 117, 123–6, 146, 150
Sympathy, 33–34, 59–64, 68, 78–79, 144, 153, 156–57, 248
Swift, Jonathan, 11, 188
Szondi, Peter, 77

Tasso, Torquato, 160
Taylor, Aline Mackenzie, 189n.
Taylor, Anya, 28n., 100
Theater, theatricality, 3–4, 14–17, 23, 56, 79–80, 108, 137, 144, 155–57, 210, 221–22, 233, 237; antitheatricalism, 121n., 234, 241–43
Theatrical Inquisitor, 101, 125, 153
Thelwall, John, 40n.
Thompson, E. P., 7, 62n., 76n.
Thorslev, Peter, 173n.
Times of London, 30n.
Tolney, Charles de, 24n., 28n.

Tooke, John Horne, 40n.
Towers, Joseph, 218
Tragedy, ix, 1, 3, 9–10, 14, 52, 86–88, 96, 99–100, 137, 139, 153, 204
Trevor-Roper, H. R., 213n.
Trilling, Lionel, 9
Triumph of Peace (James Shirley and Inigo Jones), 220–24, 232–38, 242
Turner, John, 69n.
Tyrannicide. *See* Regicide

Ubersfeld, Anne, 47n.
Uncanny, the, 49, 78, 86–88
Unconsciousness, 99, 114, 122, 125, 130

Vicinus, Martha, 74n.
Virgil (Publius Virgilius Maro), 149, 193n.
Voltaire, 116, 214

Walpole, Horace, 140n.
Wasserman, Earl, 146, 154n., 158n., 240
Watkins, Daniel P., 102n., 103–7, 197n.
Watson, Robert, 107, 121
Webb, Timothy, 79n.
Welsh, Alexander, 13, 33n.
West, Paul, 170
Wexler, Victor G., 214n.
White, Newman I., 229n.
White, R. J., 46n.
Whitlocke, Bulstrode, 212, 218, 221, 224
Wilberforce, William, 84
Will, 2, 29, 42, 46–47, 52, 56, 58, 102n., 111n., 126, 170–71, 173n., 181, 184, 194n.
Williams, Bernard, 27n.
Williams, Helen Maria, 235
Williams, Raymond, 31n., 46n., 48, 194n.
Winters, Yvor, x
Wittgenstein, Ludwig, xi, 81
Wollstonecraft, Mary, 216–17, 235
Woodings, R. B., 211–12n., 229n., 235n.
Woodring, Carl, 40n., 103, 152n., 237n.
Wordsworth, Dorothy, 64, 84
Wordsworth, Jonathan, 112–15
Wordsworth, William, 3–4, 9, 12–13, 18, 32–34, 50, 58–98, 100–103, 124, 130–31, 173; *The Borderers*, 3–4, 12, 33n., 58–98, 127–28, 147n., 198, 205; *Essays upon Epitaphs*, 84; *The Excursion*, 65, 83, 98; "Goody Blake and Harry Gill," 74; "Hart-Leap Well," 84; *Letter to the Bishop of Llandaff,* 220n.; *Lyrical Ballads* (1800), 83–84, 98, 111, 131; Note on "The Ancient Mariner," 13, 82–83; Preface to *Lyrical Ballads,* 63, 84; *The Prelude*, 3–4, 32–34, 39, 63, 65, 69–72, 83–84, 98, 106–7n., 151, 193, 224–25; "The Ruined Cottage," 39, 63, 106; *Salisbury Plain Poems,* 64n., 74; "Tintern Abbey," 64–65; *The White Doe of Rylstone,* 98
Worton, Michael, 140n.
Wynn, Charles, 51

Yack, Bernard, 195n.
Yeats, William Butler, 79
Young, Arthur, 74
Young, Edward, 36, 170n.

Zimansky, Curt R., 150n.

WITHDRAWN
from the
Alma College Library